Expository Reflections on the Letter to the Ephesians

Expository Reflections on the Letter to the Ephesians

Leon Morris

Baker Books
A Division of Baker Book House Co
Grand Rapids, Michigan 49516

© 1994 by Leon Morris

Published by Baker Books
a division of Baker Book House Company
P.O. Box 6287, Grand Rapids, MI 49516-6287

Printed in the United States of America

Library of Congress Cataloging-in-Publication Data

Morris, Leon, 1914–
   Expository reflections on the Letter to the Ephesians / Leon Morris.
     p. cm.
   Includes bibliographical references.
   ISBN 0-8010-6312-4
   1. Bible. N.T. Ephesians—Commentaries. I. Bible. N.T. Ephesians.
English. Morris. 1994. II. Title.
   BS2695.3.M674 1994
   227′.5077—dc20   93-28253

Contents

Preface

This book on Ephesians is not a commentary, as it does not deal with such questions as authorship, date, and the like. I have occasionally referred to these matters in passing, but the major thrust of the book is devotional. It is an attempt to bring to the general reader in nontechnical language some of the truths I have found as I have studied this letter.

Unless otherwise specified, I have made my own translation from the Greek. It is a fairly literal translation that is meant to bring out the apostle's meaning as I understand it, rather than to produce an elegant English version.

1

In the Heavenlies with Christ

Paul, an apostle of Christ Jesus through the will of God, to the saints who are in Ephesus and faithful ones in Christ Jesus, grace to you and peace from God our Father and the Lord Jesus Christ (Eph. 1:1–2).

In every age there have been conventional ways of writing letters. In modern western societies we would not dream of beginning a letter without writing our address and the date at the top. Then we address our letter to "Dear ——." We may be writing to a complete stranger or to our worst enemy, but that does not alter our practice. We still assure him or her or them that he or she or they are "dear" to us. And when we come to the end of the letter we write "Yours faithfully" or "Yours sincerely" or "Yours truly" or the like. It does not matter that what we have written may not be faithful or sincere or true. That is irrelevant. The point is that this is the way a letter is written in our day and in our culture.

Just as we conform to custom in our letter-writing style, so did Paul. In the society in which he lived, people had the sensible habit of beginning with the name of the writer. (When we get a letter from someone whose handwriting we do not recognize and who has neglected to put a return address on the envelope, we have to turn to the end to find out who the letter is from before we can begin reading it!) Then came "To ——" with the name of the recipient(s) and a greeting. Since that was all that was really necessary, with many letters that is all there is by way of opening.

But there would often be additions. For example, in official letters the writer would include the title of the dignitary being addressed and often a title of his own. One letter written about A.D. 25 begins: "Theon to the most honored Tyrannus very many greetings." Theon is about to ask a favor, so he addresses Tyrannus politely. Not uncommonly the writer adds an epithet to explain himself. For example, "Asclepiades, the son of Charmagon, to Portis, son of Permamis, greeting." It was customary to use the third person in the greeting, not the first person as with us. After the greeting there was often a little prayer, as in a second-century letter that goes on ". . . before all things I pray that you are in health."

Paul follows the custom of the day and begins his letter to the church at Ephesus with his name. In most of his letters he associates himself with other people in the salutation, but this letter comes from Paul alone. When we first hear of him, he was called "Saul" (Acts 7:58; 8:1; 9:1), a Hebrew name connected with the verb "to ask" (cf. 1 Sam. 1:20). But he eventually became known as "Paul" (Acts 13:9), a Latin name meaning "little." This may mean that he was a small man, or it may mean no more than that it sounds quite a lot like "Saul." Paul was a Roman citizen, which means that he would have had three names (Praenomen, Nomen, and Cognomen), but he never spells this out. Perhaps he did not want to assert his superior position in a church that had many members from the lower ranks of society. In any case, we do not know why he was usually known by his Latin name rather than his Hebrew name.

Paul usually makes his salutation the means of conveying Christian teaching, which he does here. He speaks of himself as "an apostle," a word that means "someone sent" but which in the New Testament is used of people sent by God for special purposes. Apostles headed the list of the people God has appointed or set in the church (1 Cor. 12:28). Nobody became an apostle because he thought he would like the job—notice that Paul says he is an apostle "through the will of God." Either God called someone to be an apostle or he did not. Paul constantly reminds his readers that whatever work he did was done because God had sent him. The word expresses the thought of mission, of being sent for special work, not simply sent for discipleship, a mission common to all Christians.

Paul speaks here of being an apostle "of Christ Jesus," as he generally does. When he combines these two names he most often has this order (probably 73 times, as against 18 occurrences of "Jesus Christ," setting aside the 24 passages where the manuscripts are divided). He never says why he does this, but it certainly gives prominence to the thought of "Messiah," which is what "Christ" means. "Messiah" is from the Hebrew and "Christ" from the Greek; both mean "anointed." In antiquity people might be anointed for any one of a number of reasons. For example, kings were anointed (in the Old Testament a king was often called "the Lord's anointed"), as were priests.

However, the Israelites looked for someone who would be not only *an* anointed, but *the* anointed, one who would do God's will in a very special way. It is this that the name *Christ* signifies. Paul was very fond of speaking of his Savior in this way, and he uses the word *Christ* 379 times (out of 529 times in the entire New Testament—the highest total in any non-Pauline writing is 25 in Acts). It is to Paul that we owe our habit of speaking of our Savior simply as "Christ."

The Saints

Now comes the reference to the addressees. "Saint" is our translation of *hagios*, a word that means "holy." The essential idea in holiness is that of being set apart for God. A holy place, such as a temple, is a building not to be used for secular purposes; it is set apart for the worship of God. Holy vessels are withdrawn from all other use and are used only in the service of God. Similarly, "saints" are people who belong to God. Although in popular usage saints are especially good people, this is not the idea that the Greek word expresses. Saints, of course, must live uprightly, but the essential idea here is that of belonging to God. Saints are people who have been saved through Christ and who are now numbered among the people of God. It is in this sense that Paul uses the word. Paul always uses the word in the plural; he never speaks of "Saint John" or the like, but always of "the saints" as a group. It is a way of drawing attention at one and the same time to the "belongingness" of Christians. We all belong to God and we all belong to one another.

These "saints" are also called "faithful ones in Christ Jesus," where the adjective *(pistos)* is connected with the verb that means "to believe" *(pisteuo)*. In his salutation Paul is bringing out the fact that the church members to whom he writes are believers, men and women of faith. Faith is fundamental to being a Christian, as this letter will demonstrate over and over again. Paul writes to people who belong to God, but who also have put their trust in God and therefore live by faith.

From another point of view, they are "in Christ Jesus." Paul often speaks of Christians as being "in" Christ (A. M. Hunter says that he uses this expression or "in him" or the like about 200 times). Clearly the phrase means a lot to Paul and gives expression to an important truth, but unfortunately for us the apostle never gets around to explaining what he means by the words. At least we can say that it points to the closest of unions with the Savior. Christians are people whose entire lives are bound up with Christ. "Christ Jesus" is not simply some great religious teacher of whom they have heard somewhere. He is their Savior, and they live and move and have their being in him. The connection here with "faithful ones" shows that it is by faith that we come into this close union with him. Faith makes us one with Christ; faith brings us "into" him. This also means that Christians are closely linked with one another, for only believers are in Christ and all believers are in Christ. But the main emphasis here is on relationship to the Savior, not on that to other believers.

Although, as our text runs, Paul writes to the saints "who are in Ephesus," the words "in Ephesus" are absent from some of the most ancient manuscripts of this letter. This leads many scholars to hold that the writing was originally intended as a circular letter to be sent to several churches. If so, it may well be that Ephesus was one of the churches to which it was sent and it is the Ephesian copy that has survived. However, in the first century all letters had to be laboriously written by hand, and the labor saved in omitting the name of the church for which a copy was destined was minuscule. Why should not the name be inserted in every copy sent to a church? It is better to acknowledge that we do not know why the name should have been omitted in some ancient manuscripts and to treat the letter as sent to the church at Ephesus, as most manuscripts tell us.

Grace and Peace

Typically, Paul goes on with "grace to you and peace." "Grace" is one of the great Christian words and one that Paul uses extensively (100 times out of its 155 times in the New Testament; he uses it 12 times in this letter). Paul's writings make up less than one-quarter of the New Testament, but they contain about two-thirds of the references to grace. Clearly this is a typically Pauline concept. The word is closely connected with joy; "grace" in Greek is *charis* and "joy" is *chara*. The fundamental idea in grace is "that which causes joy," and it is well that we bear this in mind. It is all too easy to think that what is solemn is necessarily dull, but this is far from true. There is, of course, a proper solemnity about the Christian way as Paul understands it. Nothing could be more solemn than the truth that sinners call down the wrath of God on themselves or that the way of salvation involved the Son of God coming to earth to die for doomed sinners and to open up to them a way of escape. But it is a very joyful thing when that way of escape is opened to sinners. And what "grace" stresses is the truth that a joyful salvation is made available at no cost to them. It is a divine gift, and a gift that brings great joy.

We must emphasize the thought of gift. Grace does not mean a contract; it means largesse.

"Peace" is also a word we must interpret carefully. Most modern English-speakers owe their understanding of peace to a classical education through which we have inherited the Greek idea of peace. For the Greeks, peace meant the *absence* of war and conflict; it was a negative idea, and that is the way we normally define the word. But the New Testament writers inherited the Hebrew idea of peace, of *shalom*. This was a gloriously positive idea. It did not mean the absence of anything, but rather the presence of something wonderful: the blessing of God in all its fullness. Of course, this does include the absence of war, and sometimes the Hebrew usage is not so very different from our own. But Paul, the Hebrew, is not saying here that he trusts that the Ephesian believers will not find themselves caught up in a war. He is speaking about the deep and abiding peace that comes when people are right with God.

We see this in that the grace and the peace of which he writes are "from God our Father and the Lord Jesus Christ." It is the gracious gift of salvation in Christ and the peace with God that comes from sin forgiven of which Paul writes. He is reminding the Ephesians of what is basic for all Christians.

Predestinated to Adoption

Blessed be the God and Father of our Lord Jesus Christ who has blessed us with the whole spiritual blessing in the heavenlies in Christ, just as he chose us in him before the foundation of the world, so that we should be holy and blameless before him in love, having foreordained us for adoption to him through Jesus Christ, according to the good pleasure of his will, for the praise of the glory of his grace which he freely bestowed on us in the Beloved (Eph. 1:3–6).

The apostle often uses long sentences, the translations of which usually break down into much shorter ones. This one goes on to verse 14, and Marcus Barth calls it "one infinitely long, heavy, and clumsy sentence, replete with dependent clauses, excurses, specifications, repetitions, and the like." But Barth does not think as badly of it as this seems to imply, for later he speaks of "the distinctness, the beauty, and the sense of the several limbs of the 'monster.'" F. R. Barry is similarly impressed; he calls it "a swirl of words with a storm of thought behind them."

Paul often begins his letters with a little prayer or an expression of thanksgiving (cf. vv. 15–16). In this passage he first ascribes blessedness to the God who has done so many wonderful things for his people. The

English verb "to bless" means "to speak well of" and may be used with either God or people as the object. In the New Testament the Greek word used here, *eulogetos,* is used only for the blessedness of God; where people are said to be "blessed," the word used is *eulogemenos.* The two different words bring out the truth that the blessedness we ascribe to God is not the same as what we have in mind when we speak of people. In God it is a natural attribute; in people it is a divine gift. The verb is often used in the sense of asking God to do good things. That is, it signifies an invoking of blessings on someone, and when God is the subject of the verb it signifies "to prosper or give blessings to." Here the first "blessed" clearly has the meaning of speaking well of God, while the second one signifies the giving of good gifts, and "blessing" refers to the good gifts that God bestows. Paul is expressing something of his joy and deep satisfaction at who God is and the wonder of the good gifts he has given his people.

Some translations avoid the difficulty of having two "blessed"s and a "blessing" in the one sentence. Thus, the Good News Bible reads, "Let us give thanks . . ." in the first place, but goes on to the "blessing" words in the following two places. So does the New International Version with "Praise be . . ." in the first place. Although such translations perhaps help us avoid using words that are abnormal for us, they have the disadvantage of hiding the play on words in the original. Paul is devoting the opening part of his letter to an emphasis on blessedness as a characteristic of the Godhead (cf. 1 Kings 1:48; Ps. 41:13; etc.) and as the result of the divine activity (cf. Gen. 22:17; Deut. 12:15; etc.).

Paul speaks of the deity as "God and Father." The first term expresses the majesty and remoteness of him who we worship and the second his love and his nearness. Both are important for a satisfying religious experience. "Your God is too small" is an accusation that may still be leveled at much that passes for Christianity. We need a sense of the greatness and the majesty of God, but with that we have the family title, "Father," because we cannot do without God's love and care. Too much emphasis on God's greatness can prevent us from appreciating his nearness. Paul preserves the balance. When he speaks of the God and Father "of our Lord Jesus Christ," he draws attention to what God has done for us in sending his Son. It is only because of the revelation of God in Christ that we know the deity as he is, so Paul speaks of him as the God and Father of *Christ,* not of us. It is true that he is our God and our Father, too, but it is only because of what God is in relation to Christ that he is what he is for us.

Paul says that God has blessed "us," which is most naturally understood of God's good gift to all his people, writer and readers alike. Some scholars hold that in this letter "you" characteristically means "you Gentiles" and "we" means "we Jews," but it is difficult to see this. Although some passages indeed may well be understood in that way, Paul mostly uses "you" to refer to the recipients of the letter and "we" inclusively of both them and himself. Then he goes on to speak of "the whole spiritual blessing." Many translations have "every spiritual blessing," which may not differ greatly, but the expression Paul uses puts its emphasis on the full divine blessing. He is not speaking of a series of separate blessings, but of one great divine blessing that lacks nothing. M. Barth says that the blessing "given 'in Christ' and described in the following eleven verses is an indivisible and perfect whole."

The Heavenlies

Paul locates this spiritual blessing "in the heavenlies," an expression he uses five times in this epistle and nowhere else. He never explains it, and we are left to work out its meaning from the general significance of the term and the way Paul uses it. J. R. W. Stott sees it as "the unseen world of spiritual reality," and this seems as good a definition as any. It is the place where Christ sits in glory (1:20), and where his people sit with him (2:6). But it is not simply "heaven," for God's people are at war with evil powers "in the heavenlies" (6:12). Those powers will not triumph, for God's manifold wisdom is made known to them "through the church" (3:10). It seems that Paul is saying that there is a conflict between God and evil, which takes place in this world but goes beyond anything we can see in this world. In the end there will be the divine triumph, a triumph in which God's people will have a place. Someone has said that the expression does not mean "heaven," but a heavenly level of life— and such a view certainly suits the present passage.

It is "in Christ" that we share that triumph and have the victory. Paul makes a good deal of use of the words "in Christ," and indeed that expression (or "in him," referring to Christ) occurs eleven times in verses 1 through 14. It is a strong expression for the union between Christ and believers. "As the root is in the soil, the branch in the vine (cf. John 15:1ff.), the fish in the sea, the bird in the air, so the place of the Christian's life is in Christ. Physically his life is in the world; spiritually it is lifted above the world to be in Christ" (F. Foulkes).

Chosen in Christ

That God "chose" us means that the divine initiative is of the first importance as we seek to understand our salvation. We would not have expected that, for it is natural for us to expect that we have the initiative, that we decide whether to be saved or not. There is a place, of course,

15

for the human will, and the New Testament never regards people as mere automatons moved about by God without regard for their own desires or the exercise of the free will God has given them. We are mistaken, however, if we see salvation as something we decide by our own choice.

I am reminded of a story I read somewhere of an old lady traveling with her granddaughter in a crowded train. There was no seat for them, so of necessity they stood. When the train stopped at a station and some people got off, the granddaughter and other passengers insisted that the old lady take one of the vacant seats. Though she protested, they took no notice and gently pushed her into it. It was not until the train got moving again that she was able to say to her granddaughter, "But dear, that was our stop!" Even with the best intentions in the world, we so often go astray.

And it can be like that not only in getting off trains at the right stop, but in our understanding of our eternal salvation. Because we like to think that we have all the say, we tend to be suspicious of such teachings as election, divine call, and predestination. It cannot be said that predestination is a wildly popular idea today. Some Christians find it completely unacceptable, saying that it reduces us to the level of puppets, people who are simply moved around as God chooses and who have no wills of our own. But this is not the way the New Testament views it. For the New Testament writers, predestination is a way of saying that the whole of our salvation, from first to last, is a work of God.

Let's look at it this way. We naturally think that we are completely free. If we are saved, we hold, it is because we have in our freedom decided to turn away from evil and to commit our lives to God and to good and to serving God. But the doctrine of predestination tells us we can never do that in our own strength and in our own wisdom. Left to ourselves, we would never make the motion of giving up evil and turning to God. It is only because God works in us first that we come to him. And because he does this good work in us, we have a deep assurance that we could never have if it all depended on ourselves. Well does the seventeenth of the Thirty-Nine Articles of the Church of England see "the godly consideration of Predestination, and our Election in Christ" as "full of sweet, pleasant, and unspeakable comfort." Here Paul tells us that God "chose" us and that he "foreordained" us, and when he says that the choosing was "before the foundation of the world" he means that the divine choice was in the eternal purpose of God. Because such a purpose will not be overthrown, this gives assurance to the people of God.

The priority of the divine act is underlined in this passage as "chose" is followed by "foreordained," "adoption," "the good pleasure of his will," "his grace," and "freely bestowed." These expressions combine to put strong emphasis on the truth that sinners are saved by the divine act.

Although there is nothing we can do that will bring about our salvation, God has acted in Christ to do all that is necessary.

We should be clear that predestination is not a doctrine that encourages spiritual laziness or complacency. We cannot reason, "Since God chose us before the world was, since our salvation is rooted in the divine purpose, it does not matter how we live." It *does* matter how we live. Predestination does not encourage moral laxity. Rather, predestination is so that we may be "holy and blameless before him" (v. 4; cf. Col. 1:22), where the two adjectives bring out the positive and the negative aspects of Christian service. Paul says it is "for the praise of the glory of his grace." If we have come to know the salvation of God, we will live out the consequences of being saved. Those who are saved live saved lives. God chose us "in him," and we are to be holy and blameless "before him." We live our lives in the presence of God, and that has to be a continuing stimulus for us to be the best that we can be.

It is not certain whether we should take the phrase "in love" with the words that precede it or with those that follow. If we take it with the preceding (which is perhaps supported by the construction in 4:2, 16), then love should be characteristic of the way we live. Love is very important in this letter, where the noun occurs ten times (a total exceeded in the New Testament only in Romans with 14 times and 1 John with 18 times). In the sense in which the New Testament writers use the term, love is known by what God did for us in Christ. As Paul puts it elsewhere, "God shows his love for us in this: while we were still sinners, Christ died for us" (Rom. 5:8). Such love is not (as in the sense in which we usually employ the term) a warm affection for the attractive or for those bound to us by some natural tie. There is nothing attractive to God in sinners who have rebelled against him! Yet, in the face of rebellion and evil, God did not turn away from sinners. Instead, he sent his Son to be their Savior, even though this meant dying for them on the cross.

And those who have been saved by the cross come to love like that, at least in some measure. They still experience the ordinary loves of life—love for spouse, family, and friends. But beyond that, they love because they have become loving people. In their measure they love as God does; they love because of what they are and not simply because they find attractiveness in some of the people they meet. Paul seems here to be saying, then, that those predestined to salvation are to show in their lives what salvation means: They are to be holy and blameless and loving.

If we take "in love" with the words that follow, Paul is saying that it was in his love that God foreordained us. This is true, as Paul makes clear elsewhere, whether or not it is what he is saying here. We should not see predestination as a grim process whereby God condemns great

17

numbers of people to eternal loss. Rather, it is the outworking of a loving purpose whereby he delivers great numbers of people for salvation. In this passage salvation is understood as "adoption to him" (Paul is the only New Testament writer to use the idea of adoption). The Jews did not practice adoption as we know it, though Hosea 11:1 comes close to it: "When Israel was a child, I loved him, and out of Egypt I called my son" (NIV). But adoption was well known in the Roman world, and the Ephesians would have had no difficulty in seeing Paul's meaning. We have no rights in the heavenly family, but God has chosen us, foreordained us, taken us into that family. This is done "through Jesus Christ." The New Testament consistently sees our salvation, however else it is viewed, as brought about by Christ. It was his atoning death that delivered sinners from their sins and cleansed them so that they might belong in the family of God.

The strong emphasis on the divine initiative is brought out further with the reference to "the good pleasure of his will" (v. 5). The Good News Bible brings out the meaning with "this was his pleasure and purpose." There are two thoughts here: that God was putting into effect what he willed, and that he took pleasure in doing so. Again we have the idea that predestination is not grim and forbidding, but joyful and attractive. This thought is continued with "the praise of the glory of his grace" (or "his glorious grace," NRSV). There is attractiveness in the wonderful grace of God, and those who see it in operation cannot but praise it.

"Glory" is a Pauline word, for the apostle uses it in all 77 times (8 times in Ephesians), whereas no other New Testament writer has it more often than John (18 times). G. Kittel points out that the significance attached to this word in the New Testament differs from its meaning in Greek, generally; in the New Testament "the word is used for the most part in a sense for which there is no Greek analogy whatever . . . it denotes 'divine and heavenly radiance,' the 'loftiness and majesty' of God, and even the 'being of God' and His world" (*TDNT*, II, p. 237). Grace is a wonderful and glorious thing, suited to heaven.

There is an emphasis on the idea of grace, for "freely bestowed" is the translation of a verb from the same root as "grace" (the verb is used elsewhere in the New Testament only in Luke 1:28). Bruce translates "be-graced" and says, "God's grace has extended to his people and enfolded them: he has 'be-graced' them." The expression underlines the truth that salvation is a free gift from God. It is brought to sinners in the saving work of Christ as a free gift, something they could never acquire by their own merits. And this gift, so freely bestowed, is given "in the Beloved" (cf. Mark 1:11; 9:7; Col. 1:13). As throughout the New Testament, there is no salvation outside Christ, but a full and wonderful salvation "in him," in what he is and what he has done.

18

2

The Mystery of God's Will

[. . . the Beloved,] in whom we have redemption through his blood, the forgiveness of our trespasses, according to the riches of his grace which he lavished on us, with all wisdom and understanding, having made known to us the mystery of his will according to his good pleasure which he set forth in him as a plan for the fullness of the times, to gather up all things in Christ, the things in heaven and the things on earth, in him in whom also we were claimed as God's own, having been foreordained according to the purpose of him who works all things according to the counsel of his will, so that we, the first to put our hope in Christ, should be for the praise of his glory, in whom you also when you heard the word of truth, the gospel of your salvation, in whom when you believed you were sealed with the Holy Spirit of promise, who is the pledge of our inheritance, for the redemption of his possession, for the praise of his glory (Eph. 1:7–14).

I have refrained from breaking up the remainder of this sentence (which began in verse 3) as most translations do to conform to normal practice in English, so that we can get something of the feel of the complicated ideas that Paul has presented here. The apostle often uses much longer sentences than those to which we are accustomed. It is part of his style.

Carrying on from the thought of the free gift made "in the Beloved," Paul goes on to the thought that we have "redemption." Here he is using a metaphor taken from the customs of ancient warfare. It was a frequent practice for the conqueror in battle to take captives who could then be made slaves and put to work in all sorts of useful service. However, if they were people of importance, they would probably not be of much use as laborers, though they might be highly valued in their homelands. In such cases the captives could be set free and restored to their rightful place by a process called redemption. A sum of money, which was called the ransom price, was paid by the vanquished to the victors, and the verb "redeem" was used for carrying the process through.

The usage was extended to other processes than that of warfare. For example, it might have been used for the freeing of slaves. There were various ways of bringing this about, but the one that concerns us here involved the slave's saving up the price of being freed. Although this would not be easy, for by definition the slave's labor belonged to the master, a determined person could set aside the few coins that would be thrown to him or her from time to time. When the full amount was in hand, it would be deposited in the treasury of a god. Then the slave and the owner would go to the temple and go through the solemn rigmarole of selling the slave to the god "for freedom." A record of the transaction might be carved in the wall of the temple, and such records as have survived show us something of what was done. This process, too, was "redemption," and the price the slave paid was the "ransom."

However it was accomplished, the thought in "redemption" is always that the person has been in a captivity from which he or she cannot break free, yet is set free on the payment of a price. The Revised English Bible translates "release" and the Good News Bible reads "set free," and there are other such renderings. While translations like these do bring out the freedom that Christ brings, they ignore the fact that "redemption" means not simply "release" but "release on payment of a price."

Paul found this a useful illustration of what happens when sinners are given their freedom by Christ, and he uses it in a number of places. His point is that we sinners are not free people. We are enslaved to sin. We might—if we try hard enough—break away from this or that sin that we have been committing, but we can never break the grip of all sin. Because in the last resort we are captives to sin and can never free ourselves from the grip of sin, when we stand before God on judgment day we will still be condemned as sinners.

Yet, says Paul, Christ has paid the price for us, the ransom, even though that price involved his death on the cross. There are, of course, other ways of looking at the salvation that Christ has wrought for us. Redemption is not the whole story, but it is an important part of it. "Redemption" emphasizes the greatness of the price paid by Christ and the freedom into which he has brought us. So here Paul speaks of us as having "redemption through his blood," where "his blood" of course means "his shed blood," "his death." Because Christ died and thus paid the price of sin, those who are "in Christ" are redeemed.

Paul immediately goes on to another way of looking at salvation and speaks of our having received "the forgiveness of our trespasses." The word rendered "forgiveness" means a letting go, a sending away or dismissal. When applied to sins it signifies that the sins are "let go"; they are no longer held against us. This brings out the freeness of the divine mercy. God simply remits our sins, refuses to hold them against us. This way of looking at our salvation is found in many parts of the New Testament, but Paul does not use it as freely as some other writers (he has this noun twice only and the corresponding verb five times, but only once in the sense of "forgive," and that in a quotation from a psalm). But he knows what it means and that it has taken place, and he brings it out from time to time as he does here. His word for "trespasses" is one that literally means "a fall beside." It is a word the apostle uses in sixteen of its nineteen New Testament occurrences. Clearly he saw as important the view that sin means a stumbling, a fall, an inability to make progress in the right direction. For believers, however, all their lapses from the right way have been dealt with. God's forgiveness in Christ has taken care of all that.

This forgiveness is no niggardly affair, and Paul proceeds to the abundance of the divine resources that brought it about. He speaks first of "the riches of his grace." "Riches" is another Pauline word (the apostle has it 15 times out of 22 New Testament occurrences, and no other New Testament writer has it more than twice). The word underlines the boundlessness of the divine wealth. "Riches" is often used of literal wealth in terms of money, but it is also employed figuratively to signify an abundance of benefits of a variety of kinds. Paul has the term five times in this letter, which equals the highest number in any New Testament book (again in 1:18; 2:7; 3:8, 16; cf. also 2:4). He uses it to bring out the abundance of grace and glory twice each, while the other occurrence of the word refers to "the unsearchable riches of Christ" (3:8). Here the emphasis is on grace, which we have already seen is a Pauline word. It matters immensely to Paul that God acts toward sinners in a joy-bringing way (for that is what "grace" means). God freely forgives them, and the language indicates something of the extravagance of the divine goodwill.

This comes out also in the verb that follows: "lavished." Strictly speaking the word refers to things that are over and above the required number and so comes to bring out the thought of abundant supply. That is the way it is with the divine grace. God gives us more than could reasonably be expected; he has "lavished" his grace on us (The Living Bible has "showered down upon us the richness of his grace").

Divine Wisdom

Paul turns from the thought of the abundance of the forgiveness that sinners receive to the divine wisdom that lies behind that abundant forgiveness. He speaks of God as acting "with all wisdom and understanding," and his first noun corresponds pretty closely to our word "wisdom." It is used of mental excellence of the highest kind. The second has to do with the exercise of the mind. "Understanding" often signifies the practical outworking of wisdom. Paul is saying not only that the way sin is dealt with results in a full and abundant forgiveness, but that it reveals something of the divine wisdom. Perhaps we should notice that it is possible that we should understand "with all wisdom and understanding" as part of the gift of God to believers, so that it is they who have such mental excellence (Abbott argues for this view). Although it is certainly true that the redeemed have a "wisdom and understanding" that they lacked before they experienced salvation, I doubt whether this is what Paul is saying here. It is also possible to take the words with the following "having made known" ("having made known in all wisdom"), but this is less likely. It is much more probable that Paul is simply exulting in the excellence of the divine nature.

This thought is carried on with "having made known to us." The idea here is that the divine wisdom proceeds along the lines of bringing knowledge to sinners. Not only does God predestine us and forgive us, he lets us know what he has done and something of the way he has done it. Paul brings out the thoughts of revelation and of that which is not revealed by using the term *mysterion,* a Greek word from which we get our word "mystery." In the ancient world it was often used of a group of "mystery" religions, which had secret rites, secret formulas, and so on. In fact, so well were their secrets kept that not very much is known about them to this day. But Paul does not use the term in that sense.

Nor is it like "mystery" in our sense of the term. With us a "mystery" is something hard to work out. We think, for example, of a mystery story, where the clues are scattered around with such gay abandon that only if we concentrate on the right ones and ignore the red herrings the writer has so thoughtfully placed before us will we be able to work it all out and exclaim triumphantly, "The butler did it!" or the like. But the Greek term does not denote something difficult to work out—it means something *impossible* to work out. It is something so mysterious that what it signifies is beyond our ability to work out—ever. In the New Testament, however, there is normally the further thought that this profound truth, which we can never work out for ourselves, has now been made known by God. It has been revealed. The word is applied, for example, to the gospel. Who would ever have worked it out that our salvation does not depend on anything that we do? Not on our prayers, our resolutions, our good lives, not on anything *we* do. It depends on God's saving action in Christ. Indeed Paul can say that Christ is himself "the mystery of God" (Col. 2:2).

This points us to Calvary and the salvation that streams from the cross, a salvation that proceeds from "his will." We must not think of salvation as something worked out by Jesus in dying for us while the Father remained aloof. It came from the will of God and was "according to his good pleasure." There is an emphasis here on the Father's plan, where the word for "plan" is one that originally signified the management of a household, though it later came to indicate administration generally: the carrying of a purpose into effect. Here it refers to the way God ordered things through the centuries and thus "a plan for the fullness of the times." There are two Greek words for "time" and, while they cannot always be distinguished in meaning, when they are differentiated the one used here often refers to "the right time," or "the significant time." Such a meaning is appropriate here. "The fullness of the times" is a difficult expression, but it appears to mean that the times of God's action in ancient Israel, illuminated by the work of the prophets, had come to their fulfillment. That era was now "full."

The expression also points to something new—the appearing of the Son of God. If the older times are now "full," that is because they have reached their consummation in Christ. Now a new era has been inaugurated in him. And in this new era "all things" are to be gathered up "in Christ," which seems to mean at least that Christ is to be head over everything there is. Nothing is excluded, and this gives us a little glimpse of the greatness Paul saw in his Savior. Not one thing is excluded. The verb rendered "gather up" is found elsewhere in the New Testament only in Romans 13:9, which speaks of "any other commandment" as summed up in the command to love. So here the apostle speaks of all things as being gathered up in Christ, as finding their destiny in Christ. Since Paul spells this out by adding "the things in heaven and the things on earth," there is to be no doubt as to the central role of the Savior.

God's Portion

From that Paul apparently moves to the thought that the redeemed have become God's own people. He uses a verb (found here only in the New Testament) that basically means "to cast lots" and thus "to choose by lot" or "to receive by lot." It may mean "we were allotted a portion," in which case it points to the wonderful gifts God has given his own. This is the way the word is taken, for example, in the Revised English Bible: "we have been given our share in the heritage." Or it may signify "we were allotted to God," claimed by God as his own, as the Good News Bible understands the passage: "God chose us to be his own people." In this context it seems that it is this second meaning that we should accept, in accordance with Old Testament passages that see God's people as his "allotted inheritance" (Deut. 32:9 NIV). In Old Testament times only Israel was God's heritage; now, in Christ, Gentiles as well as Jews make up this divine possession.

The redeemed have been "foreordained" (the same verb as in v. 5), so that we are moving again into the sphere of the working out of God's purpose. Indeed Paul goes on to refer to the foreordination as "according to the purpose of him who. . . ." That God has a purpose for his creation and that this purpose is closely linked to the work of Christ is a thought that recurs in Paul's writings. He does not think of a God who stands by helpless to do anything for us until we graciously invite him. The apostle's doctrine of foreordination means that God has a purpose for his creation and a purpose for each of us. Our coming into salvation means that God is accomplishing his purpose in us. Paul underlines this truth by going on to speak of God as working all things "according to the counsel of his will." The word for "counsel" often means "purpose," so the thought of the divine purpose is being emphasized. The expression rules out the initiative of any others; Paul is speaking of a *divine* purpose, divine from first to last.

The Christian Hope

The next words, "so that," translate a construction that conveys the idea of purpose; in this passage we cannot miss the thought that God is working out his will. The purpose concerns believers, who are described as "the first to put our hope in Christ." Up till this point Paul has largely been concerned with the past—what God purposed from the beginning and how he has worked out his purpose in Christ. But "hope" turns our attention to the future. Paul is not wrapped up in the past; he sees believers as those who press onwards with a warm and vital hope. They are seen here as "the first" to put their hope in Christ—so that they have all the excitement and the thrill of being pioneers—but Paul's use of the perfect tense in his verb for "hope" indicates that he is clear that the hope is lasting. It is something that has its origin in the past, but which continues into the present.

Most commentators see a reference here to Jews and Gentiles. The Jews are then "the first to put our hope in Christ" and the Gentiles the emphatic "you also" that comes a little later in this passage. It makes sense to see a progression like this, and it corresponds to the historical fact that the gospel was proclaimed to the Jews first (cf. Acts 11:19; cf. also "to the Jew first, and also to the Greek," Rom. 1:16). Against this there is nothing in the context to indicate that the apostle is distinguishing between Jews and Gentiles (as he clearly does in 2:11–22). It may be argued that it is difficult to think that the blessings up to verse 12 belong to the Jews only, while those in verses 13 and 14 are the prerogative of the Gentiles; therefore it may be better to understand the meaning as that all the blessings in this passage belong to all believers (cf. "our inheritance," v. 14). On the whole it seems that there is more to be said for the view that Paul speaks first of the Jews and then enlarges his horizon to take in the Gentile believers.

The aim of those who have this vital hope is that they may be "for the praise of his glory." We should not miss the order—first there is hope in Christ, then the consequence: lives lived for the glory of God. The Christianity that Paul preached, and which he exemplified in his own living out of the faith, meant living lives that would be "for the praise of his glory." This is to say that believers must so live that their manner of life shows plainly that God is central in all that they do and are. Paul does not call on believers to engage in praise of God but to be praised of God. They are singlemindedly to give themselves over to doing the will of God, so that all those who see them will praise, not the earthly servants of God, but the God whose servants they are. Paul does not speak of God at this point but of "his glory" (cf. v. 6). The servants of God are to live such lives that they will make people see God's glory in them and therefore make them praise the glorious God who does such wonderful things.

Sealed with the Holy Spirit

As Paul moves on to the work of the Holy Spirit in the lives of believers, he looks back to the commencement of the Christian lives of his correspondents. His "you" is emphatic; he is not speaking of people in general, but of "you believers." He attaches "also" to the pronoun, so he is not saying something that is true only of the recipients of his letter, but of all believers. He joins this group to the others who had heard "the word of truth." As often in Paul's writings, "word" means much more than it usually does with us. It stands here for the whole message of truth. Paul further explains this as "the gospel of your salvation." "Gospel" means "good news"—the good news that God sends, the good news that tells of salvation. Although salvation has both present and future aspects, perhaps the emphasis here is on salvation as a present reality.

Twice in this section Paul has the expression "in whom" (unless the second one means "in which," i.e., "in the gospel," but this seems less likely). Christ is at the heart of salvation, and those who are to be saved must put their trust in him. The doubled expression makes for a somewhat awkward sentence, but there is no doubting its emphasis on Christ. And, Paul says, when his correspondents believed in Jesus, they "were sealed with the Holy Spirit of promise." Sealing was very important in an age when reading was far from universal. A prominent man would choose a device for his seal that left a distinctive imprint when it was pressed into a mass of wax or the like. When people saw such an imprint they would know that the object that bore it was the property of a certain individual, and they presumably would respect the mark of ownership, especially if the man had the means to express his displeasure when people did not respect it! Or again, a man might fix his seal to a document, which meant that he had given his assent to what was written; he authenticated it.

Paul is saying that the Holy Spirit within the believer is God's seal on that person, a truth that the apostle repeats later in this letter (4:30). It is the sign that God has accepted him or her. It is the guarantee that all God's promises will be fulfilled in the believer. We may know that someone belongs to God because of the evidence that the Spirit is at work within that person's life. It is worth remembering that it was in the vicinity of Ephesus that Paul met some men who claimed to be disciples but who had not even heard that there was a Holy Spirit. This was so far from the genuine Christian experience that the apostle took steps to set things right. The men were baptized in the name of the Lord Jesus and Paul laid hands on them, after which the Holy Spirit came upon them (Acts 19:1–7). It may well be that some of this group were in the church at Ephesus when this letter was read. They would certainly have been reminded that the presence of the Holy Spirit is characteristic of all believers.

It is unusual to have the Holy Spirit described as "the Holy Spirit of promise." This expression directs attention to the fact that in times long gone by, God had promised to send his Holy Spirit, a truth of which Peter made spectacular use on the day of Pentecost when he quoted Joel 2:28–32 (Acts 2:17–21). The Holy Spirit in the life of the believer is continuing evidence that God is at work and that the ancient prophecies are being fulfilled.

Paul goes on to speak of the Holy Spirit as a "pledge" (NRSV) or "guarantee" (GNB) of our inheritance. The word *arrabon* is explained in the Bauer lexicon as a legal and commercial technical term meaning "*first instalment, deposit, down payment, pledge,* that pays a part of the purchase price in advance, and so secures a legal claim to the article in question, or makes a contract valid." Moulton and Milligan cite from the papyri a woman receiving 1,000 drachmas as *arrabona* for a cow she was selling. They also inform us that in modern Greek *arrabona* means an engagement ring. Paul is saying that the Holy Spirit within believers is wonderful now, but the present gift is no more than a beginning. It is a guarantee that God will give his people greater gifts in the future. Phillips sees the force of the passage as "until the day when God completes the redemption of what he has paid for as his own." Paul speaks of the Holy Spirit as the *arrabon* elsewhere (2 Cor. 1:22; 5:5; cf. "the first-fruits of the Spirit," Rom. 8:23).

This pledge looks forward to "the redemption of his possession." There is a sense in which our redemption has been accomplished already, and—however we understand redemption—we must recognize that the full price was paid at Calvary. In that sense redemption was completed when Christ died for his people. But the complete unfolding of all that redemption means is something that is still future. Paul is saying that the presence of God's Spirit in his people now is a guarantee that all that redemption means will in due course be realized.

The word I have translated "possession" can have the meaning "preservation" or "acquisition," but in the present passage it surely points to the redeemed as belonging wholly to God. Paul is saying that what has happened so far is a sure indication that God will see through to the end all that is involved in salvation. We belong entirely to God, and eventually all that this means will be fully accomplished. We should not miss the point that Paul has three times in the opening part of this letter taken terms used of Israel in the Old Testament and applied them to the church: "saints" (v. 1), "heritage" or "God's own" (v. 11), and "possession" (v. 14).

And it will be "for the praise of his glory." The word for "praise" is found three times in Ephesians, the most in any one book in the New Testament. All three are in this chapter (vv. 6, 12), and all three refer to the praise of the glory of God. Paul is emphasizing that in the end God's glory will be seen for what it is, and this will elicit praise from created beings. The Good News Bible makes this an exhortation: "Let us praise his glory!" But, though an admirable sentiment, this is not what Paul is saying. The words at the conclusion of verse 14 are the completion of the sentence and are thus to be taken with the preceding words. ". . . for the praise of his glory" is not a separate sentence, and there is no exhortation in this phrase.

3

The Greatness of His Power

*For this reason I also, having heard of your faith in the Lord Jesus
and your love to all the saints, do not cease giving thanks for you,
making mention of you in my prayers, that the God of our Lord
Jesus Christ, the Father of glory, may give you a spirit of wisdom
and revelation in the knowledge of him, so that, the eyes of your
heart having been enlightened, you may know what is the hope of
his calling, what are the riches of the glory of his inheritance in the
saints, and what is the exceeding greatness of his power towards
us who believe according to the working of the strength of his
might. Which he worked out in the Christ, having raised him from
the dead and having sat him at his right hand in the heavenlies,
far above all sovereignty and authority and might and lordship
and every name that is named, not only in this age but in that
which is to come. And he subjected all things under his feet and
gave him as head over all things to the church, which is his body,
the fulness of him who fills all things in all (Eph. 1:15–23).*

The next part of the letter is a prayer for its recipients
(which incidentally, with its warm tone and references to the faith and
love of the apostle's correspondents, tells against the idea that this is a
circular letter sent to several churches). "For this reason" links the prayer
that follows to the great spiritual truths that Paul has brought out in the
opening part of his letter. Those truths are not simply the object of schol-
arly debate or, on a different level, the starting point for pious conver-
sations. They are the dynamic for Christian living. Discussions at all

levels have their place, but we should not overlook the fact that Paul is looking for action as a consequence of the truths he has been outlining. It is because God is who he is and because he does what he does, specifically what he does in Christ, that his people are to engage in certain practices, such as prayer, and lines of conduct in general that differ from those accepted in the world.

The two qualities the apostle picks out in the lives of his readers are faith and love. Faith is, of course, fundamental to the Christian understanding of the spiritual life, and here it is made specific: "faith in the Lord Jesus." This expression is not as frequent as we might have expected. (It is more common to have the verb, "to believe in Jesus Christ" and with the preposition *eis,* not *en,* as here; Paul has the construction used here no more than about half a dozen times in all his letters.) The expression appears to convey the idea of faith that rests in Jesus. He is here called "the Lord Jesus," which underlines his majesty. Paul is in no doubt but that Christ is supreme over all his people. To be a Christian means to acknowledge Jesus as Lord, and that means to surrender one's whole life to him to do his good and perfect will.

Love

We saw something of the importance of love in this letter when we were looking at verse 4. The noun "love" occurs more often in Ephesians than in any other Pauline epistle except 1 Corinthians (which, of course, is much longer), while the corresponding verb "to love" is found more often in this letter than in any other Pauline writing. For some reason the apostle found it expedient to put major emphasis on love as he wrote this letter. But this expression of thanks shows that the reason he dwells on love in Ephesians is not that he thinks his correspondents are deficient in this virtue. He recognizes that they agree with him about its importance and that they put into practice their acceptance of what it means to see Christian love as so significant. The believer is to exercise love in a variety of relationships: love to God, love to Christ, love to other people. The New Testament Christian is a loving Christian, a person characterized by love.

Here Paul speaks of love to other believers, "the saints," and he says that the Ephesians love "all the saints." The word "all" is important. It is easy to slip into a concern for our own little circle while we ignore those outside it. There is a caricature of Christian praying that runs:

> *God bless me, my wife Jean,*
> *My son John, his wife Joan.*
> *Us four, no more. Amen.*

29

I don't think anyone ever really prayed that prayer, but it reminds us that it is all too easy to concentrate on our own affairs. Some sage once remarked, "A man wrapped up in himself makes a very small parcel!" And it is a not much bigger parcel when he extends the wrapping to include his nearest family and friends but no one else.

Paul was not guilty of such narrow-mindedness. He commended the wide outlook of his Ephesian friends, for he saw that their love took in all the heavenly family of which they were members. It is characteristic of Paul to think of the wider family of the whole church and not confine his remarks to their concern for the local Christians, or even those in adjacent churches.

Intercession

Paul generally tells a church to which he is writing that he prays for it (though, curiously, he does not do this in either 1 or 2 Corinthians). So here he assures the Ephesians of his prayers for them. He tells them that he never ceases to give thanks for them, which shows that he was very pleased with their spiritual progress. But he was also aware that they had needs, either in that they lacked important spiritual qualities or that they faced difficulties as they tried to serve their Lord. So Paul goes on to assure them that he makes mention of them in his prayers. The word "mention" can be used in the sense of "call to mind," "remembrance," "memory," but in the New Testament when it is joined with "making" it always refers to prayer, as here.

Paul moves to the content of his prayers for the Ephesians. He speaks first of God as "the God of our Lord Jesus Christ," which brings out the truth that when Christians know God, it is the God whom Jesus Christ has revealed that they know. This also draws attention to the genuineness of the incarnation, for the heavenly Father is Jesus' God as well as ours. We have the full title—"our Lord Jesus Christ"—as is fitting in such a prayer; it brings out something of the majesty of him whom Christians follow.

Then the apostle speaks of "the Father of glory" (an expression found only here in the New Testament), where "Father" emphasizes the nearness of God and "glory" his remoteness. God is at one and the same time the Father of all his people and the supreme ruler of all that heaven means. The word "Father" brings out the wonder of God's love for his people. Though he is so high and holy, he has been well pleased to admit people he has created into membership of his family. But, for Paul, that does not mean that God's awesomeness is in any way diminished, for he is "the Father of glory," or perhaps we should translate it as "the glorious Father." Either way, Paul is insisting on the splendor that characterizes our God.

Wisdom and Revelation

Paul's prayer is that the glorious heavenly Father will give to the Ephesians "a spirit of wisdom and revelation." There is a question here as to whether we should take "spirit" to mean the Holy Spirit (as in GNB: "the Spirit, who will make you wise and reveal God to you") or whether we should see it as equivalent to an adjective (as in REB: "the spiritual gifts of wisdom and vision"). Probably the latter is a little more likely, as it is clear that God had already given the Holy Spirit to the believers at Ephesus. But we should probably not see too great a difference between the two translations, for in either case the gift comes only through the indwelling Spirit of God; and where the Spirit is given, wisdom and revelation follow. "Wisdom" is used of the best human excellence, and the thought here will be that this excellence can come only as the Holy Spirit is at work in the believer. There is a tendency in some Christian circles to put all the emphasis on a joyful but mindless experience (being a "happy-clappy"!). This, of course, is the opposite of an equally invalid way of living out the faith, the way of concentrating on intellectualism. Paul is pointing to a balance. We should never overlook the truth that being a Spirit-filled Christian means, among other things, having "a spirit of wisdom."

With that goes "a spirit of . . . revelation." Just as it is true that the believer should aim for the highest mental excellence that the Spirit of God can give, so it is true that the believer is never in the position of being able to work out the Christian way by means of the best wisdom he or she can acquire. Christianity is a religion of revelation. It is only because God has revealed the Christian teachings that we can know them. Specifically, there is nothing about a Galilean carpenter nailed to a Roman cross that can obviously bring salvation to sinners in the modern world. But God has revealed something of the significance of that death on that cross, and it is in the light of the revelation that we come to put our trust in the crucified one. And we live out our lives in the light of the revelation, for it includes not only an understanding of the way sinners come to be saved, but also of the way saved sinners are to live out the implications of their faith.

The Knowledge of God

This wisdom and revelation take place "in the knowledge of him." The word "knowledge" here is a compound word that in the New Testament is used of religious knowledge and morality. In this letter it is used once more when it refers to "the knowledge of the Son of God" (4:13). Elsewhere it is used of the knowledge of God that sinners rejected (Rom. 1:28) and of the knowledge of God that believers accepted (Col.

31

1:10). It is also used of the knowledge of truth, which in the New Testament may well point to the truth about God (1 Tim. 2:4; 2 Tim. 3:7; Titus 1:1). Here it clearly refers to the knowledge that is to be prized above all other knowledge.

To know God has consequences. It means that "the eyes of your heart" are "enlightened." Elsewhere Paul speaks of God as making his light shine in people's hearts (2 Cor. 4:6), which is much the same thought as here, though it lacks the vivid metaphor expressed as "the eyes of your heart" ("spiritual eyesight" as F. F. Bruce puts it). The "heart" in antiquity was used metaphorically of a variety of inner states, often of intelligence (which will be behind GNB's "that your minds may be opened to see his light"). In this context it is probably not quite as definite as that, but it does point to spiritual enlightenment. "Heart" will here stand for the whole of the inner states: minds, yes, but more importantly, affections and wills as well. Paul is saying that anyone who has come to know God is a different person—becoming a Christian means the transformation of the whole of one's life.

The first thing Paul prays for in his correspondents is "hope." In modern times we seem often to have downgraded that word's meaning from the blazing certainty of the New Testament hope to nothing more than a feeble optimism. Hope was a very important concept for Paul. He uses the noun for "hope" thirty-six times and the corresponding verb nineteen times, so it obviously was a concept that meant a good deal to him. It turns up in every one of his letters except 2 Timothy. For Paul, hope represented the certainty of something not yet present: ". . . for who hopes for what he sees?" (Rom. 8:24). Because hope, as Paul understood it, rested on the certainty that Christ had brought about salvation, the apostle had confidence in the future.

Faith and hope are closely linked; as R. Bultmann says, hope along with faith "constitutes Christian existence." For most people today, hope is little more than a wish that what lies ahead will be pleasurable. But that is no way to understand the New Testament hope. That hope rested squarely on Christ's atoning work. It started with the profound truth that God had done so very much at such great cost for our salvation. It went on to the deep-seated conviction that in the light of those saving acts he would not let his purpose fail of its final achievement. Well might the writer to the Hebrews speak of hope as "an anchor for the soul" (Heb. 6:19 NIV).

Hope here is first the hope "of his calling," that is to say, the hope to which God is calling you. The idea of call in Paul's writings is more than that of an offer; it means an *effective* call, a call in which God is acting and in which he will certainly bring his will to pass. The conjunction of the two terms enables Paul to make clear that the Christian hope is solidly grounded, but that it points forward to something not seen as yet.

Paul spells out something of this as he goes on to refer to "the riches of the glory of his inheritance in the saints." Since "riches" points to abundance, the apostle is speaking of no meager or grudging gift. This is to be seen also in the word "glory," which has something of the notion of majesty or sublimity about it. Paul is writing of a wonderful future, but we should notice that he speaks not of "your" or "our" inheritance, but of "his" inheritance. This takes up the thought of verse 14 and is a further reminder that God's people belong to God. It is because they belong to God that they can be so certain of the coming glory. God will not let his people down, nor fail to effect his purpose in them and for them. They are being pointed to a glorious destiny; Paul wants them to be in no doubt but that the God who called them will not fail them in eternity.

With the foregoing, Paul now links "the exceeding greatness of his power towards us who believe" (v. 19). From the hope God has given us the apostle turns to the power behind the promise. He is not referring to God's power over all creation, nor thinking abstractly of the power of divinity. He is referring to the power that God exercises in his relationship to his people. Paul uses four different words to convey the notion of the divine power: "power," "working," "might," and "strength." Of these four words Grimm-Thayer says the first denotes "*power*, natural ability, general and inherent," the second, "*working*, power in exercise, operative power," the third, "*might*, relative and manifested power," and the fourth, "*strength*, power (esp. physical) as an endowment." It may be that this authority makes the divisions between the words too hard and fast, and it would be precarious to insist on all these definitions in detail. But what is clear is that Paul is using a multiplicity of words denoting power to bring out the truth that, however we understand "power," there is mighty power in God, and it is a power directed towards the betterment of believers. As we will see from verse 20, Paul has primarily in mind the power shown in the resurrection, a power greater by far than any power we can know here on earth.

There is no marked break in the construction here, and we could see the sentence carrying on into the following verses. It seems best, however, to see verse 19 as the conclusion of Paul's opening prayer, after which he goes into the subject matter of the letter (though this does not stop him from reverting to prayer later on, 3:14ff.). But we should perhaps notice that it is possible to take verses 19 and 20 closely together. For example, REB and GNB both carry on with the same sentence and with not even a comma to separate the two verses. It seems better—with Bruce, Barth, and others—to see verse 19 as ending a section and verse 20 as leading on to another (so NRSV).

The Exaltation of Christ

If we take "Which he worked out" (v. 20) as the beginning of a new sentence, the word "which" will refer back to the greatness of the divine power of which Paul has just been speaking. He did not say in the previous verses exactly how that power was manifested, but we see here that he had in mind primarily the resurrection of Jesus. "Worked out" is the verb from the same stem as the word translated "working" in verse 19. It shows us God strongly at work in Christ, and the particular work is that he "raised him from the dead." In the New Testament it is usually said that the Father raised Jesus rather than that Jesus rose, but it is not correct to say that this is always the case, for sometimes we read that Jesus "rose from the dead" (e.g., 1 Thess. 4:14). Whichever way the writer puts it, the resurrection is a work of divine power.

When the Father raised Christ it was not so that he might return to the earthly life he had just finished; it was to exalt him to the highest place in heaven. The Father "sat him at his right hand," and both parts of this expression are significant. Sitting is the posture of rest, and the taking up of such a posture is a way of saying that his work of salvation is complete. The older theologians delighted to speak of "the finished work of Christ," and the expression points us to a valuable truth. Nothing needs to be added to that work and indeed nothing can be added to it. And "at the right hand" means being in the place of honor; Paul is saying that there is no place higher than the place of the risen Savior (cf. Ps. 110:1).

We saw in an earlier study that Paul uses the expression "in the heavenlies" five times in this letter, but nowhere else. In this present passage it has much the same meaning as "in heaven" (though elsewhere this may not be the case—for example, when he speaks of war with evil powers "in the heavenlies," 6:12). Here on earth the Savior was slighted by earthly potentates and rejected by those who claimed to be religious leaders and faithful servants of God. But in heaven it is a different story. That is his rightful place, and there the heavenly Father has seen to it that he has the highest place of all.

Just as in verse 19 Paul had piled expression on expression to bring out the thought of the superlative power of God, so now in verse 21 he uses the same technique to underline the superiority of the risen Christ over all the celestial authorities. The word I have translated "sovereignty" has about it the idea of "first." It may be used of the beginning of all things (John 1:1), but also of first in importance (*heavenly rulers* in Rom. 8:38), the meaning it has here. "Authority" may be used of all kinds of authorities: the authority to forgive sins (Matt. 9:6), authority from the high priests (Acts 9:14), the authority of Satan (Acts 26:18), the authority of earthly rulers (Rom. 13:1–3). Yet, whatever authority can be conceived, Christ is far above it. "Might" can denote power, strength, and the like and may be used, for example, of Jesus' "mighty works" (Mark 6:2). It is also used of the power to rule (Rev. 11:17), which, of course, is its significance here. "Lordship," the function of being Lord, underlines the thought of dominion. As with the "power" words of verse 19, we should not try to put too great a difference between these various ways of alluding to sovereignty. Paul is not describing different ways in which Christ may function in heaven, but is saying that whatever sovereignty there may be in the celestial sphere, Christ is above it. He is supreme. Paul will come back to the thought of sovereignties beyond our ken here and now later in this letter (3:10; 6:12).

The "name" in antiquity was much more important than it is with us. We use it simply as a designation, a way of differentiating one person from another (and we may run into difficulties when we meet more than one person with the same name!). But in the world in which Paul lived and moved and had his being, the "name" could be used very differently. For example, we read of a reward given "to him that overcomes," namely "a white stone, and on the stone a new name written which no one knows except him who receives it" (Rev. 2:17). As we use the "name" this is absurd, for what is the use of a name no one knows? But for the writer the name stood for the whole person. The "new name" pointed to a new character that God would give him. And that nobody knew it meant that it was a wonderful secret between the named person and God. In some way the name stood for the whole person.

In this context the "name" will point to its possessor as having authority of some sort. Paul is indicating that his list is not exhaustive and, having specified four kinds of sovereignty, he adds this general expression for everything else that might be included under this heading. Whatever sovereignty Paul's readers might think of, and whatever authority was beyond their thought—whatever authority might exist anywhere—all authority is caught up in Paul's expression and subordinated to the sovereignty of the risen Christ.

Paul adds a little temporal note: "not only in this age but in that which is to come." His readers were familiar with various kinds of authority of greater or less magnitude. Paul wants them to be clear that the authority of the risen Christ is greater than that of any authority they know here and now. But he goes beyond that: Christ will have authority in the age to come. Nobody knew for sure what would happen in that age, but an age that is inaugurated by the doing away of the whole of this present age clearly implies a sovereignty of a greater magnitude than any we can know here and now. Paul subordinates all authority, of whatever sort and from whatever time, to Christ. He is absolutely supreme.

Head over the Church

Paul has been speaking of Christ's supreme authority over all things and all beings, specifically those "in the heavenlies," but now he turns his attention to the Savior's authority over the saved. First he quotes Scripture, "he subjected all things under his feet" (Ps. 8:6), a passage which originally was used of the place in creation that God has assigned to the human race, but which Paul sees as having special relevance to the risen Christ. Believers should be in no doubt as to the place occupied by their Savior. He is absolutely supreme and all things are subject to him.

While Paul is clear as to Christ's supreme authority over all that is, his great concern is with the Savior's relationship to the saved. He is in no doubt but that Christ's supremacy is of special importance to believers and speaks of him as "head over all things to the church." This is a position that the Father "gave him"; we are not to think of it as inherent in the position of Christ. Nor are we to hold that it is something that Christ achieved by his own efforts. We are to see the Father as active in the headship of Christ.

To say that Christ is "head" over the church is probably to say that he is the source of it, and certainly that he is in vital union with it. We should perhaps be on our guard here against letting our understanding of the human body dominate our exegesis. We know that the brain is situated in the head and that this is the part of the body that directs the whole. But the ancients tended to locate thought in the midriff, the diaphragm. They ascribed no directing function to the head. They could speak of the head as the beginning or source. Liddell and Scott cite it, for example, in their Lexicon in a passage that says, "Zeus is the head, Zeus is the middle, in Zeus all is completed." Clearly in this passage "the head" means "the beginning." They see it as used similarly for the source of a river and for the starting point of a period of time. We may well say that Christ is supreme over the church and that he directs it in all its ways, but this is not a truth we derive from the verses that speak of him as "head." The dominant thought here is probably that Christ is in vital contact with the church that he originated.

Not only is Jesus given as head "to the church," but Paul says that he is given as "head over all things." We should probably understand this to point us to the cosmic dimension in Christ's activities. The word "all" occurs four times in verses 22–23, and it seems that Paul is giving emphasis to the thought that the Savior is a *great* Savior, not only bringing good gifts to his own, but exercising authority throughout the whole of creation.

This is Paul's first use of "church" in this letter, a word he employs nine times in Ephesians and sixty-two times in all (which is more than half the total occurrences of the word in the New Testament). He is very interested in the thought that believers belong together. The classic expression of this is Wesley's "The Bible knows nothing of solitary religion." Christianity is not a religion to be practiced only in private. Sometimes Paul uses the term of the local church (1 Cor. 1:2, etc.) and sometimes, as here, of the church as a whole (he always has it in this wider sense in Ephesians). We should not see church membership as akin to belonging to a philosophical school or the like. There is a union between Christ and his people, and they derive their life from him. The head-body relationship signifies an organic union. It can signify other realities, and for a full understanding of the church it would be necessary to follow some of them out, but for this passage it is the organic union that is important. The church is not a group of like-minded people who gather to pursue their mutual interests. It is a group of people united with Christ.

And these people are ordinary people. The church is not made up of spiritual giants, people outstanding in their understanding of the Christian way and heroic in their living of it. In his *Screwtape Letters* C. S. Lewis has the senior devil helping the junior devil in his tempting of humans. He upbraids his assistant because he has let the man he is tempting start going to church, yet he points out that this does not mean that all is lost. Many a soul, the senior devil says, have been snatched back from the brink of salvation. So he counsels him to fasten the patient's mind on the wrong things. Let him notice "the local grocer with rather an oily expression" and other churchgoers who are not outstanding people. "Provided that any of those neighbours sing out of tune, or have boots that squeak, or double chins, or odd clothes, the patient will quite easily believe that their religion must therefore be somehow ridiculous." But Jesus takes people who sing out of tune or have boots that squeak and all the rest of it, and he makes such commonplace people into the saints of God. Church membership does not mean being a person who qualifies for a place in stained glass windows. It means trusting Christ to save us despite our manifold handicaps.

The last part of the passage (v. 23) is very difficult, and some widely different translations have been found. Some translations fit the Greek but are quite out of sympathy with New Testament teaching. Thus, although linguistically it is possible to understand the church as "the fullness" and to see the following verb as passive—with the meaning that Christ is being filled (or fulfilled)—it is impossible to think that this is Paul's meaning. The Good News Bible translates "the completion of him who himself completes all things everywhere," but it is more than doubtful whether Paul is saying that the church is "the completion" of

Christ; it is Christ who completes the church, not the church who completes Christ. Rather, we should understand the words as meaning that the church is filled by Christ in all his fullness (REB, "the fullness of him who is filling the universe in all its parts"; NIV, "the fullness of him who fills everything in every way").

4

Dead in Sin, Alive in Christ

And you did he make alive when you were dead in your tres-
passes and sins, in which you formerly walked according to the
aeon of this world, according to the ruler of the power of the air,
of the spirit which now is at work in the sons of disobedience; in
whom we also all formerly had our manner of life in the lusts of
our flesh, doing the things willed by the flesh and the mind, and
we were children of wrath by nature as also were the rest of the
people; but God, being rich in mercy, on account of his great love
with which he loved us, while we were dead in trespasses, made
us alive with Christ—by grace you have been saved (Eph. 2:1–5).

The grammar here is somewhat difficult, for the words translated "did he make alive" (2:1) do not actually occur until verse 5, so there is no subject and no verb in the opening remarks. To make respectable English we must put some such words in, and these are required by what the apostle says in verse 5. As he begins this section of the letter, Paul is putting emphasis on the plight from which the believers had been delivered before he goes on to the important truth that they had been given life. He is concerned with the Ephesians' sins and their death and pours out his concern with scant regard for grammar.

"And you" is in a prominent place, and to appreciate this we must go back a little. Paul has been speaking of the mighty divine intervention when the Father raised Christ from the dead and exalted him to the highest place. He has gone on to speak of the truth that the Father "gave him to be head over all things to the church" (1:22). Now he goes on to another divine act of raising from the dead and introduces it with "and you." This raising from the dead is the raising of the *spiritually* dead. Paul places some emphasis on the sins that had characterized the Ephesians before they became Christians and on the effect of those sins in making the Ephesians "dead." The apostle has been speaking of the whole church and the wonder of its relationship to Christ. But he is not trying to persuade his readers that they are wonderful people because they are part of a wonderful band with a wonderful relationship to the Son of God. "And you being dead" is a literal rendering of his first four words. They remind the recipients of the letter of the dreadful state in which they had been before they became Christians.

Their plight is death. Paul is not, of course, referring to ultimate spiritual death, but to the low level of life that is all that sinners know now. Every one of us knows a little of this. We can think of occasions when we have realized that we have done some evil deed or failed to do what is right. At such times we have perhaps known gloom and frustration and have been a long way from saying, "This really is living!" And we can also recall occasions when we have done the best we can and perhaps been of service to people in real need. That has enabled us to see a little of a better life. Our feelings are, of course, no reliable guide, and we must bear in mind the fact that there are evil people who exult in their sinfulness. I am saying no more than that sometimes our feelings help us to see that the ways of evil are a living death. Paul is saying that continuance in sin means the absence of real life. The person who continues in the ways of evil is dead. It does not matter that such a person may have striking achievements as the world counts achievements. If there is no awareness of God, no indwelling of God's Holy Spirit, then the person is dead with regard to spiritual life. And Paul is saying that no human achievement can compensate for the lack of response to God.

This is a lesson that our generation surely needs to learn. It is not as though we were lacking in the proof that sin does not bring real life. We are faced with our inability to achieve a just society in which crime does not pay; indeed the growth of crime empires is a frightening feature of modern states. We have no great success in managing our economic problems, so that recessions with the consequent problems of unemployment and related miseries recur. In a world where there are the resources and technical knowledge to feed everyone, many people are dying from starvation. We do not conserve natural resources, and no one knows exactly how much damage we are inflicting on our environment. As family life disintegrates, there are increasing numbers of street kids, young people who refuse to live with their families and therefore have no homes. Racism flourishes in all too many places and there is ongoing class antagonism. In most societies these days the moral values accepted by past generations have been rejected, but no adequate substitutes have replaced them. So violence flourishes—as do dishonesty, self-centeredness, intellectual arrogance, sexual promiscuity, and a host of other ills. Though we speak of creating a just and humane society, we make no progress toward achieving it.

It is a sobering thought that at no time in all its history has the human race been able to establish a society free from evil. Oppression, injustice, suffering, and other cultural ills are endemic. For thinking people, the modern world is a classic illustration of the truth that to live without God is to cut oneself off from the only life worth living. If we live without God, we sentence ourselves to a living death.

"Trespasses and sins" are two ways of characterizing the evils we do. The first word properly denotes "a falling beside," from which it comes to have a meaning like "blunder" or "misdeed." W. Michaelis points out that this differs from the breaking of a commandment, for this word "refers directly to the disruption of man's relation to God through his fault." The second word properly means "missing the mark." C. L. Mitton thinks it can be argued "that the writer by trespasses means doing those things which we ought not to have done, and by sins leaving undone those things which we ought to have done." But E. K. Simpson reverses the distinction. In any case, both agree that distinctions like those they suggest may be reading too much into the word. Certainly when Paul uses them in the plural he does not put a great deal of difference between them, and in passages like this one we should not press any difference we may discern. The two words together underline the seriousness of the plight of sinners. They bring out the truth that sinners have hopelessly disrupted right relationships with God and have failed to achieve the best at which they have aimed. And the end result of this process, the apostle says, is that they are "dead."

The Pattern of This World

Paul is fond of the metaphor of walking, a fondness he shares with John. The verb is found thirty-two times in both the Johannine writings and the Pauline epistles (eight times in Ephesians is the most in any one of Paul's letters). Paul often uses the metaphor to characterize life as a whole. It signifies steady but unspectacular progress, the kind of thing we experience as we move from day to day. Occasionally there will be significant crises in our lives, but for most of us most of the days see little that is spectacular. Paul can use the expression for steady progress in the Christian faith (Eph. 4:1; Rom. 6:4; etc.), but also for lives lived "according to the flesh" (2 Cor. 10:2) or "according to man" (i.e., "like mere man," "like natural man," 1 Cor. 3:3). In other words he can use it for steady progress in the right way or for equally steady regress into the wrong way.

Here it is the wrong way that he has in mind, for he speaks of his readers as formerly walking "according to the aeon of this world" (v. 2). The word I have translated "aeon" more usually in the New Testament means "age" and may refer to a past age, to the present age, or to an age yet to come (when it may signify something like "eternity"). But in Greek writings generally the "age" is sometimes personified and, since the next phrase refers to "the ruler," it seems probable that this is the way we should take this passage. Whether we do so or prefer to see a reference to the passing of time in the age, what is certain is that Paul is drawing attention to the world's habitual ways of thinking and living. We might speak of the "ethos" of this world, the characteristic attitude of the people of this world. Far from "walking" in the ways of this world, or the ways of the Gentiles (4:17), Paul wants believers to walk in the good works God has prepared for them (2:10), to walk worthily of their calling (4:1), to walk "in love" (5:2), as children of light (5:8), as wise people (5:15). For Paul, "walking" is a concept with far-reaching implications.

The Greek word for "world" *(kosmos)* came to have a variety of meanings. Originally it signified an ornament or decoration, a meaning that survives in "adorning" (1 Peter 3:3). It was applied to the whole universe, for the *kosmos* was for the Greeks *the* adornment. Since the world in which we live is the most significant part of the universe for us, it is not surprising that the word came to be used for "the world." From this it was a natural step to use it for the inhabitants of the world, the human race, and then for most people, the race typically. Then, as most people are not spiritually inclined, it came to denote the world in the sense in which we use "worldliness," the whole attitude of the human race in opposition to God. In this sense Grimm-Thayer defines it as "the whole circle of earthly goods, endowments, riches, advantages, pleasures, *etc.*, which, although hollow and frail and fleeting, stir desire, seduce from God and are obstacles to the cause of Christ."

It is in this last sense that Paul employs the word here. Elsewhere he sees the world as under judgment (Rom. 3:6; 1 Cor. 11:32). He sees a pattern in worldliness generally and reminds the Ephesians that before they became Christians they not only were dead in their sinfulness, but their pattern of life was one dictated by the world in which they lived and not by any such motive as a pure desire to do the will of God. Such a desire is never characteristic of the world. Of course, the world is not always sensual and obviously given over to evil. It can be very attractive, and it does have its cerebral and its altruistic aspects, but all it does is concerned with the life here and now. It never gets beyond the prudence of doing the best for life now, in this world. It is this to which Paul is objecting. He points out to the Ephesians that before they became Christians their horizon was bounded by the things of this world. They had no vision of the heavenly realities, no thought of fellowship with the one true God.

And the world continues to pressure the people of God. The world is always harsh to people who do not conform to its ways, whether they are non-Christians or Christians, and it always pressures individuals to do what others are doing. It has well been pointed out that if, for example, we live in a community where racial prejudice is commonly accepted, it is harder to resist it. So it is with other sins and, for that matter, things that are not sins. Although the world constantly pressures us all to conform to its standards, Christians must always be conscious that the world's standards are not those of Christ.

The Ruler of the Power of the Air

In their pre-Christian days, then, the Ephesians had been dead in their sins and, further, preoccupied with the affairs of this world. There is a third way of looking at their situation at that time, and Paul turns now to the role of the evil one, whom he calls first "the ruler of the power of the air." The word "ruler" signifies a person who is "the first" and is used of all kinds of rulers: magistrates, heads of nations, judges, members of the Sanhedrin, those who controlled the synagogue, and others. The word points to the supreme place of the evil one in the control he exercises over spirit beings.

"Power" is concerned with authority and may be used of any one of a variety of authorities. Like "ruler," it is concerned with the one in control and not with a subordinate whose function is to obey someone else. The control of which Paul speaks is exercised in "the air." For the people of that time, the gods were held to live in heaven while humans had their abode on earth. The air in between was regarded as the home of spirits, beings intermediate between the gods and people. Many of the spirits were seen as evil. Paul is using this popular conception to bring out the truth that Satan is served by hosts of spirit beings and that it was these spirits that had been dominant in the lives of the Ephesians before they came to know the freedom that Christ gives.

Most translations further characterize the evil one as "the spirit who now is at work in the sons of disobedience." But this does not appear to be quite what Paul is saying. The word "spirit" is in the genitive case (as is "the power"), not the accusative as is "the ruler." This means that we should not take "the spirit" as in apposition with "the ruler," as though spirit and ruler were two ways of characterizing the same being. Rather, we should understand Paul to be referring to Satan as the ruler first "of the power of the air" and then of the spirit "which now is at work. . . ." Paul appears to mean something like "the spirit of the age," and he is saying that this spirit is used by the evil one to effect his purposes, where the verb can be said to mean "be at work, operate, be effective" (Bauer). There is the thought that the spirit in question is at work with some success. The sphere of his labors is defined as in "the sons of disobedience." This means more than people who happen to be disobedient. C. Hodge points out that just as "'sons of famine' are the famished; the 'sons of Belial' are the worthless; the 'sons of disobedience' are the disobedient." The expression points to people for whom disobedience is the characteristic trait. People who wholeheartedly follow "the spirit of the age" are necessarily disobedient to what they know of the heavenly vision, for the commands of God cannot be reconciled to the impulses of the worldly-minded.

Children of Wrath

Paul now turns from the evil one and his miserable works to the plight of his dupes. Here the apostle does not take up some superior stance but classes himself with his readers. We all, he says, "formerly had our manner of life in the lusts of our flesh." "Formerly" looks back to pre-Christian days—before he came to know the saving power of Christ, Paul was just as much entangled in sin as anyone else. He makes it clear that the Ephesians to whom he writes were in the same condemnation. He is not leaving open the possibility that there might be some people who escaped the bondage of which he writes. We were "all" in this position.

The apostle is not referring to occasional lapses but to a way of life. His verb (which, interestingly, in some contexts has meanings like "turn back," Acts 5:22; 15:16) came to have the meaning "behave," a meaning that is well attested in the papyri. This earlier manner of life, Paul says, was lived "in the lusts of our flesh." The word for "lusts" is neutral in Greek generally, and it simply refers to strong desires, good or bad. We occasionally find the term used in a good sense in the New Testament, as when Paul speaks of his strong desire to see the Thessalonians again (1 Thess. 2:17). But in the overwhelming majority of cases the strong desire is for something evil, as here. Although the expression "the lusts of the flesh" quite often means sexual desire, it can also signify other strong longings.

Paul goes on to bring out his meaning by saying that the lusts of which he was speaking were "willed by [more literally, "doing the wills of"] the flesh and the minds." Paul recognizes that there are some lusts that refer specifically to bodily functions, and it is possible for us to sin by giving way to such lusts. But if we think we are in control of ourselves in respect to lusts like this, that does not mean that we are safe from the temptation to lust. There are lusts of the mind, intellectual lusts, perfectly respectable lusts in the eyes of our community (and perhaps of ourselves, too). The word for "minds" is usually in the singular (this is the only occurrence of the plural in the New Testament). The plural may be meant here in the sense of "thoughts," or the plurality of "minds" may come from the fact that there is a plurality of people, each of whom has a mind. But after the singular "the flesh" we would certainly have expected "the mind." Whatever the reason, Paul is saying that any strong desire that leads us away from God is to be reckoned as a lust; and when we constantly are found "doing the things willed by the flesh and the minds," we are falling below the level that is demanded of us and are sinning against God.

That puts us into the class of "children of wrath" (cf. "sons of disobedience" 2:2; 5:6) and this "by nature" (Paul puts "by nature" between "children" and "of wrath," an unexpected order of words, putting some emphasis on "by nature"). Those who so naturally yield to the lusts of the flesh and of the mind must expect the consequences of what they do. Paul is saying that they necessarily become the objects of the divine wrath.

There is a tendency in recent times to play down the idea of the wrath of God. C. H. Dodd is often quoted for his view that in the teaching of Jesus, "anger as an attitude of God to men disappears, and His love and mercy become all-embracing" and that Paul takes up much the same position. The apostle uses the concept of the wrath of God, according to Dodd, "not to describe the attitude of God to man, but to describe an inevitable process of cause and effect in a moral universe" (*Moffatt New Testament Commentary on Romans*, p. 23). But this is the way a modern scholar understand things, not the way the New Testament writers, and specifically Paul, think of God's attitude to evil. When Paul says that "the wrath of God is revealed from heaven against every impiety and unrighteousness of men" (Rom. 1:18), he is not referring to an impersonal process, but to the well-known divine hostility to every evil (cf. Rom. 3:5; 9:22; etc.). In the present passage he is making it clear that sinners are in a no-good situation. Because, being sinners, they can expect nothing but the divine wrath, Paul can speak of them as "children of wrath." Their sinful lives and the divine wrath go so closely together that the link between them may be likened to the tie that binds a family together.

The reference to the plight of "the rest of the people" is a reminder of the universality of sin. It is not a matter afflicting the occasional person here and there but something in which we are all involved. There is a story told of a small boy who on his first day at school handed a black-edged envelope to his teacher. She opened it and found it contained a card with the printed words: "A Message of Sympathy—to tell you that my thoughts and heartfelt sympathy are with you." The boy's mother had then written, "Thank you and good luck!" No doubt she loved the lad, but she knew what he was capable of. And, somewhat like that mother, but in a far broader sense, Paul is pointing out that wrongdoing is universal in the human race.

A God of Mercy and Love

"But God . . ." writes Paul. The sin of the race, with its bringing down on sinners the inevitable retribution, is not the last word. Paul immediately turns from it to the God in whom he had put his trust. In any situation it is a mistake to overlook the fact of God: the God who is interested in his people and who takes action to meet their needs. Sin is real, and the wrath of God is real. But also real and most important in the situation in which sinners find themselves is the fact that God is "rich in mercy." This is a thought we find repeatedly in the Old Testament Scriptures (e.g., Gen. 19:19; Ps. 23:6), and there is a wonderful passage in which the prophet tells us that God "delights in mercy" (Micah 7:18). Indeed it might be said that mercy is at the heart of Old Testament religion, for the covenant that God made with Israel is fundamental and the covenant is never seen as based on Israel's merit—it springs from God's mercy (cf. Isa. 63:7). The people could plead the mercy of God (Ps. 79:8–9), yet sinners have no claim on God, a thought implied in the very concept of mercy.

With the thought of the divine mercy Paul joins that of the divine love, and he will go on to speak of God's grace and of his kindness. This joining of four wonderful qualities brings home to us something of the kind of God our Father is. We are mistaken if we think of him as a rather stern judge, so that we must be on our guard all the time lest we offend him. He *is* a judge, of course, and that aspect of his being and his work is not overlooked in the New Testament. But the writers of the early Christian books were thrilled with the truth that Christ had brought them to see: that the qualities that mark out our God are qualities like mercy and love and grace and kindness. It is important to recognize this as we seek to serve our God.

Here Paul speaks of God's love as "his great love" and proceeds to emphasize this thought by adding "with which he loved us." As we noticed in the comment on 1:4, love is specially prominent in this letter. It is a central topic for Paul and he reverts to it again and again. For Paul, the sinner who had earlier persecuted the church of God, it was a striking fact that God's love extended to the persecutor, and he keeps coming back to that fundamental fact. So now the apostle links mercy to love. He does not say that God "loves" us (though that is implied) but that he "loved" us. It is possible that, in using the past tense, he is looking back to the event that so signally demonstrates that God loves sinners: the death of Jesus on Calvary's cross. That is at the heart of Paul's understanding of love (Rom. 5:8).

Death and Life—and Grace

Paul has spoken of the plight of sinners and reverts to it now by drawing attention to the end results—"we were dead in trespasses." This is not the death that we all undergo at the end of our mortal life, but a state of estrangement from God, which means the absence of all life that is worth calling life. Once more Paul sees our sins as "trespasses" (as in 1:7; 2:1). Our "stumblings," our "falls beside" the path, are no minor and excusable lapses, but culpable failures to keep to the right way. And the result, Paul says, is that we are "dead." He leaves his readers in no doubt as to the terrible fate of sinners. We should notice further that he does not say "we will die because of trespasses" but "we were dead in trespasses." That unforgiven sinners will in the end suffer unpleasant consequences is not for Paul in doubt, but at this point that is not what he is saying. He is referring to the life that sinners live here and now, a life that comes so far short of the life God intends for his people that it can be called death. It is the absence of *real* life, that eternal life of which the New Testament says so much.

We learn something important about the divine forgiveness from this phrase. Sometimes when people offend us we are tempted to take up the position that we are ready to forgive them when they show that they are fit to be forgiven (as F. R. Barry puts it). We do not retaliate, perhaps, but that is as far as it goes. But God forgives us when we are not fit to be forgiven, when we are "dead in trespasses" and sins.

In that situation the mercy of God prevailed and God "made us alive with Christ." The compound verb "made alive with" is found elsewhere in the New Testament only once (Col. 2:13). The life of the Christian is real vitality, the life that is life indeed. Often it is spoken of as "eternal life," which does not mean only that it takes place after death in this world; it refers to the quality of the life God bestows on those who come to him in faith. It is a gift that believers receive here and now. Though they are assured that they have nothing to fear after death, life with Christ means more than that. Believers have nothing to fear before death either, for they are given a wonderful new life here and now. This life, Paul says, is "with Christ." Some manuscripts read "in Christ" but, while this is true and is affirmed elsewhere, it appears to be not what Paul is saying here. He is making the point that our life is a life we live with the Savior, which of course is a wonderful way of looking at salvation.

Clarence Macartney tells the story of the conversion of Colonel James Gardiner, an officer and the son of an officer. He was a daring soldier, but his many narrow escapes from death never made him think seriously about eternal issues or lead him to abandon the licentious life he espoused. Gardiner was so given over to this way of life that he said that omnipotence itself could not reform him without destroying his body and giving him another. On a certain Sunday evening in 1719 he had an assignation with a married woman at midnight, but as he sat in his rooms waiting for the time to go by he chanced to pick up a book given to him by his mother when he left home, a book called *The Christian Soldier, or Heaven Taken by Storm.* As he read, he says, there was a sudden blaze of light, and when he looked up he saw Christ on his cross surrounded with glory. There came a voice, "Oh, sinner, did I suffer this for thee, and are these the returns?" Philip Doddridge, from whom Macartney took the story, held that this was a dream; Macartney is not sure. But what is certain is that from that time on Gardiner was a different man. Although it took time for him to appreciate the wonder of forgiveness, he cast himself straightaway on the mercy of God and never went back to his old way of life. Not all believers have such a sudden and spectacular conversion, but all have the basic experience of ceasing to rely on their own feeble efforts and coming to accept the mercy and the forgiveness that Christ brings.

Paul now breaks his construction to interpose "by grace you have been saved." As we saw in earlier studies, "grace" is one of the great Christian words and one for which Paul has a special liking. He keeps coming back to the thought that we owe everything to God's free favor, to his grace. Here he puts the result in the terse "you have been saved." The verb is in the perfect tense, which indicates a continuing stake— that salvation took place in the past but it continues on. We should also notice the abrupt change of subject. From verse 2:3 on, Paul has spoken in the first person plural, with a succession of things "we" did or which happened to "us." Now he makes salvation personal to the Ephesians with "you" have been saved. It is important for them to be reminded both of the fact of their salvation and that it is due to the sheer grace of God. Indeed that is a profitable reflection for Christians at any time.

5

Created for Good Works

*And he raised us with him and sat us with him in the heavenlies
in Christ Jesus in order that he might show in the ages that are
coming the exceeding riches of his grace in kindness toward us in
Christ Jesus. For by grace you have been saved through faith, and
this not of yourselves; it is God's gift, not of works, so that no one
may boast. For we are his workmanship created in Christ Jesus
for good works which God prepared beforehand so that we may
walk in them (Eph. 2:6–10).*

A feature of Ephesians is what has been called the "withness" of the letter. In addition to the two Greek prepositions meaning
"with," Paul uses quite a number of compound words where the first
element is "with." He has two of them here: "He with-raised us and with-
sat us . . ." and in the previous verse he has just used the verb "with-
quickened us." It is not easy to bring out the force of this feature of the
epistle, for we do not go in for such compounds in English. But we must
not miss the emphasis Paul is placing on the truths that Christians belong
together and that they belong with Christ. He could have said simply
that God raised believers from the death of sin, but it is important that
he raised them with one another and with Christ. He could have said
that God sat believers in the heavenly places, but it is important for Paul
that God sat them *with* one another and *with* Christ. We who are saved
belong with one another and we belong with Christ.

We should understand being raised in terms of what Paul said a verse
or two back about the plight of sinners: They were dead in their tres-

passes but they have been made alive with Christ (2:5). Part of Paul's understanding of salvation is that where there was death there is now life. Anyone who continually gives way to temptations to do what is wrong and to leave undone what is right is not living at all. Those who do this sort of thing go through the motions of living, but in fact they are dead in all that matters. To be raised from that death demands a miracle, and the miracle occurs every time a sinner comes to trust the Christ who died to put away our sins.

Seated in the Heavenlies

Not only were believers raised with Christ, but they are "seated-with" him. As we saw in the comments on 1:20, sitting is the posture of rest. That Christ ascended into heaven and sat at the right hand of the Father is one of the great teachings of the New Testament. It points to "the finished work of Christ"; nothing needs to be added to his work of bringing salvation to sinners and nothing *can* be added to it. To speak of Christ as seated, which is the posture of rest, brings this out. As this point Paul is adding the thought that the saved enjoy rest with the Savior; they share the blessedness of his finished work. Just as Christ's being seated in the heavenlies signifies that his work of salvation is perfectly completed, so their being "seated-with" him means that for each of them salvation is perfectly completed. The saved rest in the finished work of their Savior. Salvation is perfectly completed for each of us, so rest in that finished work. And we do this "in the heavenlies," which means that we do so in the highest and most delightful region of all.

We saw in the note on 1:3 that the expression "the heavenlies" refers to the realm of spiritual realities. Now we find that this has significance for believers here and now; believers are already "in the heavenlies" in Christ. They already partake to some extent in the life that is proper to heaven, for they are one with their Savior in their new life. Christ died for their sins and then was raised from the dead; Paul is saying now that believers are one with Christ in his dying and in his rising. Elsewhere he says, "one died for all, therefore all died" (2 Cor. 5:14), which surely links the saved with the Savior in his death. Now the apostle says that when Christ rose, believers were "raised-with" him, which just as surely links them with the Savior in his rising. God's saving work in Christ has brought them into a new way of living. Believers have died to a whole way of life and have risen to a new way.

This does not mean that the saved are ethically perfect here and now, but it means that there is nothing lacking to the perfection of the salvation they have received. They are not "half-saved" or the like. As far as the old sinful way before they came to know Christ is concerned, they are dead. They died to that old way when they were united with Christ.

Now that this has happened, Paul is saying, nothing needs to be added to bring them salvation. They have salvation now. He could have gone on to say that all eternity remains for believers to explore the implications of what salvation means, or that even here and now they may make progress in the Christian way so that they become more mature as Christians as the years go by. But at this point the apostle is not concerned with developing such truths. At this point in his argument he is simply making it clear that believers are one with Christ now—"in the heavenlies" they know what it is to die to an old way of life and to rise to a new one in Christ.

There is, of course, a sense in which the heavenly life is not attained until we reach heaven, and until that happens we can do no more than look for it. "If you were raised with Christ," Paul can say, "seek the things above where Christ is, sitting at God's right hand" (Col. 3:1). The full enjoyment of heaven is not here and now, and the prospect of heaven, Paul tells the Colossians, is a spur to godly living. But in another sense what we experience here and now is a true foretaste of what awaits us in heaven, and that is what the apostle is telling the Ephesians. Incidentally, the use of the expression "in the heavenlies" in this context shows plainly that we should not understand it to be another way of saying "in heaven." It can refer to things happening here and now, though, of course, when used in this way the words indicate a heavenly quality in this present life.

Elsewhere Paul says that Christians must not be conformed to this world; they must be transformed by the renewal of their mind (Rom. 12:2). Something like that is what he is saying here. The life of believers is "in the heavenlies" right now. Their citizenship is in heaven (Phil. 3:20). We should be clear that this is essential to an understanding of what being a Christian means. Christians do not simply think of Jesus as a great religious teacher or as a great and good man. Many who have no allegiance to Christ and who would not number themselves among his followers can hold such views. They see him as an admirable person but no more. But Paul is speaking of Christ as one who has brought salvation to sinners and who has even more for the saved when they pass from this life.

As we have seen, the apostle has emphasized the thought of community by using verbs compounded with the preposition "with." Interestingly, he proceeds to add, "in Christ Jesus." This is perhaps a remarkable piece of physiology, but the important point for us is that the apostle adds to his previous teaching the thought of union with Christ who is the head. From one point of view we have fellowship with him; from another we are united to him. Both truths are important.

The Riches of God's Grace

Paul next introduces the note of purpose (v. 7). God intended not only that believers should experience his wonderful grace, but that this grace should be made manifest. Although the apostle does not say to whom it should be shown, he makes it clear that this was to be done in such a way that it would be visible. But though he does not say to whom it would be shown, he indicates something of the permanence of the display by adding "in the ages that are coming." Paul is interested in "the ages," and he uses the word for "age" thirty-eight times in all. He can speak of this present age as an age dominated by the evil one, but he can also look beyond this to the time when God will intervene and bring to an end the world as we know it and usher in the final state of affairs.

Some commentators hold that "the ages that are coming" are the ages in the history of the world (which may be supported by the use of the present tense), while others see a reference to the ages after the second advent of Christ. It is probably not wise to try to be too precise in this matter, when Paul has not chosen to delimit the expression. He may well include both. At this point he is not defining the time of which he writes with precision but speaking generally of all the ages yet to come (though, of course, the ages of eternity will be much more significant than those now, on this earth). Paul uses a compound verb, "come upon" (which I have translated as "are coming"), and he may be intending his readers to think of the ages as "coming upon them," not simply of the passage of time.

And in these ages believers will be demonstrating "the exceeding riches of his grace in kindness." The verb I have translated as "exceeding" was used in 1:19 of "the exceeding greatness of his power," and it will be used again of the greatness of the love of Christ "exceeding knowledge" (3:19). Now Paul uses it to bring out the truth that the riches of God's grace are boundless. God's grace is not rationed out, so to speak, so that when we have received a certain amount it is cut off. Nor can we say that if we slip into sin it is cut off. God's grace is exceedingly great, and it is lavished on sinful and imperfect people. The apostle does not want his readers to miss this point. No matter how great our sin, God's grace is more than sufficient to meet our need.

E. K. Simpson makes another important point when he says succinctly, "Grace is glory in the bud." Grace is wonderful now, but it points forward to the glory of heaven that we will experience in due course. Paul adds that this grace is exercised "in kindness." Paul is not drawing a picture of a stern and unyielding God who is determined to punish all sorts of people. He is a God of grace, a God of mercy, and here a God of kindness: "kindness toward us in Christ Jesus." Paul does not think of the divine kindness as confined to the denizens of heaven; it overflows to people here on earth. And that it is exercised "in Christ Jesus" turns our thoughts to the saving work that Christ accomplished.

Saved by Grace

Next, in verse 8, Paul repeats from verse 5 the truth that "by grace you have been saved." This time "grace" has the definite article: "the grace," the grace just mentioned, the well-known grace of God. The apostle emphasizes the fact that salvation is a gift; it does not come to us through any effort of our own. He highlights this by piling one expression on another, every one of which brings out the truth that we do nothing to deserve salvation. First, salvation is "by grace"; it is only because God is a God of grace that we know this experience. Then believers are "saved," where the passive points to something done for them; it is not "you save yourselves." Further, it is "through faith," a gift made to those who trust God. Explicitly, "this" is "not of yourselves"; nothing that sinners do brings their salvation (some commentators take "this" to refer to "grace" or to "faith," but the grammar does not favor these views since both "grace" and "faith" are feminine forms, while "this" is neuter. Paul is pointing to the whole process as the gift of God). Then salvation is "God's gift," not originating in anyone else and not obtained other than as a gift. This is underlined with "not of works" (v. 9); we may engage in good works of many kinds, but none of them merits salvation. And "no one may boast"; the fact that salvation is a free gift takes away all opportunity for the saved to say, "I did it myself. What a good person am I!" We are "his workmanship" (v. 10); again there is the thought that it is God who made the saved what they are. "Created" brings out yet again the thought of the divine activity. Finally, even when the saved manage to perform good works of any sort, those good works are works that "God prepared beforehand."

This emphasis on salvation as a free gift of divine grace cuts clean across the natural human tendency to think of salvation (however that be understood) as due to human effort. When we realize that some people will be saved and some not, it is the most natural thing in the world to see the distinction as one made on account of our good deeds. We see this in all sorts of religions. The primitive savage, worried by disaster of some sort, sees the situation as demanding that he *do* something. So he offers a choice sacrifice and trusts that now his god will be appeased and become favorably inclined. But this approach is not confined to primitive people. It makes its appearance even in the most sophisticated of religions.

In Paul's time there were religions we know as the "mystery religions." Those admitted to them were bound by oath not to reveal the mysteries, and so well were the oaths kept that to this day we cannot be sure of all that was done. We can say, however, that candidates for admission were put through a horrifying initiation process and brought out of this into an experience of peace. But to get this peace they had to *do* something—go through the prescribed process. A little later, Gnosticism appeared. Although some scholars think this was as early as New Testament times, this does not appear to be well grounded. Whenever it appeared, Gnosticism put a strong emphasis on knowledge (the term "Gnosticism" derives from the Greek word *gnosis*, "knowledge"). For salvation it was necessary to "know." There were several Gnostic systems, but they all put knowledge as the route that leads to salvation.

Indeed in all religions many people, perhaps most, see salvation, with whatever differences salvation is understood, as the result of human endeavor. For example, popular Judaism in Paul's day, while it paid due deference to God's choice of his "chosen people," in practice often put emphasis on the keeping of the law. Jesus' parable of the Pharisee and the tax collector depicts the Pharisee as emphasizing his superiority to other people on the grounds of what he did not do and then of what he did do. This is a picture of religious man as he all too often is. The Muslim, while he insists that Allah is the All-Merciful, in practice insists that for salvation it is necessary to do certain things. He must say the simple creed, "There is no God but God and Mohammed is the prophet of God," say prayers, abstain from certain foods and drinks, and if possible, make the pilgrimage to Mecca. It is all a question of what one *does*.

Buddhism is a very different religion; it sees heaven in terms, not of houris and sensual delights, but of the bliss of nothingness. But to attain this bliss it is necessary that the Buddhist come in the right way. He must endeavor to do nothing, think nothing, and even *be* nothing. And when he succeeds he has attained the blissful state of nirvana, "nothingness."

We do not need to go far afield to find this emphasis on what the individual worshiper *does*. For example, who has not met the Roman Catholic who believes that faithful attendance at Mass is the way to salvation? Or the Protestant who holds that if you live a good life you will go to heaven when you die? Even those modern skeptics who reject the religion of their fathers and profess atheism or agnosticism often give themselves over to good causes of one kind or another and find their "salvation" in so doing. Life, for them, would be a poor affair if it were spent wholly in selfish pursuits.

Even when we are trying to expound the teaching of Scripture we may find the temptation to call upon "salvation by works." I recall hearing a powerful sermon from an evangelical as Good Friday approached. He exulted in the cross and went into detail as he described what happened to Jesus at that time. After speaking of the sufferings that Jesus endured and the humiliations heaped upon him, he pointed out that all this has an important lesson for us. "All this Jesus bore for you," he said. "Therefore, what should you do for him?"

Now I do not deny that his question is an important one nor that we should all ask it of ourselves. But it is not this that Paul had in mind when he spoke of the preaching of the cross as foolishness (1 Cor. 1:18, 21). The apostle was talking about the cross as the means of paying the price for our sins; he was referring to the salvation that Christ makes available for sinners by dying in their stead. He was talking about salvation by grace. Many people shy away from such a message to one that makes more "sense" to them, a message that we can and must follow the example of the Christ. There is a certain element of truth in this, for the saved must live saved lives. But none of this alters the fact that Paul was talking about salvation by grace. He was not saying that we must bravely do the best we can (true though that is); he was saying that Christ died to bring us salvation as God's free gift.

It can scarcely be denied that in the modern church we often encounter the idea that salvation depends on what we do. It may or may not be articulated, but for many who profess to be Christians what matters is the ceaseless round of church activities. Being a Christian for them means attending church services and playing a full part in church organizations. It means running the youth club or bringing outsiders into the fellowship. Or perhaps it means being sacramentalists; the prime duty then is to partake of the blessed sacrament, and those who follow this way look to find salvation because of their merit in diligent preparation for it and faithful reception. Others are convinced that the church has misunderstood the thrust of the gospel, so they opt for the "social gospel" or "religionless Christianity" or "liberation theology"—the list of things the church has failed to do and which these enthusiasts now commend is endless. Now I am not denying that there is much that is useful in many such activities. I am denying that the center of Christianity is anywhere else than in the cross of Jesus, where the love of God brought free salvation to sinners.

Wherever we look we find an emphasis on what we do. For the whole human race it seems that this is the way we enter salvation, however we understand that term (and indeed whether we use it or not). So Paul's emphasis on salvation as God's free gift is unusual as well as important. He is not stating a truism but drawing attention to the Christian way as one that is completely new and so revolutionary that to this day many people find difficulty in understanding it. Paradoxically, many very humble and insignificant people enter readily into an understanding of this profound truth. They cast themselves unreservedly on the grace of God and come to know the peace that passes understanding where more sophisticated people raise problems. And reject grace.

The Teaching of Jesus

Although this book is about the teaching of Paul in one letter, it is worth turning aside for a moment to notice that what the apostle is emphasizing in this place is also emphasized in the teaching of Jesus. Grace features in a number of parables; for example, the Prodigal Son (Luke 15:11–32). That story brings before us a young man who forsook family ties, collected all his inheritance money, and in a foreign land wasted the lot in riotous living. Reduced to utter poverty he returned home, hoping for nothing more than employment as a servant. But he was received rapturously and given the warmest of welcomes.

So with the story of the Pharisee and the tax collector (Luke 18:9–14). Both went to the temple to pray. The Pharisee preened himself in the presence of God. He drew attention to evils from which he abstained and to good works which he practiced. He came short of congratulating God on the excellence of his servant, but not by much. The tax collector had no good works to commend him, but he flung himself on the divine compassion, praying, "God, be merciful to me, the sinner." Jesus said, "I tell you, this man went down to his house justified rather than the other, for everyone that exalts himself will be humbled and he that humbles himself will be exalted" (Luke 18:14).

Another parable that stresses the thought of grace is that of the laborers in the vineyard (Matt. 20:1–16). Jesus spoke of the owner of a vineyard who hired laborers to work for him for a denarius a day (the normal rate of pay). Later he hired others, even as late as an hour before time for the end of the day's work, but without specifying how much he would pay them. At day's end he paid these latecomers a denarius each, which led those who had toiled all day to expect that they would get more. They did not. Not unnaturally they complained, but the employer pointed out that he had done them no wrong; they had received the wage they had agreed on. If he chose to give others the same amount, he was free to do so.

It has been pointed out that it would have been quite possible for the owner of the vineyard to pay each of the laborers exactly the amount that his labor entitled him to. There was a little coin, the pondion, that was worth one-twelfth of a denarius. The man could have paid those who worked for one hour one pondion, those who worked three hours three pondia, and so on. But, as T. W. Manson points out, "There is no such thing as a twelfth part of the love of God." What Jesus is saying is that the whole of the mighty love of God is poured out on undeserving sinners. We receive from him not according to our merits, but according to his wonderful love and grace.

God's Workmanship

Salvation, then, does not come from anything we do: it is "not of yourselves." Paul goes on to insist that it is "God's gift" and adds once more that it is "not of works." It is fundamental to the way the New Testament writers see the salvation of sinners that they do not bring this blessed state about by their own endeavors. Paul goes on to give some part of the purpose of this: "so that no one may boast." Boasting may puff us up but it does not build us up (cf. "Knowledge puffs up, but love builds up," 1 Cor. 8:1 NIV). Simpson cites W. Gurnall for a timely reminder of one aspect of living out the Christian life: the gospel "cuts the very comb of pride. When thou hast thy best suit on, Christian, remember who paid for it!"

"We are his workmanship" (2:10) points us to the truth that, just as we can claim no merit for the putting away of our sins, so we can claim none for our works of Christian service. In the Greek "his" is the first word in the sentence; this puts some emphasis on the fact that what we are is due to what God has done in us. It is *his* workmanship that results in our new creation to do good works. Left to ourselves we would live for ourselves, but those who are saved enter a new life. They can be said to be born again (John 3), to live by faith (Gal. 2:20), to have all things made new (2 Cor. 5:17), and there are other ways of bringing out the truth that the Christian life is distinctively new. Here the thought is that God has thoroughly remade us; we are the result of his creating activity. The Greek word for workmanship is *poiema*, from which we get our word "poem." Is this not a hint at the beauty of the life God brings us? The word occurs elsewhere in the New Testament only in Romans 1:20, where again it refers to God's works of creation. A number of commentators think that the word is appropriate for a work of art and see a reference to God's masterpiece. The Jerusalem Bible translates, "We are God's work of art. . . ."

To put the same thing in another way, we are "created," the word normally used for God's creating all things (Matt. 19:4; Mark 13:19; etc.). What God has done in the saved is more than a little moral revolution. As Paul puts it elsewhere, "If anyone is in Christ, there is a new creation; the old things have passed away, look they have become new!" (2 Cor.

5:17). God has done something astonishingly new in believers: he has created in them a new life. This life is "in Christ Jesus"—the believer is not an independent entity, living to himself or herself and looking primarily for personal gain or personal pleasure.

The object of the new creation is "good works," and believers should never lose sight of that. There is evil in plenty in this work, but it is not meant that Christ's people should add to it. Rather, they must resist evil and overcome it. They are delivered from bondage to evil, and the new creation that God has created in them is so that they may do good. Paul does not say in what the good works consist, but there is plenty of scope for them in a world like this. And that God has them "prepared beforehand" indicates that his forethought extends to the life of every believer. "So that we may walk in them" is another use of the verb "walk" to indicate a continuing practice. Believers are to be consistent in living their new lives in accordance with the divine direction.

It is important that we take notice of this. The Bible teaches plainly that there is nothing we can do to merit our salvation. We must rely wholly on what Christ has done for us. It is easy to go on from there to reason, "Then it does not matter how we live! Christ will save us from the consequences of any evil we commit." But this is fallacious reasoning. The living of good lives is not the cause of our salvation, but it is certainly the result. When we put our trust in Christ, as Paul has been saying throughout this section, we are re-created. We enter new life, where we do the good works God has prepared for us to do.

6

Peace, Perfect Peace

Therefore remember that formerly you, the Gentiles in the flesh, who are called "uncircumcision" by that which is called "circumcision" in the flesh made with hands, that you were at that time without Christ, alienated from the citizenship of Israel and strangers from the covenants of the promise, not having hope and without God in the world. But now in Christ Jesus you who formerly were far off have been made near in the blood of Christ (Eph. 2:11–13).

Paul next proceeds to draw some conclusions. His "therefore" introduces a consequence of what has just been said; he is not starting off on a completely new line of instruction, but indicating that what follows is a deduction from what he has just said. "Formerly" is a general term, but in this place it clearly points back to the days before his readers had been converted to Christianity. Since his correspondents have been saved by grace and since that involves being God's workmanship—made for good works—a conclusion may be drawn.

What is unexpected is the nature of that conclusion, and it is introduced by a call to remember their former state as "the Gentiles in the flesh." Although "the flesh" is often used in a derogatory fashion for what is opposed to the Spirit of God or even to the spirit of man, here it may signify no more than that circumcision is concerned with the physical body. All the more is this the case in that Paul goes on to speak of the readers as called "uncircumcision" by what "is called 'circumcision.'" There is a certain emphasis on name-calling, though with the implication that this sort of thing is done away in Christ. Divisions that matter so much to people entrenched in their bitterly contested religious or secular positions mean nothing when those people come to Christ.

The division between Jews and Gentiles was one of the most bitter divisions in the ancient world. The Jews were very proud of their status as the people of God, the one nation in covenant relationship with the only God there is. So they often treated people of other nations with disdain. And this, of course, provoked a reaction from those they despised. Why should Jews put on airs and claim superiority to everyone else? All too often the result was ill feeling between the circumcised Jews and the uncircumcised Gentiles.

Paul recognizes this ill feeling, but his references to "in the flesh" and "made with hands" may be part of his way of making the point that the division that meant so much to many people of his day did not matter at all in the sight of God. Circumcision, which was so highly esteemed by Jewish controversialists, was in fact a work done "in the flesh." Whatever spiritual meaning might be seen in circumcision when rightly performed in accordance with the divine command, in itself it was a fleshly act. Both those who accepted it and those who did not should bear this in mind. Elsewhere Paul can refer to the unimportance of physical circumcision in comparison with the "circumcision not made with hands," which Jews and Gentiles share alike (Col. 2:11). That is not his point here, but it may well have been in the back of his mind as he reminds his readers of a very bitter division in their past.

The Jews then were very strict in their carrying out of the regulations that their male children be circumcised and very proud of their status as "the circumcised." To speak of Gentiles as "uncircumcised" was to draw attention to the fact that they lacked the mark of membership in the people of God, the people in covenant relationship with God. Paul saw the atonement God has brought about in Christ as of central importance, and the corollary of this was that circumcision mattered very little. He makes his position clear when writing to the Galatians: "In Christ Jesus neither circumcision nor uncircumcision avails anything, but faith working through love" (Gal. 5:6). "Circumcision is nothing," he tells the Corinthians, "and uncircumcision is nothing, but the keeping of God's commandments" (1 Cor. 7:19). God, he says, "will justify the circumcision out of faith and the uncircumcision through faith" (Rom. 3:30). Since God saves people in Christ and since all that people need do is believe, there is no point in putting emphasis on such an external rite as circumcision. But that does not alter the fact that in pre-Christian days there had been a very real division; the Gentiles, lacking the mark of the covenant, had been "aliens" as far as the people of God were concerned.

Without Christ

Paul is not unmindful of the contention between the circumcised and the uncircumcised, but what matters to him is not that in those early days the Ephesians had been without circumcision, but that they had been "without Christ" (2:12). For Paul, the very central truth was that Christ is the Savior. By his death on the cross, Christ brought salvation unto all who believed. By definition, those Jews who simply viewed themselves as "the circumcised ones" and had no interest in what God had done in Jesus were outside salvation. So were Gentiles who had never believed in Jesus. They did not know the saving work of Christ, and being "without Christ" they were in dire peril.

Paul proceeds to spell out that peril. His Gentile readers had been "alienated from the citizenship of Israel"; they had had no part with the people of God. The verb "alienated" indicates that they were with the enemies of God's people rather than allied to that people. There was a gulf between the circumcised and those outside of Israel.

The apostle goes on to speak of "the citizenship" of Israel. The word is used elsewhere in the New Testament only in Acts 22:28, where it refers to Roman citizenship. It can also signify "government" or be used for the constitution of a state. Here it is often rendered "commonwealth," but this translation overlooks the fact that there were some Gentiles who lived in the land of Israel but did not belong to the people of God, and that there were Jews outside the land who were governed by other people but were genuine members of the people of God. The Good News Bible renders "did not belong to God's chosen people." Jews everywhere held firmly that they and they alone had membership in the people of God. Membership in that people did not depend on the place where they lived. Here Paul is clearly using the expression figuratively for the privileged position of Israel in the divine plan. This gave the Jews a profound sense of their unique place, and it is not surprising that they saw themselves as set apart for God in a way that no other nation was.

With that, Paul links "strangers from the covenants of the promise." In the Old Testament a number of covenants between God and people are mentioned, such as his covenant with Noah (Gen. 9:8–17; Paul may not have included this covenant in his expression, for it was a covenant with all people, not just the Jews) and that with Abraham (Gen. 17:2–21; cf. Lev. 26:42). But specially important was his covenant with the people of Israel, a covenant made with blood (Exod. 24:8). This covenant solemnly set the nation apart to be God's people in a way that other people were not, and Jews looked back to this covenant as profoundly important. There were also other covenants recorded in the Old Testament, and the effect of them all is to bind Israel to God with strong ties.

61

Such covenants did not include people like the Ephesians, and Paul says that they were "strangers" to the covenants.

Though the word "covenants" is plural and refers to a multiplicity of occasions when God entered into agreements with his people, the word "promise" is singular and is preceded by the article: "*the* promise." It would of course have been possible to use the plural, for all God's covenants are "covenants of promise," and promises were an integral part of covenants like those God made with Israel. Covenants that men made with other men were usually different. They were agreements of the "You do this for me and I will do that for you" variety. But there is nothing people can do that will add to the possessions of the great God, nor is there any service they can render that will improve things for God. Any covenant with God must necessarily be one-sided; such covenants mean that God promises to do such and such things for his people. They can, it is true, pledge themselves to be faithful in serving him (e.g., Exod. 24:3), but even if they carry out their pledge fully they confer no benefit on God. The promises of God are what distinguish God's covenants from all other covenants.

But here the singular is significant. While a multitude of divine promises find expression in the various covenants, what really mattered was the one great promise that underlay them all: God's promise to send his Messiah (Gen. 12:2–3; 13:14–15; Dan. 9:25, 27; etc.). It is *the* promise that underlay the covenants and made them so significant.

People who have no part in the covenants are characterized as without hope and without God. As we saw in the notes on 1:18, hope is a very important part of the Christian life as Paul understands it. People in the lower classes in the first-century Roman Empire had little to hope for. Their present lot was circumscribed by the harsh conditions under which they lived, and they usually saw no prospect of a bettering of that lot. Indeed for people at large there was little hope. There was no widespread concept of a beautiful life beyond the grave, so there was little to look forward to in some future life. And the Greek cyclical view of history meant that the race as a whole was going nowhere. Where is there room for hope in such a philosophy? J. G. Strelan cites Sophocles, who put "the Gentile view succinctly when he said that the best thing to happen to a man is never to be born; the next best thing is to be born and to die immediately."

For Christians, it was important that hope sustained them despite the harsh conditions in which they lived. They might not have much in the way of amenities in this life, but they had a living hope. The God whom Paul preached was a God of love, one who had provided for the salvation of the lowliest of his people by sending his Son to die for them on the cross. Believers could expect divine intervention as God worked out his purposes in the affairs of communities. And, if the worse came to the worst and there were no spectacular interventions on behalf of any individual member of the church, there was still the hope of everlasting life. They could look forward to deliverance from the hardships of this life in due course, in the certainty that they would live forevermore in the blessing of their heavenly Father. Occasionally in the Old Testament we come across the thought that the Gentiles have hope in the one God (e.g., Isa. 11:10). Rightly read, the Scriptures that the Jews valued so highly pointed to God's provision for the Gentiles.

C. L. Mitton reminds us that there are those without hope in the modern world: "In our own time Bertrand Russell spoke of himself similarly as without hope and without God, and it was in recognition of this that he wrote: 'Only on the firm foundation of unyielding despair can the soul's habitation henceforth be safely built.'" Mitton adds, "Some may be able to produce such stoic courage, but all too often human life begins to go to pieces in so bleak a world." It is still the case that to be without hope in a world like this is the ultimate disaster.

Besides being without hope, these Gentiles had been "without God in the world." They may have worshiped deities of some sort but these were not really gods. Unlike Israel, the Gentiles had no knowledge of the one true God and thus their situation was a hopeless one. This is the only occurrence of the word *atheos* in the New Testament. Abbott points out that in Greek generally the term may mean "atheist," or "impious," or "godless," or "without God's help." Here it will signify "not knowing God." Whatever deities the Greeks may have worshiped, they had no knowledge of the one true God and thus were in very deed "without God in the world."

"But now" (2:13) introduces a new state of affairs and one in marked contrast to the earlier state. At that earlier time they had lacked hope and the knowledge of God; they had been far off from the place of blessing. But now things are different. They have responded to the gospel and this has changed everything. "In Christ Jesus" has replaced "without Christ." This familiar Pauline expression for being a true Christian means that everything has been changed. Specifically, their previous state of alienation has been cancelled. Paul does not explain what he means by "far off" or "made near," but his words may be a reminiscence of Isaiah 57:19 (which speaks of "Peace, peace, to those far and near"); it is clear that he is speaking of the relationship of his Gentile converts to God. In their earlier state they had been a long way from God. Now they "have been made near." Paul does not say they have come near or the like; the passive points to something done for them, not to any achievement of their own. "In the blood of Christ" brings out once more the centrality of the atoning work of Christ. It was because Christ died for them that they have had their alienation ended and have been brought near to God.

Christ Is Our Peace

For he is our peace who made both one and in his flesh destroyed the party-wall that separates, the enmity, having nullified the law of commandments in ordinances, so that he might make the two in him to be one new man, making peace, and so that he might reconcile the two to God in one body through the cross, having slain the enmity in it. And he came and preached peace to you who were far off and peace to them who were near, because through him we both have introduction to the Father in one Spirit (Eph. 2:14–18).

In a magnificent turn of phrase Paul says not simply that Christ brings peace, but that he *is* our peace. This fulfills a prophecy in which Micah says of the Messiah, "He will be their peace" (Micah 5:5). Barth draws attention to Paul's emphatic pronoun and translates, "He is in person the peace between us." Certainly there is an emphasis on what Christ himself has done. We should perhaps be on our guard here, for peace may be understood in more ways than one. The Greeks tended to see peace as negative; it was the absence of war. When a given nation found itself without a war on its hands, it was at peace. And this is the way we still tend to see it, for our education has taken this concept from the Greek classics and it never occurs to us that peace means anything else.

But Paul and most of the other New Testament writers were Hebrews, and for them "peace" was *shalom*, a word for which a standard Hebrew lexicon gives the meanings, "completeness, soundness, welfare, peace." We find the notion of completeness in the passage in which Jeremiah speaks of Judah as "wholly carried into exile" (Jer. 13:19); we would not use the term "peace" ("peace carried into exile"?) in such a connection. Nor would we use it as the psalmist does in saying "there is no peace in my bones" (Ps. 38:3), or when Joseph asked his brothers about their "welfare" (Gen. 43:27). When Paul used the word "peace," then, he was using a term that he and his whole nation understood to have a rich and full meaning. Where the Greeks saw peace as the absence of warfare and strife, the Hebrews did not see it as the absence of anything. It was the presence of something, something wonderful. It conveyed the notions of completeness, soundness, and the like, the well-rounded life. It pointed to the blessing of God poured out on his people.

To say, then, that Christ "is our peace" does not mean simply that Christ has delivered us from warfare and strife. It means that he has enriched our lives by bringing us completeness, well-roundedness, abundant blessing. And when Paul says that he *is* our peace, this identifies Christ with the peace more clearly than if he had said simply that Christ brings peace. We should not miss the point that Paul sees the Messiah (not the Father) as effecting reconciliation. His work is described both positively, he "made both one," and negatively, "destroyed the party-wall that separates." Chrysostom is impressed with the making of both one, which he sees as "not by knitting us to them, but by knitting both them and us into one." He illustrates the process by thinking of two statues, one of silver and the other of lead. But when they are melted down "the two shall come out gold." Clearly, though Chrysostom is giving his imagination full reign, he is making a valid point. The end result is infinitely more precious than the contribution either of the two groups brings to it.

The "party-wall" denotes a wall within a house, a partition, whereas "that separates" is really another noun, which seems to have the notion of protection rather than simply separation. Barth sees the combination as pointing to some such thing as "a ghetto wall, the Iron Curtain, The Berlin Wall, a racial barrier, or a railroad track that separates the right from the wrong side of the city." The passing of time has made some of Barth's illustrations out of date, but we get the general idea clearly enough. There had been a strong and bitter division between Jews and Gentiles, a division that Christ had overcome in his death, thus making peace.

It is possible that Paul has in mind the wall in the temple at Jerusalem that marked the limits to which Gentiles could go. An inscription carved in the wall read: "Let no foreigner enter within the screen and enclosure surrounding the sanctuary. Whosoever is taken so doing will be the cause that death overtaketh him" (cited from Deissmann, *Light from the Ancient East,* [London: Hodder and Stoughton, 1927], p. 80). The regulation seems to have been strictly enforced, and indeed Paul in due course was arrested and eventually taken into custody by the Romans when the Jerusalem mob thought he had infringed it (Acts 21:28ff.).

The unity that binds believers matters a good deal to Paul, as we see from his letters as a whole. Wherever he encountered disunity he denounced it and urged believers to come to agreement. It is part of the gospel as he understood it. Since we owe our whole salvation to Christ it ill becomes us to assert ourselves against our fellow believers, who in any case are in the same position as we are. That believers are "all one in Christ Jesus" (Gal. 3:28) is important for Paul, and he brings this out here as part of the way he understands the Christian peace.

He goes on to say that Christ "destroyed the party-wall that separates," and since he says that Christ did this "in his flesh," he is surely looking again at the atoning work our Lord accomplished at Calvary. Christ, Paul says, "destroyed [the verb means "loosed," but "loosing" a wall means loosening the bonds that keep its constituent parts together and thus destroying it] the party-wall that separates." The word for "party-wall" is a rare one; it is not found elsewhere in the New Testament and does not appear to be attested in pre-Christian Greek. The equivalent masculine form is found in one inscription (Paul's word is neuter), while in a fragment of Eratosthenes the word is used figuratively but not of an actual wall. Clearly the word was not one in common use. As we noted above, it denotes a partition, an inner wall.

Paul is emphasizing the fact that prior to the saving work of Christ there had been a division between Jews and Gentiles, a strong division that effectively prevented friendship or fellowship between them. They were separated by a wall neither of them could break down. But now Christ has destroyed the wall. This, of course, was not in the sense that the physical barrier in the temple was removed. That did not take place until the destruction of Jerusalem in A.D. 70. But now that Christ has died to put away our sins and to make peace between God and sinners, there is no barrier between Jews and Gentiles. In the most important sense the wall has gone. Together in Christ, Jews and Gentiles have free access to the heavenly Father.

Then Paul's imagery changes, and what separates Jew and Gentile is now described as "the enmity." It is, of course, possible for people to agree to differ and for them both to see the differences as comparatively minor, so that there is goodwill on both sides of a divide. But this was not the case with the Jew-Gentile divide. The Jews saw themselves as the people of God and all Gentiles as the objects of the divine wrath; the Gentiles saw the Jews as arrogantly claiming a monopoly of the divine blessing. There was no meeting of minds; instead, there was mutual contempt. Well might Paul speak of "the enmity," since there was strong hostility on both sides.

The Commandments

For the Jews, the commandments of God were very important. They prided themselves on the fact that God had made his commandments known to them, and they saw this as a wonderful treasure that God had entrusted to his people. The commandments were meant to be obeyed and they formed a "law." When Paul speaks of "the law of commandments" (2:15), he is referring to the law that God had given his people Israel, a law that found expression in a series of commandments (the Jews counted 613 commandments in The Law, the books Genesis through Deuteronomy). While it was possible to regard the law as the way to salvation and make keeping the commandments the way to life, it seems that many Jews simply delighted in the law, as a mark of God's favor to them. Of all the nations of the world it was this nation only to which God had entrusted the law!

But Paul seems to have in mind at this point those Jews who thought of the commandments as the way to salvation. Christ "nullified the law of commandments." Paul made it clear that people are not saved by the keeping of commandments (elsewhere he points out that no one keeps all God's commandments). When Christ died to put away our sins, he "nullified the law of commandments in ordinances." In the light of the cross no one could say that salvation comes from what we do: the cross has "nullified" the lawkeeping way. Law as a way of salvation has been totally destroyed. The word translated "ordinances" is used of decrees of the Romans (Luke 2:1) and of the apostles (Acts 16:4). It refers to any binding decree and comes in fittingly at this point.

Reconciliation

Paul brings out the aim of all this by speaking of it as reconciliation. He speaks first of the unity that binds all believers: Jews and Gentiles in Christ are made to be "one new man." This expression emphasizes the closeness of the unity that binds believers together. They may have many differences, as Jews and Gentiles did. But the unity transcends all such differences; in the light of the unity the differences may be set aside. So Paul says that Christ makes the two into "one new man." This is a strong expression for the doing away of enmity. If instead of two people at odds with one another we have "one new man," then obviously all hostility has gone. This is indeed "making peace."

The purpose of this is "that he might reconcile the two to God" (2:16). Reconciliation is a way of looking at what was done on Calvary that evidently appealed to Paul, for he uses the concept a number of times. It presupposes a state of hostility. When there is such a state of enmity it can be done away only if the root cause of the hostility is dealt with. Failing that, there may be an uneasy state of truce, but there cannot be real peace. Paul sees the cause of the enmity between God and sinners as sin. It is sin that disrupts fellowship between God and those he has created, and Scripture makes it plain that sinners face the wrath of God. We must not think that God is no more than mildly displeased when we do wrong. He is angry. And if we are not to face some very unpleasant consequences, something has to be done about our wrongdoing.

And something *has* been done. The Son of God came to this earth and lived a perfect life (showing us how we ought to live). Then he died on Calvary's cross. Paul can say that Christ "died for our sins according to the Scriptures" (1 Cor. 15:3), or that Christ "died for ungodly people" (Rom. 5:6), or that God shows his love in that "while we were still sinners, Christ died for us" (Rom. 5:8). Throughout the New Testament it is clear that the death of Jesus is regarded as a death for sinners and a death that put away sin. This means that it removed the cause of the divine enmity; in other words it effected reconciliation: Christ "having slain the enmity in it."

Paul says that the death on the cross was "so that he might reconcile the two to God in one body through the cross." Here "the two" are, of course Jew and Gentile, and that they are now "in one body" indicates the perfection of the reconciliation. Paul speaks of the church as "the body of Christ" and this one body includes both Jews and Gentiles. There are not two bodies, one for the ancient people of God and the other for more recent converts from Gentile nations. The apostle is very emphatically making the point that, whereas there had been enmity between God and sinners and between Jews and Gentiles, all the enmity has been done away in the cross. When Paul speaks of Christ as "having slain the enmity," he means that enmity is no longer a force; it has been destroyed. "In it" means "in the cross," which was the means God used to bring about reconciliation.

Now Paul thinks of Christ not only as the one who effected peace by his death, but as the one who preaches peace (2:17—the verb is connected with "gospel," so could we say he "gospels peace"?). There is a public proclamation of peace as well as an effective bringing of it about. The expression is influenced by an Old Testament passage in which God says, "Peace, peace, to those far and near" (Isa. 57:19). So Christ is pictured as preaching the good news of peace both to "you who were far off" (i.e., the Gentiles) and to "them who were near" (the Jews). For both Gentile and Jew the way to God is the way of reconciliation brought about by the death of Jesus.

Paul adds a reason in verse 18. It is through Christ that both Jews and Gentiles have their introduction to the Father. It is important that our introduction is to "the Father," the very highest of all. And it is interesting that this takes place "in one Spirit." The New Testament does not usually link the Spirit with the atonement, but this expression makes it clear that all three persons of the Trinity are concerned in the process that brings salvation. "Introduction" is here explained as "to the Father," though the term is used absolutely in 3:12, and it is explained as introduction "by faith into this grace in which we stand" (Rom. 5:2). However the term is used, it brings out the fact that whereas our sin had cut us off from access to the highest, Christ has now made the way open for all who come in faith. At this point there is some emphasis on the fact that this applies to Gentiles as well as to Jews. In making salvation available through the atoning work of Christ, God has made it open to all believers and has removed the distinctions caused by the great religious barrier between Jews and Gentiles.

Wholeness and the Modern Community

Paul's emphasis on peace, *shalom,* is just as important for us who live in the modern western world as for those who lived in the first-century Roman Empire. For example, those of us who live in any great metropolis mostly find that the sense of community has gone. Though there are so many people gathered together with whom theoretically we could have a rich and full experience, in practice we know very few people and often they have much the same outlook as we have. The richness of the modern community is difficult to experience. And even when we have some activity that unites us temporarily, it tends to fragment life. Thus we may have "Road Safety Week" or "Apprenticeship Week" or "Education Week" or a period of time devoted to any one of a number of other worthy concepts. But to concentrate for a time on just one object in this way, desirable though it may be to emphasize its importance, is to fragment life. *Shalom* directs our attention to life as a well-rounded whole.

We manage to break up the compartments into which we divide life. Thus, although we see education as very important, we divide our learning into separated units. Since we have as a rule no integration, we see each subject as an entity on its own, certainly not as part of a well-rounded whole into which other subjects fit. Likewise we give lip service to the concept that a number of institutions are involved in our education—home, church, school, community affairs, jobs—but again there is no integration. The concept of *shalom* would have us combining all our learning experiences into one integrated whole, but most of us do not rise to this, so life is a series of isolated units.

Wholeness in Theology

There is a special temptation to compartmentalize our faith for those of us who are Christians. To begin with, we may become specialists in one part of Scripture. The big divide is, of course, into students of the Old Testament and of the New. But then we narrow that down and become specialists in the Pentateuch or the Psalms or the Prophets. Or we put our attention into the Synoptic Gospels or the Pauline writings or some other restricted field. While there is nothing wrong with such specialism (it is difficult to be on top of the literature in all aspects of biblical studies!), there is danger in cutting ourselves off from whole sections of the Bible.

We must beware, too, of minimizing sin by fragmentalizing our nature. Thus it is easy to see sin as something concerned with the flesh, but without relevance to our minds. We can spin fine theories about our subconscious and think of our bodies as pure and wholesome. And there are other ways of coming to the conclusion that the evil we do is not really our fault and that accordingly we are not really culpable. But wholeness applies to every area of our life. Each of us is one person and all aspects of our personhood belong to us. We cannot say that we sin with this or that part of our being, while the rest of us is innocent.

Again, there are people these days who are depressed about Christian teaching. They are happy enough to accept the fact that the church has some important things to say about Christian ethics, but they see as irrelevant anything to do with Christian doctrine. It is important to see that there is a wholeness here, too. The New Testament writers teach that such and such doctrines are true; *therefore* believers must live in a certain way. The ethics and the doctrines are bound up together. We neglect either at our peril.

Somewhere I came up against an apocryphal story that illustrates my point. It concerns a scientist who is said to have trained a flea so that when he placed it on the palm of one hand and held the other nearby, he could call "Jump" and the flea would jump to the other hand. One day he is said to have put the unfortunate creature under anesthetic and cut off its legs. Then he put it on his hand and called "Jump." Nothing happened. Nor did anything occur when he repeated his command. "Well," said the scientist, "that just proves my theory that fleas can't hear when their legs are cut off!" Even without scientific training we feel that there is something wrong with the reasoning in this fable. And so it is with those who want to separate Christian doctrine and Christian behavior. No matter how learnedly the case is argued, we must feel that there is something defective in their reasoning. Christian doctrine and Christian living belong together. They form a unity. There is a wholeness about the Christian life.

Wholeness in Living

Non-Christians and Christians alike should bear in mind that there is a "wholeness" about our lives. All that we do comes together to make up one life. Different aspects of our personalities come to the fore when we move from home to work to social life and so on. But each of us is one person, and unless the life we live is characterized by wholeness we come short of real living. For example, in these materialistic days some people are wholly given over to making money, to being successful in the business world. They forget that "man shall not live by bread alone" (Matt. 4:4; Luke 4:4). It is possible to be very well off materially and yet very impoverished spiritually. Thoreau is reputed to have said, "A man is rich in proportion to the number of things he can afford to let alone," a truth we neglect at our peril. If we must constantly seek gratification in material possessions, our lives are very impoverished. It is what we are, deep down, that speaks of real riches or real poverty.

It is a pity that so many of us fail to reckon with this. Considering the level of education open to everybody in modern democracies, the riches that open up to us, and what technology has made available to us (e.g., the best music and literature in the world is within reach of us all), it is curious that so many of us content ourselves with comics and the like. Or if we do get serious, we tend to mindlessly follow some leader rather than think for ourselves. Dictatorships are out of fashion in most countries, but it is still quite possible for us to find someone in our own circle to whom we turn for authoritative guidance.

I like the story of the American general who was making a speech in Korea. He did not know the local language, so he had an interpreter by his side to render what he said into Korean. At one stage he told a joke and was intrigued when the interpreter put it into the local language in very few words. Since the audience laughed heartily, it had evidently gone over well. Afterwards, as the general was talking to the interpreter, he commented on the fact and asked, "How could you tell my joke in so few words?" The interpreter responded, "I knew the people would not understand the joke, so I simply said, 'The general has told a joke. Everybody laugh!' And they did." And that is the trouble with much of our modern living. We laugh, not because we appreciate the humor and are genuinely amused, but because it is the party line to be amused. And we accept all sorts of positions because they are accepted in the group to which we belong.

Instead, it is important to practice wholeness in our living. Someone has said there is a God-shaped blank in the heart of every one of us, and unless we see that God fills it we are always going to be in trouble of some sort. True Christians, people who genuinely trust God, have God at the center of their lives. When God is in control of all that we do, we know genuine wholeness of living. He is our peace.

7

A Holy Temple

Therefore you are no longer foreigners and resident aliens, but you are fellow-citizens with the saints and members of God's household, having been built on the foundation of the apostles and prophets, the cornerstone being Christ Jesus himself in whom every structure being fitted together grows into a holy temple in the Lord, in whom you also are being built together into a dwelling-place for God in the Spirit (Eph. 2:19–22).

Therefore" renders two Greek words with similar meanings: "wherefore therefore," a construction used by Paul alone in the New Testament. We do not use such an expression in English, but we should not miss the fact that Paul is putting strong emphasis on the logical connection of what follows with what has gone before (2:11–18). Because of what Christ has done in bringing peace and in bringing both Gentiles and Jews to the Father, certain consequences necessarily follow. This was crystal clear to Paul, but it was far from clear to some people in the early church. Now Paul proceeds to make it plain for his readers.

The apostle points to an important change in status that had taken place when his correspondents were converted: they were "no longer" what they had been before. Though the word I have translated "foreigners" can mean "strangers" (and NRSV and some other translations have that term here), "foreigners" is surely the meaning in this passage, as it is in the lament over the destruction of Jerusalem: "Our inheritance has been turned over to aliens" (Lam. 5:2 NIV). In that passage we see something of the notion of enemy aliens and, while this nuance is not always present, the word lends itself to such a meaning. Barth can say, "A 'stranger' could be, and sometimes was, treated as an outlaw or spy (Gen. 19:1–10)."

To this word for foreigners is added "resident aliens," people of another nation residing in one's community. Such people were there on sufferance; they did not enjoy full rights to membership of the community and were not assured of the full protection of the law, which meant that they lived precarious lives. They could, for example, be expelled from the community, and they had no right of appeal against such a sentence. They were second-class citizens.

The combination of terms points to people who might well feel themselves under a very great handicap. We should bear in mind that the first Christians were all Jews and that Jews as a whole had a rather harsh attitude toward those of other nations. Were they not God's chosen people? Did they not stand in a relation to God shared by no other people? The Jews were oppressed by the Romans, who did not understand their religion or their claim that there is only one God, but they looked down on their conquerors. They despised idolaters, which meant all the nations with which they came in contact. They did not see Christians as faithful Jews, and, for example, the Jews in Corinth could say of Paul, "Contrary to the law does this man persuade men to worship God" (Acts 18:13). They might practice hospitality to strangers, but that would only be to those of their own race and religion. Those who were not were usually firmly rejected.

The first Christians were, of course, all Jews and many of them shared the Jewish attitude toward outsiders. We see something of their hesitation to receive Gentiles in the fact that Peter needed a special vision before he would go to the lodging of the centurion Cornelius and bring the message of salvation to that Gentile. He commented to the people in the house where Cornelius was, "You are well aware that it is unlawful for a Jewish man to associate with a man of another nation or visit him" (Acts 10:28). Again, after converts had been made in Antioch, some Jewish Christians from Judea came and taught that "unless you have been circumcised according to the custom of Moses you cannot be saved" (Acts 15:1). This question was referred to the apostles and elders in Jerusalem, and when they met there were some believers who said, "It is necessary to circumcise them [the Gentiles] and command them to keep the law of Moses" (Acts 15:5). Although the meeting decided against this point of view, there can be no doubt that it was strongly held by some Jewish Christians.

Paul's letters make it plain that his attitude to Gentile Christians was not shared by all the church. For him the keeping or non-keeping of

73

Jewish law made no difference, but for some other early Christians the fact that this law was the law of God meant that Gentile believers must keep it. Because they did not see, as Paul did, that the coming of Christ meant a profound change in the way we are to see the law, it was all the more important that Paul should make it clear that the gospel did not countenance any distinction between Jewish and Gentile believers. All who are saved are saved solely on account of Christ's saving work; nothing can be added to that.

But when Gentiles were converted they found themselves members in a group of believers where there were many Jewish ideas. Their Savior had been a Jew. Their Scriptures were the Jewish Scriptures. Their apostles, the most important people in the church, were Jews. Some of the membership looked down on Gentile converts. It would have been easy for Gentiles to see themselves as second-class citizens in a church with such strong Jewish connections. They lived in a world where resident aliens were well known and were regarded as second class citizens. They knew that proselytes to Judaism were often looked down on by Jews proud of their Jewish ancestry.

The difficulties of their position are illustrated by the incident to which Paul refers in Galatians 2:11–13. Peter had apparently been quite happy to eat meals with Gentile believers (something strict Jews would never do). Why should he not, considering the vision he had had which led him to evangelize and baptize Cornelius and his household? But when "some from James" came and refused table fellowship, Peter became afraid and withdrew from that fellowship. There was evidently such a furor that "the rest of the Jews" also withdrew and even Barnabas was carried along with them. Paul goes on to say that he argued strongly against Peter (vv. 14–21), and evidently in the end he carried the day. The incident shows us the kind of tension that could arise when strong Jewish Christians tried to impose Jewish ways of living on Gentile believers.

Here Paul is combating ideas like this. Because of what Christ has done, the Ephesian believers (and for that matter all other believers) are no longer to be seen as "foreigners" or as "resident aliens." "No longer" points to a new state of affairs. Before Christ came they had been from a Jewish point of view foreigners and aliens (resident or otherwise). But not any more. The coming of the Savior and specifically his atoning death brought salvation. That there was no other way of forgiveness of sins meant that in the sight of God Jews and Gentiles had the same standing. Gentiles shared in the blessings Christ brought just as fully as any other members of the church. Being a Jew gave no special privileges to sinners who had been redeemed by the death of the Savior.

Paul is calling on his readers to focus on the thing that really mattered. So often we allow ourselves to be distracted from the central point as we give ourselves over to concentrating on nonessentials. I recall reading of an examination paper set by the air force for potential pilots. One question read: "You are piloting a light aircraft and the Queen of England falls out of the back of the aircraft. What is the first thing you would do?" The answers given covered a wide range. One hopeful young man wrote, "Swoop down and try to catch her." A pessimist said only, "Suicide," and another, "Disappear." The answer the examiners were looking for, of course, was "Adjust controls to compensate for loss of weight in the rear section." It is important to concentrate on the essentials. It does not matter *who* falls out of a light aircraft; the pilot's business is with the controls of his plane.

So it is with God's people. What matters is that Christ has died to bring us salvation. Whether we are Jew or Gentile does not matter; salvation is the same for us all. We are to look to Christ and to Christ alone for our salvation and for all that is involved in our Christian life. We must not let ourselves be distracted by such disputes as the relative places of Jews and Gentiles and the extent to which the ritual practices of one group of Christians should affect another group.

F. F. Bruce points out that in the Qumran scrolls there is the thought of the community as forming a sanctuary. They formed "a most holy dwelling for Aaron . . . and a house of perfection and truth in Israel." He points out that for the men of Qumran, "Aaron" signifies the priests in the community and "Israel" the lay members. This means that the words quoted signify that "the laity constituted the holy place and the priesthood the holy of holies." But Paul is not differentiating between one class of believers and another. For him the kind of differentiation taken for granted at Qumran was impossible. He is arguing strongly that all believers, Gentiles as well as Jews, are as one in God's sight. All are caught up in the holy temple and there is no differentiation, as though one group were more holy than another.

God's People

Paul then uses a number of pieces of imagery to bring out the exalted status of the Ephesian believers. He speaks of them first as "fellow-citizens with the saints." The Greek word for "citizen" *(polites)* is connected with that for "city" *(polis)*, which reminds us that at that time citizenship tended to be connected with a city rather than with a country. Thus Paul could speak of himself as a citizen of Tarsus (Acts 21:39). But it was possible also to have a wider citizenship, and Paul was also a Roman citizen (Acts 22:27), a citizen of the vast Roman Empire. This citizenship gave him certain rights and privileges that operated anywhere within the Roman Empire, rights and privileges that did not apply to people who lived in the empire but who had never been given the privilege of Roman citizenship. Paul understood what citizenship meant and he valued his earthly citizenships.

But here he is speaking of a much more important citizenship. He and the Ephesian Christians were both "fellow-citizens with the saints." This signifies that they belonged with the holy people; their citizenship is a higher citizenship than that of any earthly city or state. Elsewhere Paul can say "our citizenship is in heaven" (Phil. 3:20), and that is in mind here. "The saints," as commonly used in the New Testament, refers to the people of God. The word *hagios,* "holy," means "set apart for God." It is used in many religions and may refer to things, such as temples or objects used in worship, or to people, in which case it signifies that the people in question have a special relationship to the deity. In modern times the term "holy" is often used in the sense "outstandingly righteous," but we should be clear that this is not the sense in which it is used in the New Testament. Among the early Christians it is a customary word for believers, for the characteristic of "the saints" is that they belong to God.

We should not miss the point that Christians belong together. John Wesley's dictum, "The Bible knows nothing of solitary religion" is often quoted, and it has relevance here. Those who are converted are not a series of holy hermits. They are "fellow-citizens with the saints." We Christians belong together in the body of Christ, the household of God, the "holy temple in the Lord" of which Paul is about to speak. This was important for all Gentile believers in the first century, and it is important for all believers still.

The point that Paul is making here is that the Ephesians share with all other Christians the fact that they belong to God. They are not to think that the Jews, those who formed Jesus' kinship by race, had any priority with God. It is those who have been saved by Christ, from whatever earthly nation they may come, who are "the saints," the holy ones. Without distinction they all belong to God, and the Ephesians are left in no doubt of their status.

A second way of looking at their position, says Paul, is that they are "members of God's household." In antiquity a household would denote the members of a family, and it could also include servants and the like. Noah's household included his three sons and their wives (Gen. 7:1, 7). It is recorded that Abraham had three hundred and eighteen men who were "born in his household" (Gen. 14:14), so the term could have an extended meaning. However widely enlarged, the term has about it the air of a family unit.

Paul is saying that the Ephesian believers are in intimate relationship with God. They belong to his household and there can be no higher privilege than that. This is a closer relationship than that of citizenship.

A member of a family is tied much more closely to the head of that family than is a citizen to a head of state. Either relationship may be used to bring out Christian truth, but we should not miss the advance when Paul moves from the idea of state to that of family.

We should bear this in mind when we are oppressed with the ordinariness of most Christian living. We hear stories of great Christians of the past or for that matter of the present (when they are usually missionaries toiling against great odds in difficult situations in backward countries or giving themselves in ministry to slum-dwellers or the like). We admire such Christians. We marvel at the grace of God so manifest in their lives—and we wonder why all these wonderful things happen to other people but not to us. It is important to bear in mind that the life of the Christian is not necessarily a series of mountaintop experiences as we toil against fearful odds. For most of us, life is one ordinary day after another. But even in the ordinariness of life we belong to God. We are members of his household, whatever our place in life and whatever our experiences. There is a place for the grace of God in the most ordinary of lives.

A Holy Building

Paul moves to a different metaphor with the thought that his correspondents have "been built on the foundation of the apostles and prophets" (2:20). It is possible to understand the Greek as meaning "the foundation that is the apostles and prophets," but it is perhaps better to take it to signify "the foundation laid by the apostles and prophets." Stott points out that both apostles and prophets were "groups with a teaching role" and argues, "it seems clear that what constitutes the church's foundation is neither their person nor their office but their instruction."

The apostles were the really important people in the early church. Originally the term was applied to twelve disciples whom Jesus chose and associated with himself throughout his ministry (Matt. 10:1–2). The word "apostle" means "one sent," and Mark tells us that Jesus chose the Twelve "that they might be with him and that he might send them to preach" (Mark 3:14 NIV). The early chapters of Acts shows that they took a leading part in the life and work of the early church, Peter being especially prominent. But it is interesting that the Twelve are only rarely mentioned after the Gospels (Acts 6:2; 1 Cor. 15:5; Rev. 21:14), though there are also a couple of references to "the eleven" (Acts 1:26; 2:14).

But "apostle" does not apply solely to the Twelve. Paul frequently claims the title for himself, and sometimes in such a way as to show that he saw it as important. But if it is clear that it does not refer solely to the original Twelve, it is not clear exactly who could claim the title nor how apostles were chosen. Barnabas is called an apostle along with Paul (Acts 14:14), and reasoning from the "we" of 1 Thessalonians 2:7 we probably should include Silvanus (Silas). James the brother of our Lord was an apostle (Gal. 1:19). It may well be that there were other apostles, but those who wrote the books of our New Testament were not interested in giving us a list, nor in telling us exactly what either the qualifications or the duties of an apostle were. Nevertheless, we can certainly say that the apostles were the most important of the leaders of the early church.

It is not clear whether we should understand "prophets" as referring to the great figures of the Old Testament or to the prophets of the early church of whom Paul has a good deal to say in 1 Corinthians 14. The fact that he prefixes "apostles" seems to show that he is thinking primarily of these prophets (cf. 3:5), though the Old Testament prophets may not be completely out of mind. Clearly he is referring to people who spoke the word of God: inspired men. Anything built on what they said was soundly based.

Even though it seems plain enough that "the prophets" here are not the great prophets of the Old Testament, it is worth noticing that it matters a good deal to Paul that there is a continuity between the great teachers of the Old Testament and the Christians. He often appeals to the great prophets of old. They pointed forward to the coming of the Messiah, and in that sense the church may perhaps be said to be built on what they said. But this does not seem to be the apostle's thought at this point.

The Cornerstone

The important place in this building is not that occupied by the apostles and prophets, but by Jesus Christ. Paul speaks of him as "the cornerstone," a term that sets us a puzzle by reason of our ignorance of the technical terms used for buildings in antiquity. That "corner" is used in the expression indicates that the stone is at a corner of a building, but there is dispute as to whether its place is at the base or at the top of the wall. Many hold the meaning to be "keystone," an important stone at the top of a wall; it holds two walls together and thus completes the structure. Alternatively the term may indicate a large stone in the foundations. A heavy and large stone would determine the positions of two walls and thus of the whole building. This latter view is supported by an Old Testament passage that speaks of "a tested stone, a precious cornerstone for a sure foundation: (Isa. 28:16 NIV). This clearly presupposes that the "cornerstone" is in the foundation rather than at the summit of a building. Against "keystone" is the difficulty of fitting this into what

Paul is saying. Since the keystone is at the top of the edifice, it presupposes a completed building. If this is the meaning, Christ has as yet no place in the building. But Paul is describing a building in the process of erection and ascribing the most significant place to Christ. While we cannot be absolutely certain of its position, the cornerstone is clearly regarded as the most important stone in the building, and the probability is that it is the foundation, the great stone determining the position of the whole building.

This cornerstone, Paul says, is "Christ Jesus himself." Depending on the way we take the previous expressions, there are two ways of understanding all this. Paul might be saying that the church is built on the apostles and prophets who are its foundation ("a building that has the apostles and prophets for its foundations" JB) and that Christ is the keystone, the last and greatest stone that holds the whole together. Against this is the fact that apart from this verse the New Testament never seems to regard the apostles themselves as the foundation on which the church is built (in Rev. 21:14 the names of the twelve apostles are on the foundations of the walls of the heavenly city, but the apostles themselves are not said to *be* the foundations). The New Testament regards their preaching in this way (Rom. 15:20; 1 Cor. 3:10–11), but not the apostles themselves.

Alternatively we could understand Paul to be saying that the church is built on the foundation given in the preaching of the apostles and prophets (cf. "we preach Christ crucified," 1 Cor 1:23; "I laid a foundation," 1 Cor 3:10) and that this means that Christ himself is the foundation, the cornerstone (cf. "other foundation can no one lay than that which is laid, which is Jesus Christ," 1 Cor 3:11). While there will always be dispute as to the better way of taking the passage, it seems to me that there is more to be said for the second way: Christ is the foundation.

A Holy Temple in the Lord

The thought of Christ as the foundation leads on to that of the building erected on that foundation (2:21). This is preceded by "in whom" where we might possibly have expected "on whom." There is, of course, truth in both ways of putting it. "On whom" would carry on the thought that the church is built on the sure foundation of Christ. But Paul often speaks of believers as "in" Christ, so it is natural for him to draw attention to this truth even while he is going on to the thought of the church as a building erected on the perfect foundation of Christ.

But while being "in Christ" is important for Paul, that is not what is being emphasized here. Rather his thought is that—though there are many members of the church, each making his or her own contribution to the great edifice—the varied contributions do not mean chaos, for the great building is held together by Christ. "Every structure" is not quite what we would have expected. Perhaps the idea is that each piece of the building, though it may be distinguished from other pieces, nevertheless forms part of one great edifice (*Phillips*, "In Him each separate piece of building properly fitting into its neighbour . . ."). W. Lock draws attention to the New York cathedral, where there are chapels round about the central shrine, each having its own individuality, while together they make up one great edifice.

Here the apostle employs an unusual word (found only in this letter in the New Testament and not cited anywhere before Paul) which I have translated "being fitted together." It, says Barth, "is derived from the Greek noun *harmos*, which generally denotes a fitting or connection. In architecture the noun describes either a joint or a junction of two stones, or the sides of the stones that were so worked as to fit together." Barth also thinks that the verb "may be Paul's creation." Later in the letter Paul will use it for a body being fitted together (4:16; cf. 4:12), just as in this passage he has the thought of a building growing. Obviously the apostle has no objection to mixing architectural and biological metaphors. The point that he is making here is that every member of the church fits harmoniously into the mighty edifice. With our limited vision we may not see how this is done or even that it *is* done, but Paul has the grand vision of the mighty God at work erecting a magnificent building. Every part of it, no matter how small and apparently insignificant, has its place in the great edifice, and it all fits together. Perhaps we should notice that the Greek verb is compounded with the preposition "with." This is a feature of Ephesians (I have noted fourteen such compounds in these six chapters). Paul is insistent that believers belong "with" one another.

Having used proper architectural terms ("being fitted together"), Paul moves on to biological language when he says that the building "grows." He does not see the church as static, a group of people chosen out of the world for salvation, who then remain as a select group. Rather, Paul has a dynamic conception of the church: it is a living, growing organism. Even when he is using architectural metaphors to bring out some aspects of its being, he swings easily into an expression that indicates that it is alive. It grows as all living things grow.

Perhaps we should notice another grammatical point. The verb "grows" is used in a transitive sense in classical Greek, like our expression "to grow flowers" or the like. But here there is no object and the meaning may be, as some expositors hold, that Paul is thinking of the church as having a responsibility for its growth. There is nothing automatic about the growth of the church as there is about the growth of a crop (in Mark 4:28 the evangelist uses the word *automate*, "automatic").

The church has a responsibility for its growth in holiness and in numbers. We are not to think of it as growing exactly as a building grows, where everything depends on what the workmen do. The church grows because of the life within itself, not because of some equivalent of the workmen who erect a building.

A Temple for God

The result of the growth of the church is that it becomes "a holy temple in the Lord." In a temple in antiquity there were many rooms and courtyards, since a temple had a variety of functions and required a number of rooms and even buildings accordingly. The most important place, the place where it was held that the deity was specially present and where worship was offered, was denoted by a special word, and it is this word that Paul uses here. He is talking about the "shrine," the holy place into which the church is growing.

It is a thousand pities that the modern church so often concentrates on what we might liken to the outer rooms (or even the courtyards!), as opposed to the sanctuary. It is easy to busy ourselves with what we see as good works, good works of many kinds, but good works that lead neither the doers nor those for whom they are done any nearer to God. I recall hearing one gentleman who was somewhat depressed at the way the church with which he was familiar was behaving say, "It's the business of the church to feed the saints, not to amuse the goats!" That the church is a sanctuary should never be overlooked. Later the apostle will say that the church builds itself up in love (4:16), but we should not overlook the fact that love as the New Testament knows it is a *holy* love.

A Dwelling-Place for God

Paul repeats "in whom"—"in whom every structure grows . . . in whom you also are being built together." We are not to miss the emphasis on Christ, nor should we miss the "you also" in verse 22. When Paul speaks of the wonderful things Christ has done and of the magnificent church that he has set in being, these Gentile believers must see that they are included in the divine plan. Just as the believing members among the Jews, the ancient people of God, belonged in the "holy temple in the Lord," so do these Ephesians Gentile believers. Here Paul is emphasizing their place in the people of God.

He speaks of them as "being built together," and his verb is not common, being found here only in the New Testament. Elsewhere it is used of people sharing with one another in putting up a building and of the combining of different materials in building. This is a vivid metaphor for the uniting of Jews and Gentiles in the church, the people of God, the place where God dwells. Strictly the verb used here for "build" means "build a house," though, of course, it may be used of building other edifices. But "build a house" is specially appropriate here, where Paul goes on to the thought that the edifice is "a dwelling-place for God." The verb could theoretically be seen as imperative, "Be built together . . ." but the context makes this unlikely. At this point Paul is pointing out the blessings the Gentiles believers enjoy, not exhorting them to further endeavor.

What is being built is "a dwelling-place," where Paul uses another rare word (again in the New Testament only in Rev. 18:2). There is little doubt that Paul is talking about the church as God's dwelling, just as he has already spoken of it as a building and a holy temple. Perhaps we should notice that the writer of the Epistle of Barnabas says, "the habitation of our hearts is a shrine holy to the Lord" (*Barnabas* 6:15), and the language appears to be an echo of this passage. But while there is truth in saying that the hearts of believers form a holy shrine, it does not appear that this is what Paul is saying. He is surely speaking once more of the church. It is the church that is the place where God has his "dwelling-place in the Spirit."

The precise meaning we should attach to "in the Spirit" is disputed. It is usually taken to refer to the Holy Spirit, but this may be understood in more ways than one. It may signify that it is God the Holy Spirit who dwells in the habitation of which Paul has been speaking. Or it may refer to the building materials used in the making of the dwelling-place to give the meaning that it is only the people in whom the Spirit is actively at work who form the dwelling-place (cf. 1 Cor. 3:16). Another suggestion is that we should take the term to describe the dwelling-place as spiritual rather than as referring to the Holy Spirit. On this view the dwelling-place is not built with physical materials. It is not made with hands (2 Cor. 5:1); it is a spiritual house (cf. 1 Peter 2:5). Since no convincing reason seems to have been urged to rule out any of these, it is possible that Paul is deliberately using an expression that may be understood in more ways than one.

8

The Mystery of Christ

For this reason I Paul, the prisoner of Christ Jesus for the sake of you, the Gentiles—inasmuch as you have heard of the administration of the grace of God that was given to me for you, that the mystery was made known to me by way of revelation, even as I wrote to you briefly above, which, when you have read, you are able to perceive my understanding in the mystery of Christ, which in other generations was not made known to the sons of men as it has now been revealed to his holy apostles and prophets in the Spirit, that the Gentiles are fellow-heirs and fellow-members of the body and fellow-partakers of the promise in Christ Jesus through the gospel, of which I became a minister according to the free gift of the grace of God that was given to me according to the working of his power (Eph. 3:1–7).

For this reason" (3:1) carries on the argument—having dealt with the thought of the holy temple, Paul is prepared to move on to the next part of this thought. He intends to make a very personal statement and emphasizes this with his emphatic "I Paul" (he has a similar emphatic "I" in 1:15; 4:1; 5:32). Elsewhere the apostle uses this emphatic expression to make a personal statement in a letter that others join with him in writing (1 Thess. 2:18) and in a personal statement of readiness to pay some money (Philem. 19). It emphasizes his personal activity. Here he seems to be beginning to say that it is he, Paul, the man in prison for the sake of the Gentiles, who prays for the Gentiles (the sentence is carried on in 3:14).

This is not meant to introduce a piece of common Christian knowledge, or even something that the rank and file may not know but which is well known to Christian leaders. It points to something of which Paul wants to speak, but in which he does not associate other people. There is no doubt that the apostle was an outstanding thinker among the leaders of the early church, and there are many things in his letters to which other Christian leaders may not have been ready to give a wholehearted assent. And there were many facets of Christian teaching into which Paul had entered wholeheartedly but which were far from being Christian commonplaces. So Paul makes it clear that what he is about to write comes out of his own personal understanding of the Christian way. Other Christian leaders may or may not have put it the way Paul does.

We should notice further that understanding implies thought. Paul does not see the Christian message as the repetition of some form of words; the gospel cannot be reduced to a formula. As B. F. Westcott put it, "It had cost him thought and it claimed thought." We should always bear in mind that Jesus told his followers that they are to love God with all their mind, as well as with all their heart and soul and strength (Mark 12:30).

Paul points out that he is "the prisoner of Christ Jesus" (the name "Jesus" is omitted from some manuscripts, but it is well attested and there is no good reason for doubting that Paul inserted the name). In earlier days Paul had put people into prison for following Jesus. Now he knows what it is like to suffer in that way. He almost certainly includes in his meaning the fact that he has been taken captive by his Savior (he is the prisoner "of" Christ) and that he lives only to do the will of Christ. That he was utterly devoted to his Savior is clear from all his writings. But it is probable that on this occasion he is writing from a physical prison, in which case he is saying also that he is in jail on account of his service of the Master. In this case the meaning will be something like the "prisoner for Christ Jesus" (as NRSV translates). Paul is in jail, but not because of any criminal act; it is because of his faithfulness to Christ.

From another point of view Paul's imprisonment is "for the sake of you, the Gentiles." Had he remained a loyal and practicing Jew, making no attempt to evangelize the Gentiles, he would have been safe from Roman arresting officers. But when he went out to preach the gospel in Gentile cities in response to what he saw as his mission as a Christian, he could and did run foul of the authorities.

This arose partly because of his essential message and partly because of the consequences of its being received. The Romans were tolerant of many religions, but they understood a legitimate religion to be a nation's traditional religion. The Christians, however, preached that the gods of the nations were not really gods at all. There is only one God. To the

Romans this appeared suspiciously like atheism, and they found no way of seeing it as a legitimate religion to be included in the broad spectrum of national religions under Roman toleration.

The consequences of the preaching were also important for the Romans themselves. Nobody likes being told that their gods are no gods, and to the Romans it was self-evident that their gods were more powerful than any other gods. Had not their gods enabled them to conquer the world? But the new little sect outrageously rejected the religion of the powerful Romans and said that the deities the Romans worshiped were no gods at all.

It was the same with other people's religions. Wherever people became believers, those who resisted the Christian message tended to be outraged. Those committed to the old ways would not tolerate people who left their traditional religions and followed the newfangled way the Christians preached. From Acts we see the kind of rioting and violence that could follow when some people accepted the Christian message.

At first, Christians seem to have come under the general shelter of Roman toleration, apparently being seen as a peculiar variety of Judaism. But, of course, many Jews denounced them, and in any case there was no reason in Roman eyes for a Jewish form of religion to be preached among the Gentiles. Because that did not accord with what they saw as right and proper, Christians were arrested. And Paul, of course, as a successful preacher of the new religion and one who won many converts, was an obvious target for police action.

But here Paul insists that his imprisonment was not on account of any crime. He was a prisoner "for the sake of you, the Gentiles." Had he been content to practice his Christianity quietly at home, he would have been unmolested by the authorities. But when he took the gospel to the Gentiles he ran foul of the authorities, and it was this that brought about his imprisonment at the time of his writing this letter. He does not say "you Gentiles," but "you, the Gentiles," which may indicate that he was thinking of his calling to preach the gospel to all Gentiles, not only to those at Ephesus.

The Administration of Grace

The mention of "Gentiles" apparently caused a break in the apostle's chain of thought. It is immediately after this that the construction is broken. Some students think that there has simply been an omission of the verb "to be" and understand Paul to be saying, "For this reason I Paul am a prisoner. . . ." Others take the sentence to mean "I Paul, a prisoner for Christ Jesus, am a prisoner for the sake of you Gentiles. . . ."

85

But it is better to take the words as they stand without inserting anything, in which case the apostle is deferring what he was about to say and breaking off into some information about what it meant that he was the apostle of the Gentiles. The parenthesis appears to go on to the end of 3:13, with the main argument resumed in verse 14 with the same words as we have at the beginning of verse 1. Some see the parenthesis as ending at verse 7, and others at the end of the chapter, but verse 13 seems more likely, with the use at the beginning of verse 14 of the words with which Paul begins the chapter. This whole section is one long sentence, another of those long sentences so characteristic of this letter.

Paul's correspondents would know that he had preached to them, but they might perhaps not know that his whole calling was to preach to people like them. He says, "inasmuch as you have heard . . . (v. 2), and the way Paul expresses this seems to imply that they had indeed heard this (cf. NIV, "Surely you have heard . . ."). He was making sure that they knew of his position. Evangelizing Gentiles was not a chance occurrence that happened to take place in Ephesus, but something that would inevitably occur wherever Paul was. He had been chosen by God to evangelize Gentiles, and he was diligent in being obedient to his call.

He says that "the administration of the grace of God" has been entrusted to him, where the word I have translated "administration" is the one rendered "plan" in 1:10. As we noticed there, it refers to the management of a household, from which it comes to signify management or administration generally. Paul is saying that God had entrusted him with the task of an orderly preaching of the gospel of God's grace. This was something that he did characteristically, not haphazardly. It was a duty entrusted to him and one he must duly discharge. Paul took preaching to the Gentiles very seriously. It was not a task he chose, but a divine commission. In another letter he can say: "necessity is laid upon me: woe to me if I do not preach the gospel," and he adds that if he does this willingly he has a reward, but if he is unwilling he must still preach it (1 Cor. 9:16–17). He cannot escape the obligation to present the gospel.

This task involved proclaiming "the grace of God." As we have noticed earlier, "grace" is one of Paul's important words. He comes back to it again and again. So it is not surprising that when he is referring to the task he daily performs for God, it is grace that immediately comes to light. The gospel Paul incessantly proclaimed was a gospel that stressed the grace of God that brought salvation freely to penitent sinners, sinners among the Gentiles as freely as those among the Jews. And Paul sees this grace as given to him, not in order that he might luxuriate in it and take delight on the freeness of the pardon God had given him with no thought for others. No. It was given to Paul "for you." There is nothing selfish about the gospel. Paul saw grace as something God meant his hearers to receive, and specifically this was the case with the Gentiles. It was necessary for Paul to live and to preach in such a way that his hearers came to know God's grace just as he did.

The Mystery

The apostle goes on to speak of his understanding of "the mystery" (3:3), a term he has used in 1:9. There we saw that it does not denote a mystery in our sense of the term: a puzzle hard to work out. A mystery, for Paul, was something impossible for people to work out, but which God has now made known. Paul says here that it has been made known "by way of revelation"; that is, of course, the only way a "mystery" could become known to us. In the earlier passage the mystery concerned the purpose of God to bring everything, whether in heaven or on earth, under the headship of Christ. Here it is not so much the headship of Christ that is in mind as the truth that the gospel applies to Gentiles just as freely as it does to Jews, the ancient people of God. Paul came to know this truth "by way of revelation." That the Gentiles shared as fully in God's salvation as did the Jews was a blinding new truth for a Jew, and it is not surprising that it came to Paul by way of revelation. A Pharisee of the Pharisees would never have worked out such a truth for himself. The word "mystery" recurs in verses 4 and 9, so it is much in Paul's mind at this stage of his argument.

We should not miss Paul's reference in verse 4 to his "understanding" with regard to the mystery. He was not concerned with a parrotlike proclamation of the gospel. His mind was involved, and he spoke to people like the Ephesians out of the fact that he had come to an understanding of what God was doing. All his writings make it plain that he well knew the importance of thinking through what the gospel is and what it demands from those who accept it. And he looked for his readers to understand what the Christian message is and what it demands of them.

Paul says that he wrote to the Ephesians "briefly" about this (v. 3), by which he apparently means that he has done this earlier in this letter. The expression I have translated "I wrote above" could be rendered "I wrote before." But we have no reason for thinking he had written to the Ephesians before this, and the words apply well to the earlier part of the letter in which he has indicated the essence of the gospel. When his correspondents read that part of the letter, they will be able to see for themselves Paul's understanding of the mystery. "Read" in verse 4 translates a present participle and has a meaning like "as you read," "while reading." The reading in question would probably be in a public reading of Paul's letter, since not many of the rank-and-file Ephesians would have been able to read.

Something new came into the world when Jesus made his appearance. "In other generations" this was not known to people (v. 5), but Jesus finally brought the way of salvation that God had purposed through eternity. "The sons of men" is a normal Old Testament expression for "people" (though in the New Testament it occurs elsewhere only in Mark 3:28). Paul does not minimize the importance of the Old Testament revelation. He quotes from it often, and invariably with reverence and acceptance. But he is clear that with the coming of Jesus, God had done something new and surpassingly wonderful.

This, Paul goes on, "has now been revealed to his holy apostles and prophets in the Spirit." The precise functions of the apostles and prophets in the New Testament church are not clear. Obviously the New Testament writers knew quite well what both did and so did their readers. There was thus no point in writing it all down, and we are left to guess. But the apostles were certainly the leaders of the church, and it was important that they should know such things. That they were "holy" means, of course, that they were set apart for God. They belonged to him in all that they were and did. The expression is the same as that applied to all Christians, for all were "saints"—and the suggestion of some that the writer here ascribes a special degree of holiness to the apostles and prophets lacks foundation. That Paul can ascribe to the apostles and prophets the revelation that the Gentiles were full members of the church shows that this was not a private opinion of his own. It was accepted by the leaders of the church because divine revelation had shown it to be so.

Paul speaks of the truth as being revealed to them. We should not think of this as something that happened to the apostles all at one time as a group, for there is evidence that Paul's making of converts from among the Gentiles did not at first win universal approval (see Gal. 2). But in time the apostles and others in the church came to see that this was right (Acts 15), and Paul ascribes this to revelation. We know little about the way the prophets came to see this truth, but Paul is clear that they did. And he ascribes the revelation to "the Spirit." God's Holy Spirit was at work in the church, and among other things he revealed truth to people like apostles and prophets. Paul, then, is making it clear that the acceptance of Gentiles as full members of the church with the same rights and duties as Jewish members was something due to divine revelation, not a man-made custom.

Gentile Believers

The revelation was that Gentiles were received into the church in the same way as Jews (v. 6). There was to be no difference. Paul says the Gentiles "are," not that they "will be," sharers with Jewish believers or "should be fellow-heirs," as the King James Version translates. The way Paul puts it, there is certainty about the present status of the Gentiles. He uses three words with the preposition meaning "together with" prefixed to bring out this point, and I have tried to convey his meaning by prefixing "fellow" to each of them. Both J. Armitage Robinson and M. Barth translate with "co-heirs, concorporate, and co-partakers," and the first and third members reflect the Greek well. But "concorporate"! Moffatt does better with "co-heirs, companions, and co-partners." Some translations put the word "together" after each expression, as "heirs together," "members together," and "sharers together," while others abandon the attempt to reflect Paul's expressions precisely.

Whichever way we tackle the problem of translation, the point that Paul is making with some emphasis is that Gentile converts belong right up there with Jewish believers. We are not to think of "Christians, Class 1" and "Christians, Class 2." Paul is saying not only that the Gentiles may be saved by the atoning work of Christ, but that when they are saved they are on the same level as Jewish believers. C. Hodge comments, "The hand is not in the body by permission of the eye, nor the eye by permission of the hand. Neither is the Gentile in the church by courtesy of the Jew, nor the Jew by courtesy of the Gentiles. They are one body."

The threefold expression puts emphasis on the fact that all believers belong together and that no one group has a superiority over others. "Fellow-heirs" echoes Old Testament passages that speak of Israel as receiving an inheritance from God. This is just as true of Gentile believers as of the ancient people of God. "Fellow-members of the body" is one word in the Greek and expresses very concisely the thought that Gentiles have their place in the body of Christ, just as Jews do. Preference is given to neither, but the two belong together. "Fellow-partakers of the promise in Christ Jesus through the gospel" brings out the truth that Gentiles are the recipients of the divine promise just as much as are others. Salvation is not the result of Gentiles making a big effort, which turns out to be the same as the effort made by the Jews. Both Jews and Gentiles depend on the promise God has made in Christ, a promise expressed in "the gospel." The good news is the same for both groups.

That the Gentiles had their place in God's scheme of things and that they would receive blessing from God is brought out in the Old Testament. As early as the time of Abraham it was said that in the patriarch "all the families of the earth" would be blessed (Gen. 12:3; cf. also the relevant passages cited in Rom. 15:9–12). What is not made clear in the Old Testament (and was hidden "from the ages and from the generations," Col. 1:26) but is abundantly plain in Paul's exposition of the gospel is that salvation in Christ means equality: Gentile believers are on the same level as Jewish believers.

Paul—A Minister

The apostle rounds off this section of his argument by reminding his readers of his own position. First he became "a minister" (v. 7). His word is not ecclesiastical in origin, but secular. It denoted a table waiter and from this came to be used of any lowly servant. The Christians took up the word and used it for a deacon, the lowliest ecclesiastical servant. When it comes to the gospel, Paul does not see himself as occupying any important place; his place is that of a lowly servant (he uses this form of expression again in Col. 1:23). Elsewhere he speaks of himself as a minister of the new covenant (2 Cor. 3:6), as a minister of God (2 Cor. 6:4), and as a minister of Christ (2 Cor. 11:23). His lowly service has many aspects.

Then he goes on to the thought that he was a minister, not because he decided that was a good thing to be, but because God gave him the gift. Being a lowly servant of the gospel does not mean that he has accepted a depressing burden. In other places Paul can make it plain enough that the ministry he exercised was demanding, but there he speaks of it as "the free gift of the grace of God." The wonderful thing that had happened to him was that God had pardoned his sins, especially his sin of imprisoning and executing Christians, and had not only pardoned him but had given him a place of service as a minister. We should not miss the piling up of expressions in this verse: "free gift," "grace," "given," "the working," "his power." Paul was very conscious that in his ministry he owed everything to God, and each of these expressions brings out the point.

And his gift of ministry was a gift of grace. We have noticed before that "grace" is one of Paul's favorite words. He uses it again and again. God did not give him the gift of being a member of the ministry because he had merited it in some way. That would be a complete misunderstanding of Paul's meaning. Rather, he saw his function as an outworking of the divine grace. It was wonderful that the mighty God had freely chosen Paul and not only chosen him, but had given him the exciting gift of becoming a minister.

He finishes his description of this event with the note of power. The gift was "according to the working of his [God's] power," where the first noun is that from which we derive our word "energy" and the second the one that gives us "dynamite." The ministry to which Paul was called was no namby-pamby thing; it was to be exercised according to the mighty power of God.

9

The Multi-Colored Wisdom of God

To me, the very least of all saints, was this grace given, to preach to the Gentiles the gospel of the unsearchable riches of Christ and to bring to light for all people what is the administration of the mystery which has been kept hidden for ages in God who created all things, in order that through the church there might now be made known to the sovereignties and the authorities in the heavenlies the multi-colored wisdom of God according to his eternal purpose which he accomplished in Christ Jesus our Lord, in whom we have boldness and approach in confidence through faith in him. Therefore I ask that you do not faint at my afflictions on your behalf, which are your glory (Eph. 3:8–13).

Paul has just spoken of the working out of the mighty power of God, and that leads on to the thought that God's great power is effective in the lowliest of people. Now he speaks of himself as "the very least of all saints" (3:8). Actually he puts a comparative ending onto a superlative, which is scarcely grammatical; it is as though we were to say in English, "the leaster" (F. F. Bruce suggests "lessermost"). Paul's refusal to be bound by strict grammar emphasizes his point that he is a very lowly person. He sees himself as less significant than any other of the followers of Jesus. Characteristically, he refers to them as "saints," "holy ones." They are those who are set apart for God, people who belong to God in a special way. All the redeemed are "holy ones," so Paul does not hesitate to include himself in the number. But he remembers his past and sees his rank among them as the lowest of all.

Elsewhere he calls himself "the least of the apostles" and explains, "I am not worthy to be called an apostle because I persecuted the church of God." He adds, "but by the grace of God I am what I am," and this grace he sees as "not in vain," because he labored more abundantly than all of them. He goes on, "but not I, but the grace of God which is with me" (1 Cor. 15:9–10). This passage enables us to see something of Paul's understanding of his place in God's scheme of things. He could never forget that he had been a persecutor of God's people, and that kept him humble. (Perhaps that was in his mind when he spoke of sinners and added, "of whom I am chief" [1 Tim. 1:15].) But neither could he ever forget that God's grace prevails over every human situation. He keeps coming back to the thought of grace, and grace certainly had worked wonders in and through this humble apostle.

Characteristically in introducing his task, Paul speaks of the "grace" that was given to him. He could have said that Christ had called him to preach or that God had chosen him, but grace is such an important concept for the apostle that it comes as no surprise that he refers to grace as the motivation and power behind his preaching of the gospel.

Also characteristically, he speaks of his preaching "to the Gentiles." That was his particular piece of service, and he recognized the grace of God as behind it all. We may doubt whether he would have chosen this work for himself. He agonized over the spiritual plight of his own nation (Rom. 9–11), but, while he has some moving references to Gentiles, there is nothing equivalent to this. God, however, called him to be the apostle to the Gentiles, and Paul took this call with full seriousness. His verb "to preach" means "to bring good news." It is used in this sense, for example, in 1 Thessalonians 3:6, where Paul says that Timothy brought him "good news" about the faith and love of his Thessalonian converts. But for Christians there was no good news to compare to the good news of what God had done in Christ to bring salvation to sinners, and the verb became the ordinary one for the preaching of the gospel. It is in this way that Paul uses it here, and he specifically brings out the point that his special calling was to bring the gospel to the Gentiles.

He speaks of "the unsearchable riches of Christ" as the content of his preaching, where "unsearchable" is the translation of another of Paul's vivid words. In the Greek translation of the Old Testament it is used of God's works in Job 5:9; 9:10. It is a compound made up of the negative prefix, the preposition meaning "out," and a noun that signifies "track" or "footstep." It thus signifies "what cannot be tracked out" or possibly "footprints that cannot be tracked out." For Mitton, the word "suggests the picture of a reservoir so deep that soundings cannot reach the bottom of it. No limit can, therefore, be put to its resources." This is a help-ful comment, but the imagery is not that of a reservoir. It is that of fol-lowing tracks. Lock sees the meaning as "The tracks of His footsteps go in so many directions that no man can follow them all up," and this may be what is meant. Paul is saying picturesquely that the riches in Christ that are made known by the gospel are greater than we can ever track down or search out. It is no poverty-stricken gospel that Paul proclaims, but one that is rich beyond all human need and beyond all human telling.

Not only was it Paul's business to gain converts among the Gentiles, but in the process of doing this he was playing his part in bringing out the wisdom of God before the whole heavenly order. He begins his approach to this section of his argument with "and to bring to light for all people what is the administration . . ." (v. 9). The New International Version reads "to make plain" in the opening part of this expression and this is certainly part of the meaning, but it misses the fact that Paul's verb means "to give light" and thus "to enlighten." Although the NIV expresses a truth, we should not miss the connection with "light." Paul is bringing out the truth that apart from the gospel, people live in dark-ness. The gospel can be spoken of as uncountable riches, but it may also be seen as the bringing of light into the darkness of evil. "It is the God who said, 'Out of darkness light shall shine' who made his light shine in our hearts to illuminate them with the knowledge of the glory of God in the face of Jesus Christ" (2 Cor. 4:6).

Paul moves on to the universality of the gospel with his "for all people" (we could translate "to enlighten all people"). This is another concept that means a great deal to him. The gospel as he understood it was no minuscule message for a small, unimportant group. It was God's answer to the need of the whole world. This had not been made known until Paul's own day. For centuries the Jews had seen themselves as God's own people and had recognized from their Scriptures that God would bring blessing on the Gentiles. However, they had not come to see that God would bring Jews and Gentiles together in one body as he was now doing in the church. The universal application of the gospel was a new thing in the world.

The apostle does not say that the gospel was being brought to light but that all people could now see "what is the administration of the mystery." We have seen the word "administration" in verse 2 of this chapter. It is an important word for Paul, and the truth it conveys was important for the Ephesians. "Mystery" is another word we have seen before (1:9; 3:3, 4). It points us to the truth that the gospel is not something that people could ever have worked out for themselves but is known as God has revealed it. That the mystery was not known previously is emphasized with the statement that it "has been kept hidden for ages in God." Paul was not repeating a series of hackneyed truths that everyone had known previously; he was proclaiming a "mystery" that God had only just made known. The gospel could not, of course, be proclaimed until Christ had died for sinners, for this is the very heart of the Good News. There could be prophecies about this or that aspect of the gospel in earlier days, and Paul constantly draws attention to the fulfillment of prophecy in the gospel he proclaimed. But the fullness of the gospel itself—the message that Christ had died to bring salvation to Gentiles as well as to Jews— could not be proclaimed until these times had come.

That the mystery was hidden in God "who created all things" points to the divine purpose that runs through the universe. First, the mystery was "hidden in God," where the perfect tense in the verb "hidden" indicates continuity and security. This was not something carelessly covered over that might easily be discovered. It was so securely hidden that people could never discover it by themselves. "For ages," literally "from the ages," points to the truth that from the earliest age right through to the present time the mystery had been kept hidden. And that it was hidden "in God" means that it was hidden where no created being could stumble upon it accidentally or even find it by diligent and purposeful search. When Paul adds that it was hidden in the God "who created all things" he makes it clear that there was no way created beings could come at this truth until God was ready to disclose it. Paul might not know why God had chosen this particular time to reveal it, but he was certain that God's secret was such that no created being could penetrate it until God was ready to make it known.

The Divine Wisdom

Paul mentions the church nine times in this letter (a total exceeded in his epistles only in 1 Corinthians). The word may be used of the local congregation, but in this letter it always signifies the church universal. Clearly the church was much in the apostle's thought at this time, and from the present passage we can see something of the importance he attached to it. He is speaking of the divine wisdom and says that this is to be made known "through the church" (v. 10). This is perhaps surprising. The church in Paul's day was not a group of the world's outstanding people. The apostle reminds the Corinthians that there were "not many wise according to the flesh, not many mighty, not many well born" in their number and that, on the contrary, God has chosen the world's foolish ones and weak ones, the world's lowly and despised ones (1 Cor. 1:26–28). But God has never depended on the world's great ones, and Paul is now saying that it is through the group of apparently insignificant people that make up the church that God's wisdom will be displayed.

We should give this more attention than we usually do. For many people the church is an irrelevancy. They may see Jesus as a wonderful teacher, perhaps they may even trust him as their Savior, but they see the church mainly in terms of its deficiencies. They find it easy to criticize the church, concentrating on the divisions, the pettiness, and the narrow-mindedness that have too often been its mark. Because they find no inspiration in the local groups of Christians whom they know, in the end they disregard the church. It is a pity that we so often give this kind of impression. But it does not alter the fact that the church of God is made up of perfectly ordinary people, with only this to distinguish them from others: they have been saved by Christ, with all the consequences that salvation means. Paul saw the church, with all its failings, as the body of Christ and as God's demonstration of his wisdom and his power before those in the heavenlies. We ignore this to our loss.

The divine wisdom will be made known to "the sovereignties and the authorities," where Paul makes use again of two of the expressions he used in 1:21. Here they clearly refer to spirit beings—they are "in the heavenlies" (see comments on 1:3)—but the apostle does not stay to specify closely which ones he has in mind. Some students hold that he means the spirits that are opposed to God, evil spirits (from 6:12 we see that there is evil "in the heavenlies"), but others see the reference as including all spirit beings, good or bad (cf. Paul's reference to "thrones or lordships or sovereignties or authorities" [Col. 1:16]). Whichever way we take it, Paul sees the function of the church as extending far beyond the petty concerns of this life. What God is doing in the church has its repercussions throughout the spirit world. John Stott quotes J. A. Mackay, "the history of the Christian church becomes a graduate school for angels."

God's wisdom is "multi-colored," and Paul's word really means "multi-variegated" ("many-splendored"?). It is an unusual word to be used in such a connection, but then Paul is talking about an unusual wisdom. F. F. Bruce points out that the first attested use of the word is in Euripides, where it refers to a "many-colored cloaks," and he draws attention to a passage in the apocryphal *Wisdom of Solomon*, in which we read that in wisdom "there is a spirit that is intelligent, holy, unique, manifold, subtle, mobile, clear, unpolluted, distinct, invulnerable, loving the good, keen, irresistible, beneficent, humane, steadfast, sure, free from anxiety, all-powerful, overseeing all, and penetrating through all spirits that are intelligent and pure and most subtle" (Wisd. of Sol. 7:22–23). Paul expresses himself more concisely, but his unusual word underlines the fact that the divine wisdom has many aspects.

Perhaps we should notice a striking interpretation of the expression given by Gregory of Nyssa, who speaks of the wisdom of God as "producing contraries by contraries; by death, life; by dishonour, glory; by sin, righteousness; by a curse, blessing; by weakness, power. The invisible is manifested in flesh. He redeems captives, Himself the purchaser, and Himself the price" (cited by Abbott). Paul may not have meant all this by his one word, but it is an interesting and valuable reflection on aspects of the divine wisdom.

This multi-faceted wisdom is seen in the outworking of God's "eternal purpose" (v. 11). Paul is greatly interested in the divine purpose (he uses the word "purpose" in exactly half of its New Testament occurrences, six out of twelve). It is important for him that God is working out his purpose in the events of human history. We should perhaps notice the point made by W. Sanday and A. C. Headlam that Paul does not use the ordinary word for purpose: "No previous instance of the word *prothesis* in this sense seems to be quoted. The conception is worked out by the Apostle with greater force and originality than by any previous writer, and hence he needs a new word to express it." The German scholar C. Maurer similarly says that Paul uses the word "in a wholly new sense when he uses it for the primal decision of God whereby the saving event in Christ and the resultant way of the community to eschatological glorifying are established and set in motion."

We should be clear that when Paul talks about the outworking of the divine purpose he is not saying that something is occurring similar to the accomplishment of human purposes. He is saying that the purpose of God is so grand, so far-reaching, so unexpected, that the ordinary word for "purpose" will not do. God is doing something far greater than anything we see in human purposes.

And that purpose is worked out in Christ. Paul speaks of it as "accomplished in Christ Jesus our Lord." In the Greek there is an article before "Christ" and some students hold that we should understand the expression as "accomplished in the Christ, Jesus our Lord." This is a possible understanding of the Greek, but there seems no great difference in meaning. We could translate the verb as "did"; it is normally used in this way. However we translate, Paul is making it clear that, in what Christ did, the divine purpose was brought to its fulfillment. We should notice the use of the aorist tense, which points to a deed accomplished in the past. It is, of course, true that a great deal of that purpose awaits the future. But it is also true that the central thing is Christ's saving work in dying on the cross for sinners. Since that has been done, the rest will inevitably follow, and the apostle can speak of the great over-arching purpose of God as "accomplished." Because of Calvary, God's people need have no qualms about the future. Since God in Christ has done so much, the final outworking of his purpose is certain.

Confidence

Because of what Christ has done, we have confidence (v. 12). Paul introduces this thought with "in whom," one of his characteristic concepts. He uses the idea of being "in Christ" perhaps as many as two hundred times; certainly the usage is frequent throughout the Pauline writings. Christians live and move and have their being in Christ. They are not separate from him in anything they do. Paul is saying here that it is only as we are "in" Christ that we "have boldness and approach in confidence." The state of being in Christ is clearly of the greatest importance.

Then Paul says we have "boldness." In Greek the word is made up of two words, the first meaning "all" and the second "speech." It denotes our attitude when we have "all speech," when we feel quite at home and the words flow freely. With this Paul links what I have translated as "approach." The word is often taken to mean "access" (so, for example, NRSV), but this scarcely seems adequate. "Access" seems to mean that the way is open and that we may come when we will, and the word on occasion can have much this meaning. But the word strictly has the idea of "a bringing to"—there is the thought of an introducer, which "access" does not have. Paul is saying that it is through Christ that we come, not that we may come of ourselves. It is because of Christ's atoning work that we have both boldness and a Savior who brings us to the Father.

As Paul goes on to the thought of confidence, it is not certain whether he means (a) that we have boldness, and (b) that we approach in confidence, or whether both boldness and approach are in confidence. But in any case there is no great difference. Confidence is important for Paul; he uses the word six times and is the only New Testament writer to employ the term (and it is used only once in the Greek translation of the Old Testament). It is thus very much a Pauline word in Scripture, and it draws attention to an important part of the Christian life. Forgiven sinners do not come to God hesitantly, wondering about their likely reception. They rest not on their own achievement but on what Christ has done for them, and for that reason they come full of confidence.

With this is linked "faith in him [Christ]." Faith is the basic Christian quality and one to which Paul constantly reverts. So central is faith for Christians that they may be called simply "believers," people who have put their trust in Jesus Christ. Christian faith means the abandonment of trust in one's own achievements and a coming to rely on what Christ has done to bring us salvation.

Perhaps we should notice that in Greek the same word is used for both "faith" and "faithfulness," and some scholars hold that we should see the latter meaning here. In that case Paul is saying that we should approach God in confidence because of Christ's faithfulness. There is truth in this, but in this passage it seems that Paul is referring, rather, to faith in Christ.

The Greek that opens verse 13 might be interpreted in more ways than one. The verb "ask" may be used either of prayer or of a request to humans. Paul may be asking the Ephesians not to faint at his sufferings ("I beg you, then, not to be discouraged," GNB), or praying that the Ephesians should not faint ("I pray therefore that you may not lose heart," NRSV), or he may be asking God that he himself should not faint ("I ask that what I am having to suffer for your sake may not make me lose heart," *Goodspeed*). On the whole it seems that the first way of taking it is to be preferred. There is nothing in the context to indicate a prayer, and the argument of the whole section makes it unlikely that Paul is referring to a possible fainting of his own. He is afraid that the Ephesians might faint at his sufferings, not that he himself would do this.

"Therefore" in this verse draws a conclusion from the great truths to which the apostle has just drawn attention. Because God has done such wonderful things through Christ, because he has demonstrated even to the spirit powers the fulfillment of his eternal purpose, the Ephesians should be encouraged and not give way to gloom. They might well have been depressed at Paul's imprisonment and at all that he had had to suffer. They might have concluded that this new religion was unable to stand up to the might of Rome. Paul has made them see that such a conclusion is shallow and not in accordance with the facts. God has been working out a great eternal purpose, and the seemingly powerful Romans are nothing greater than players of bit parts. In their stupidity they may convince themselves that they can do as they will with the Christians, even blot out the whole Christian movement with their persecutions. But that is shallow thinking. It concentrates on what humans are doing and overlooks the far more significant fact that God is active and that he is working out his purpose through the crucified Christ and through those who have come to salvation through faith in that Christ.

So Paul urges his readers not to "faint" at what was befalling him. The verb "faint" may be used in the sense of becoming physically weary but also signifies losing heart, and there is no doubting that this is its meaning here. The Greek word underlying "afflictions" has the notion of pressure. It is used, for example, of pressing grapes, when it denotes pressure to the point of bursting. We should be clear that Paul is not speaking of some minor irritation, but of severe hardship, pressure to the bursting point. Here he makes it clear to the Ephesians that he was in deep trouble.

Interestingly, he says that this is "on your behalf." We would have no trouble in seeing the apostle's sufferings as an example for other people or as a way of demonstrating his depth of commitment or the like. But

Paul sees what he is suffering as in some way a help to the Ephesians. Elsewhere he speaks of his sufferings as filling up what was lacking in the sufferings of Christ "on behalf of his body, which is the church" (Col. 1:24). We should not think of Paul as grimly putting up with the afflictions that came his way, knowing that he could not escape but rebelling all the way. No. For Paul, the sufferings attendant on his mission were meaningful. They related to the sufferings of Christ, and they related to the needs of fellow-believers. They were part of the way in which the great divine purpose was set forward. As Dietrich Bonhoeffer put it, "To endure the cross is not a tragedy: it is the suffering which is the fruit of an exclusive allegiance to Jesus Christ. When it comes, it is not an accident, but a necessity. It is not the sort of suffering which is inseparable from this mortal life, but the suffering which is an essential part of the specifically Christian life. It is not suffering *per se* but suffering-and-rejection, and not rejection for any cause or conviction of our own, but rejection for the sake of Christ" (Bonhoeffer, *The Cost of Discipleship*, p. 78).

Another aspect of suffering that we should not overlook is revealed in a remark Paul made to the Corinthians. He wrote to them of the "momentary light affliction" as working for us "an eternal weight of glory beyond measure" (2 Cor. 4:17). The Ephesians should not miss the fact that Paul's afflictions were working towards that glory. Indeed Paul uses that very word "glory" in this passage to bring out the point that his sufferings on behalf of other Christians were in some way their glory. The Ephesians might well be shocked and grieved by what they knew of Paul's sufferings, but the apostle does not want them to lose sight of the more significant facts that in some way those sufferings set forward the divine purpose and that in some way they brought glory for people like those first readers of this letter.

10

To Know the Love of Christ

For this reason I bow my knees to the Father, from whom every family in heaven and on earth is named, in order that he may give you according to the riches of his glory to be strengthened in the inner man with power through his Spirit, that Christ may dwell in your hearts through faith, so that, being rooted and grounded in love, you may be strong to grasp together with all the saints what is the breadth and length and height and depth and to know the love of Christ that surpasses knowledge so that you may be filled to (the measure of) all the fullness of God (Eph. 3:14–19).

"For this reason" in 3:14 takes up the same expression used in verse 1 of this chapter and proceeds with the argument that Paul then broke off. The "reason" for what Paul is about to write is the state of the Ephesians as outlined at the end of chapter 2: their being built together spiritually so that they are God's household in the Spirit. Because of their position, and because they are still being built together in the divine household, Paul looks for them to make further progress and he prays for them.

"I bow my knees to the Father" must be taken to mean "I kneel in prayer to God." This is not the usual way of saying "I kneel" (which is rather "I place the knees," as, for example, in Acts 7:60), but there can be no doubt about the meaning. Kneeling was not the usual posture for prayer (Barth speaks here of "this extraordinary attitude of prayer"). As a general rule people stood when they prayed. Thus Jesus said, "When you stand praying" (Mark 11:25), which indicates that this was the ordinary way of praying. Again, in his parable of the Pharisee and the tax collector, both men stood—the Pharisee "stood and prayed to himself" while the tax man "stood at a distance" (Luke 18:11, 13). But sometimes at especially solemn times people prayed on their knees, as Jesus did in Gethsemane (Luke 22:41) and Stephen did when he was being stoned (Acts 7:60). Calvin remarks, "Not that prayer always requires kneeling, but because this sign of reverence is commonly employed, especially where prayer is not perfunctory, but serious." Every time Scripture speaks of prayer offered kneeling the occasion is serious.

Paul's prayer is directed "to the Father" where "the" Father points us to the one Father of all. People sometimes referred to the father of a nation or a tribe or some other group, but in the simple expression "the Father" we cannot limit the application to any one group. The term "Father" also indicates that the apostle is not praying to some remote and disinterested deity but to someone who loves his people. Paul sees God as a loving Father who will surely respond to the prayer of even the lowliest of his servants (as Paul held he himself was, v. 8), so prayer may confidently be addressed to him.

Considering his strong argument for the unity of Jewish and Gentile believers in chapter 2, we might have expected the apostle to go on "from whom the whole family . . ." and indeed this is what the King James Version and some other translations read (v. 15). But this would require the definite article in the Greek and Paul does not use it here. H. C. G. Moule and others argue that the language of the Greek New Testament is "less precise" than that of classical Greek and therefore that the meaning of KJV should be accepted. But the natural way to understand what the apostle writes is "every family," as most modern translations agree.

The word I have translated "family" denotes people descended from a common ancestor. It is sometimes translated "fatherhood"(*Phillips* and others), but this is not its meaning. Foulkes cites Allan for the view that the term means "any father-headed group," and that seems to be the meaning. In both the other places where it occurs in the New Testament (Luke 2:4; Acts 3:25) it signifies "family," people who have a common father. Outside the New Testament it is sometimes used for a larger group, a clan, a tribe, or even a nation; it can signify any group with a common ancestor. Moulton and Milligan see its meaning here as "a group of persons united by descent from a common father or ancestor." This should surely be accepted; "family"—those in relationship to the Father—is surely in mind at this point.

"Every family in heaven" recalls the fact that the rabbis sometimes referred to "the family above" when they spoke of angels. If this is what Paul has in mind, it would seem to signify that there are different groups among the angels (which, of course, is not impossible, though we have no other evidence for it). It is probably not wise, however, to pry too closely into what the apostle is saying about heaven. His point is that God is "Father" in the sense that every fatherhood, in heaven as on earth, derives from him. He is the source of all fatherhood, wherever it may be. We should not think that human fatherhood is the standard, that we start from what we know about fatherhood from our human families and apply that to God. Paul is saying that God is the source of all father-hood and that it is only as we know God as Father that we know what fatherhood really means.

"On earth" points to all those groups on earth who stand in a right relationship to the heavenly Father (Jewish Christians and Gentile Chris-tians?). The primary thought with respect both to the families on earth and those in heaven is that of relationship to the Father, not the divisions between the groups. Wherever it is, every family "is named," gets its name as "family," from God. Paul is consistent in seeing the divine initiative. Some have suggested that the meaning here is "gets its name as 'sons of God,'" but "gets its name as family" seems more likely. In antiquity the name was, of course, very important; the name and the quality it signi-fied went together. To be given a name meant more than to acquire a des-ignation; it meant to acquire whatever the name signified. Here we should probably understand the apostle to be saying that every family gets its status as family from the fact that God names it as such.

Membership in the divine family is not aimless, and Paul proceeds to the purpose ("in order that," v. 16) of his bowing the knees in prayer or perhaps the content of his prayer. We might also discern a reference to the purpose of God in admitting people as family members, but, while it is true that the divine purpose is fulfilled when God names people in his heavenly family, in this passage Paul seems, rather, to be giving the con-tent of his prayer. He asks God to give the members of the family the gift of being "strengthened in the inner man" (literally "into the inner man," which indicates the direction he wants the gift to take). It is consistent New Testament teaching that we are not able to serve God acceptably in our own strength. All too easily we give way to stronger forces or simply succumb to what we see as desirable in the temptations we encounter along the way. To walk in the ways of God we need a strength more than our own, and Paul prays that his converts may know that strength.

Divine Power

The aid for which Paul looks is "with power" and is "through his Spirit." This appears to be a way of asking for the divine power to be exercised through the Holy Spirit. Some have seen the "power" as the power of the converts and suggest that Paul is asking that God will give them the power they need. But this means something like praying that they may be "strengthened with strength," which is tautology and does not appear to be the probable meaning. It is much more likely that it is God's power that is in mind and that Paul looks for that power to be set in motion through the Holy Spirit. Calvin points out that we should not try to separate Christ and the Holy Spirit: "We are partakers of the Holy Spirit to the extent that we share in Christ; for the Spirit will be found nowhere but in Christ, on whom He is said to have rested for that purpose. Nor can Christ be separated from His Spirit; for then He would be, so to say, dead, and empty of His power."

Paul asks further that the gift may be given "according to the riches of his glory," which points us to an exceedingly strong power. Human power at best is puny. It is said that in the early days of World War II when there were bombing raids on Britain, there were grave fears that magnificent old buildings would be destroyed. Special arrangements were made to protect many of them, and Winston Churchill explained to the Archbishop of Canterbury in some detail what had been done to safeguard Canterbury Cathedral. "We are sure," the Prime Minister ended, "that the cathedral is safe from anything but a direct hit." The Archbishop replied gloomily, "But what if there is a direct hit?" "My dear Archbishop," said Churchill testily, "that you must regard as a direct summons!" The story reminds us that even with the best will in the world there is always a limit to what people can do in this life. But Paul is not writing about what people can do in this life by putting forward their best effort. He is pointing the Ephesians to the truth that believers do not depend on power as this world knows power, but on the power that is "according to the riches of [God's] glory." That power enables them to do what they could never do in their own strength.

The "glory" of God stands for all that is magnificent in the heavenly realm, and "according to the riches" of this glory looks for an exercise of the divine power that is in accordance with the wealth of heaven. It is no niggardly salvation for which Paul prays. It is a depressing fact of life that in every age people have found it much easier to go along with the low standards of the society in which they live than to accept the divine standards and put their energies into the service of God and therefore of their fellows. This has been so from the beginning, and Paul prays to God for strength to be given to the converts. He does not want them to be content with the low standards and poor achievements that the worldly-minded accept as the norm.

The apostle looks for Christ to "dwell" in the hearts of the Ephesian Christians (v. 17). The verb he uses here is not very common in the Pauline writings (three times only). It indicates a permanent settlement, not a casual visit or even a temporary sojourn. The "heart," of course, stands for the whole of the inner being: thoughts, will, emotions, and whatever else there may be at the center of what we are. If Christ dwells in our hearts he is at the very center of our being and exercises his influence over all that we do and are.

This is not some physical or mechanical form of dwelling, but something that takes place "through faith." As we have seen in earlier passages, faith is for Paul a concept of central importance, and here he sees it as the means "through" which the divine indwelling takes place. The apostle uses a variety of constructions with "believe" and "faith." He may refer to believing that . . . , to believing Christ, to believing in Christ, to faith in Christ, to faith on Christ, and so on. The way he puts it here indicates that the gift is one that is appropriated and *can* be appropriated only in faith. Faith is not a merit that is rewarded with the gift. Rather, the gift is of such a kind that it can be received only by faith.

In my younger days it was common to have Sunday school picnics, times when the whole Sunday school was taken off for a day of recreation and rejoicing. I remember one such day when at lunchtime it was my task to carry round a four-gallon container of a cool drink and fill up the mugs that the children had brought. I came to one energetic boy who had evidently spent the morning running hard and was now obviously hot, out of breath, and thirsty. Indeed, I thought that at that moment he probably had Australia's No. 1 Thirst. Though I had gallons of refreshing liquid that I was eager to give to him, he had no mug, no means of receiving what I was offering. Fortunately we were able to find a mug somewhere, so the lad did not perish in the wilderness.

The boy's mug was not a way of earning his drink. It was no more than the means by which he could receive it. And faith is something like that. Without faith we cannot receive the gift God offers. But when we do believe, that does not mean that we earn salvation. Faith is no more, and of course no less, than the means whereby we receive God's good gift.

Love

Paul moves on to the necessity for love in the Christian life. He has spoken of this virtue before (see comments on 1:4), but now he brings out the fundamental importance of love with the use of two metaphors that stress its significance. His word order puts emphasis on love by putting the word "love" first: literally, "in love being rooted and founded." Paul looks for the Ephesians to be "rooted" in love. Just as the roots are of the utmost importance for plants, so love is of the utmost importance for believers. Love is the root that sustains them and through which their spiritual nourishment is derived, and the use of the perfect tense in the participle points to something that is permanent. The verb properly applies to plant life, but in Greek writings it is sometimes used in other ways; the lexicons cite its use, for example, of a bridge, among other things. The usage is not unlike that in English, where "rooted" is often used of things other than plant life. But the metaphor takes it point from the absolute necessity of the roots if the plant is to live, let alone flourish. Paul does not envisage a mere occasional loving impulse; he sees love as at all times basic to Christian living.

With "rooted" Paul links "grounded," thus combining agricultural and architectural imagery. Here the metaphor is taken from laying the foundation of a building. Again the apostle uses the perfect passive participle, which indicates what is permanent. A solid, well-laid foundation is a necessity if a building is to last. Paul is saying that love is that foundation for the believer. The use of the two metaphors perhaps means that Paul does not wish to take either as exclusively indicating the reality. Each draws attention to an important aspect, and the combination of the root and the foundation imagery puts special emphasis on the importance of love in the Christian life. It is not too much to say that love is the source of the Christian's strength and the firm foundation on which the Christian's life is established (cf. Knox, "may your lives be rooted in love, founded on love"; REB felicitously reads "With deep roots and firm foundations").

From the derivation of nourishment (the root) and the base on which everything else is built (the foundation), Paul turns to mental strength (v. 18). He speaks of his prayer that the Ephesians may be strong in understanding. We should not miss the point that Paul expects his friends at Ephesus to think hard about their religion. Christians all too easily emphasize the "spiritual" and concentrate on their devotional life. Of course, nobody would minimize the importance of the devotional life; Christianity without it would not be Christianity. But this is also the case with the intellectual aspect of the faith. Christians are expected to use the brains that God has given them and to think through the implications of the great central truths to which they are committed. Here the verb "be strong" is not the simple verb but a compound that seems to mean "that you may be fully strong" or the like. Paul is referring to something more than an ability simply to cope; he looks for the believer to have abundant strength. We see this also in the verb "to grasp," which has a meaning like "to seize" or "to lay hold of." When one "grasps a truth one is not hesitantly wondering; the verb points to sure knowledge. Such sure knowledge, of course, does not spring from human ability, which is why Paul makes it the object of prayer.

This comprehension takes place "together with all the saints." As we have seen, Paul puts a good deal of emphasis on the Christian community. Though his letters amount to no more than about a quarter of the New Testament, more than half the references to the church in the New Testament are found in them. In addition, as here, he often refers to "the saints." In fact he uses this expression (with or without the article) forty times, which is more than in all the rest of the New Testament put together. For the apostle, the Christian religion is not something to be practiced in our solitariness, but something to be lived out with other believers. It has, of course, something to say about our solitariness, and if we are not committed to Christ when we are alone we are not committed. But Christians are a society; their life together is important.

Paul is not saying that we should be Christian only when we are in company with other believers. Rather, he is saying that it is only in company with other believers that we can enter into the fullness of what the Christian way means. We know something of love in what God has done to us personally, but we know the fullness of love only when we see what God has done in "all the saints." The words rule out any suggestion that there may be a spiritual elite who looks down on the rank and file of church membership. That is impossible in genuine Christianity. All believers need all the other believers to enter into the full understanding of the love of God.

E. K. Simpson has a wonderful turn of phrase regarding Paul's insistence on the place of every Christian in this prayer: "The ancient mystagogues restricted their choicest teachings to an esoteric circle, industriously sifted from the vulgar herd of auditors, admission to which was counted in itself no small privilege. But Paul reckons every convert a candidate for honours, or he would not have offered such an exalted prayer on their behalf." We should not miss the great importance of the lowliest of God's people.

Paul goes on to speak of comprehending "what is the breadth and length and height and depth," which is surely a way of emphasizing totality; an object has three dimensions, but Paul puts in a fourth. Look at it as you will, he is saying, the whole is known. The expression also underlines the vastness of what there is to be known.

But what is it that is to be known in this way? Paul does not say explicitly. Some commentators think he is referring back to the mystery that featured so much in the earlier part of the chapter, others that it is the temple, which has occupied Paul earlier (cf. 2:21); still others hold that it may be the grace of God or the love of God. But there seems no reason why any one of these should be referred to, and it seems unlikely that Paul would speak of any of them in this way. Abbott cites references from the early Christian writers who seem often to have discerned a reference here to the cross of Christ, but this seems fanciful.

It is much more likely that we are to see the words as referring to "the love of Christ," which immediately follows. The New International Version takes this meaning and renders "to grasp how wise and long and high and deep is the love of Christ." This, however, turns a series of nouns into adjectives and overlooks the fact that "the love of Christ" is the object of the verb "to know," not an addition to the words about dimensions. We may say that our best understanding is that Paul has in mind "the love of Christ" when he speaks of his four dimensions, but that does not give us the license to translate in a way that remodels the way he has expressed himself.

Paradoxically, the prayer is that the Ephesians may "know the love of Christ that surpasses knowledge" (v. 19). This does not mean, as some have urged, that love in itself surpasses knowledge. Rather, Paul is saying that the love of Christ is so great that no one can ever know it all. No matter how much we know of the love of Christ, there is always more to know. Although the expression "the love of Christ" can sometimes mean our love for Christ, there is not the slightest doubt that here it means *his* love for us. Paul is saying that we never come to know all that love. No matter how fully we enter into Christ's love for us, there is always something more to be known. At the same time we should notice that Paul does not specify who is loved by "the love of Christ." Paul is not emphasizing that this love is directed toward the church or to believers generally or to the Ephesians. All these and more will, of course, be included. But by the way Paul expresses himself the emphasis is on Christ as the loving one, rather than on any specific recipients.

The prayer ends with "that you may be filled" and then literally "into all the fullness of God." I have taken this to mean that it is the fullness of God that gives us the measure of the fullness with which we have been filled; we are filled up to the measure of the divine fullness. It is possible, however, to leave out the reference to measure and to understand the passage to mean " that you may be filled with all the fullness of God" (so NRSV). There is probably no great difference in meaning, with NRSV more in our modern idiom and my translation closer to the Greek.

Glory to God

Now to him who is able to do superabundantly more than all that we ask or imagine according to the power that works within us, to him be the glory in the church and in Christ Jesus to all the generations for ever and ever, Amen (Eph. 3:20–21).

Paul breaks off to ascribe glory to God, though without using the word "God"; he prefers to speak of what God can do, but the terms in which he does this leave us in no doubt that he is referring to God. He speaks first of God's power, saying that God is "able," has the power, where Paul's verb is that from which we get our word "dynamite." He uses a noun from the same root a little later when he speaks of "the power" that works in us, a word play difficult to reproduce in English. The apostle leaves no doubt about the mighty ability of God. His adverb "superabundantly" is a compound that starts from a word meaning "over and above." To this, two prepositions are prefixed, the first of which has the meaning of completeness and the second, "more, beyond." The result is a very expressive compound to indicate what is abundantly more. Paul uses it again in 1 Thessalonians 3:10; 5:13, but it does not seem to be cited anywhere else. Abbott takes from Ellicott the point that there are twenty-eight words compounded with hyper (the preposition used here) and of these "twenty-two are found in St. Paul's Epistles and Heb., and twenty of these are found there alone." The point of this piece of linguistics is that Paul is fond of words expressing the idea of abundance and uses them cheerfully even though many of them are used by nobody else. Which leaves us wondering whether he coined them because the words people generally used were not expressive enough for him.

Paul frequently exhorts his readers to pray and often prays himself, but now he says that God can do far more than we ever ask. Our praying is apt to be limited by what we think is possible. Even though we do not consciously set a limit to what we ask from God, yet being finite beings we pray as finite beings do. We have no conception of what almighty power can do. Paul says it goes beyond our knowledge and understanding: God's power is capable of doing more than we can even imagine! Paul is advocating prayer to a God who is greater by far than our feeble imaginations can stretch. Prayer is not concerned only with what we can think up; prayer is directed to the omnipotent God, and he answers, not according to our puny petitions, but according to his mighty omnipotence.

And that power is already at work within believers! Paul goes on to speak of the power "that works within us." He does not stop to spell this out, for at this point he is concerned with God and the greatness of God, not with what happens in the hearts and lives of believers. But his correspondence as a whole makes it very clear that the power of God had done great things in those who had been converted to Christianity and that it continued to do great things. Paul was not satisfied with a mini-mouse kind of Christianity. He saw it as important that the humblest believer should make abundant use of the power of God that was at work in every believer. So, while he speaks here of God as working unimaginable things, those things are akin to what happens in all believers, Paul and his readers alike ("within us").

"To him" then "the glory—" (v. 21). It is natural to supply "be"—"to him be glory"—though we could, of course, understand the words as "to him is the glory." But in a doxology it seems more likely that we should understand "be." Paul is not unmindful of the glory that people ascribe to God here and now, but he is looking forward to the fullest ascription of glory at the end of all things. Paul has used the word "glory" five times in chapter 1 and now three times in this chapter. He is in no doubt as to the glory that is to be associated with God.

It is perhaps surprising that he speaks of glory "in the church" before that "in Christ Jesus" (though we should notice that a little later in this letter "one body," i.e. the church, comes before "one Lord" [4:4–5], or that the church is the bride of Christ [5:31–32], so that the two are closely connected). Paul prefers to use an ascending order in this place. Some manuscripts omit "and," which would give the meaning "in the church that is in Christ Jesus." But, while it is true that the church is in Christ, this does not appear to be what Paul is saying at this point. He sees glory in what Christ has done in believers and he sees glory in his Savior and he looks for both glories to continue.

Paul speaks of the glory as continuing "to all the generations." No matter how long the human race lasts on this earth glory is to be ascribed to the church and to Christ. The expression "to all the generations" means literally "of the age of the ages, amen." Hodge translates it "to all the generations of an eternity of ages." This seems to signify one vast "age" that takes in all the ages. We think of an infinity of moments as making up one age; Paul is referring to an age so vast that every "moment" in it is what we would call an age. But we should probably not try to analyze the expression too closely. Paul is using exuberant language and pointing to glory that will never cease. Similar doxologies are found in a number of places, but nowhere else do we have exactly the same wording as here.

11

The Unity of the Spirit

I beseech you therefore, I the prisoner in the Lord, that you walk worthily of the calling with which you were called, with all lowliness and meekness, with long-suffering, bearing with one another in love, being diligent to keep the unity of the Spirit in the bond of peace. There is one body and one Spirit just as you were also called in one hope of your calling; one Lord, one faith, one baptism, one God and Father of all, who is over all and through all and in all (Eph. 4:1–6).

Quite often Paul begins a letter with a solid doctrinal section in which he discourses on important Christian truths, after which he turns to the kind of conduct that befits people who accept those truths. He passes from what we must believe to what we must do. He does that in this letter. Some object that the earlier chapters of this letter are praise rather than doctrine, but, while there is something in that, it is still the case that even while Paul is calling his readers to praise God he is teaching them. Throughout the earlier part of the letter he has been teaching the Ephesians (and us) important truths about God and Christ and the church. Now he turns to the kind of conduct that ought to characterize people who accept those truths. His "therefore" (4:1) is important. Because the things he has been saying in the earlier chapters are true, *therefore* the Ephesians should live in such-and-such a way. Doctrine for Paul is not a collection of abstract ideas, important only for dry-as-dust theologians in their studies. Doctrine is the systematic setting forth of truths, important truths that Christians live by. Doctrine, truly under-stood, leads to action; faith and works belong together.

That right doctrine leads to right conduct is important and is a truth we sometimes overlook. I recall a conference of bush pastors I once attended. We had gathered at a small hospital, and on a sunny day in winter we brought chairs outside and enjoyed the sunshine as we dis-cussed our profound business. We heard later that the small daughter of a lady who came that day to help with the hospital's laundry dismissed us contemptuously: "They are supposed to be having a conference and all they are doing is talking!" I hope this was not a true evaluation of that particular conference, but such a description might be applied to a good deal that Christians do. We are better at talking than at living out the faith. Paul will not let us forget that what we *do* is important, more important than what we say.

Though Paul sees right conduct as very important, indeed the nec-essary outcome of the truths he has expounded in the opening chap-ters, he does not bluster or dictate. We might expect that he would com-mand the Ephesians to do this or that, but he begins this section of the letter with "I beseech you." Paul leaves no doubt as to what he wants his readers to do, but he leaves no doubt either that he wants this to be in accordance with their own resolution. He advises and requests, but in the end they must live their own lives and therefore come to their own decision.

Yet Paul leaves no doubt as to the importance with which he regards his request. He uses the emphatic "I" (as in 3:1) and reminds his read-ers that he is "the prisoner in the Lord" and therefore one whose advice should be taken with full seriousness. His appeal does not come from one whose circumstances are comfortable, but from one who himself suffers for the Lord. In his earlier reference to his imprisonment he spoke of himself as "the prisoner of Christ Jesus for the sake of you, the Gentiles" (3:1), but here he is the prisoner "in the Lord," an expres-sion that Paul uses more than forty times. It is not dissimilar to this frequent use of "in Christ" (which may occur as often as 200 times), though C. F. D. Moule suggests that there may be a difference, at least on some occasions. Moule points out that "in Christ" is often used with statements and "in the Lord" with exhortations or commands. He sees "in Christ" as used when Paul is speaking of Christ's saving work and "in the Lord" with its working out in human conduct. "In short, if one uses the familiar Christian cliché, 'Become what you are!', then one may say that what you are is 'in Christ', and what you are to become is 'in the Lord'" (Moule, *The Origin of Christology*, [London: Cambridge University Press, 1977], p. 59). Whether or not Moule's distinction can be shown elsewhere, it certainly applies here. Paul is urging the Ephesian Christians to become more fully what they are—people redeemed by the precious blood of Jesus in order that they may serve God faithfully.

Paul first urges his appeal in general terms. He asks the Ephesians to "walk worthily" of their calling. We have seen that Paul often uses the metaphor of walking to indicate steady progress in the path of life (see comments on 2:2), and here he is clearly exhorting his friends to make a consistent advance along the Christian way. All Christians would surely agree that this is the right thing to do, but, without putting it into words, many reach a plateau in their Christian experience and are content to stay there. Paul wants the Ephesians to keep pressing on. Christians have never done enough in the Lord's service. They never reach a high point when they can say, "I need do no more!" They must continue to "walk," to make progress in the path of service.

Paul goes on to speak of walking "worthily of the calling with which you were called," where the conjunction of two words from the same root puts emphasis on the idea of call. The noun "call" is almost confined to Paul in the New Testament (he uses it nine times out of the New Testament total of eleven), and, while he has no such preponderance with the verb, the fact that he uses it thirty-three times shows that it is an important word for the apostle. It matters to Paul that Christians have been called by God. Their "walk," their whole manner of life, should be "worthy" of their call. The fact that they have been the objects of a divine call must affect everything they do. It is easy to think that since God has called us we need make no great effort in the Christian way. Paul is not of this opinion. Rather, he sees the divine call as the incentive and the standard for Christian living. This call puts Christian living on the highest plane.

It often seems to believers that they are Christians because they have made up their minds that this is the way they want to go. They may indeed have done this, but on Paul's view this would be only because there has already been a divine work within them. It is important for the apostle that God is always the initiator in the work of salvation. God took the initiative in sending his Son to die to put away our sins, and God continues with the initiative in calling us out of our self-centered lives into lives of service. Relating the divine initiative to human freedom is an intricate process, and no way of doing this has commended itself to Christians as a whole. But that does not matter. What does matter is that we recognize that we owe everything to God and that he took the initiative in bringing us to salvation. It is that divine initiative on which Paul is placing emphasis at this point.

Lowliness

It is natural to the human race to be self-assertive. We all instinctively try to get the best for ourselves. In every walk of life people try to reach what they see as the top and to attain what they see as prosperity. It is easy for this natural tendency to be nourished in such a way that people become selfish, concentrating on what will be to their own advantage. Christians feel this temptation just as much as other people do. It is not natural for the human race to be lowly or humble.

But Christianity is not another example of the outworking of this human tendency. At the heart of Christianity is the cross, the cross on which the Son of God laid down his precious life. For sinners! And when sinners in faith accept the salvation he offers, there is no room for human merit. All who are saved—rich and poor, civilized and uncivilized, educated and uneducated, oppressors and oppressed, slaves and free—are saved not because of any achievement of their own but because Christ has died for them. As the hymnwriter has put it:

> *No merit of my own I claim*
> *But humbly lean on Jesus' name.*

In the light of this there is no room for pride in the Christian, and the New Testament often rebukes any such attitude. So Paul here specifically calls on the Ephesians to show "all lowliness and meekness" (v. 2) in the walk that issues from their divine call.

It appears to have been a new thing in the ancient world to see lowliness as a virtue. The word Paul uses here seems to have been rarely used by Greek speakers in general, and when they did they saw its meaning (and also that of related words that they did use more often) not as a virtue but as a defect. Thus the Jewish historian Josephus uses it of the "meanness" of Galba when he refused a gift to the praetorians that had been promised in his name (*War,* IV, 494). Trench finds "few and exceptional" the occasions when the word group is used for anything "which is not grovelling, slavish and mean-spirited." Paul is not simply reproducing a common first-century attitude. He is flying in the face of accepted values when he advocates a way of life that accorded indeed with Jesus (who was "meek and lowly of heart," Matt. 11:29), but that was rejected by the thinkers of the day. J. Armitage Robinson comments, "To the Greek mind humility was little else than a vice of nature. It was weak and mean-spirited; it was the temper of the slave; it was inconsistent with that self-respect which every true man owed to himself." But Christians are called to have the same mind as Christ, "who humbled himself" (Phil. 2:8).

The same must be said, of course, of Paul's call to "meekness" (a word he uses in eight of its eleven New Testament occurrences). This was not a quality that was highly esteemed in the first-century Roman Empire. The first concerns of both the Romans and their subject peoples were to set forward their personal aims regardless of the consequences to other people. "In the thinking of the Jew loftiness was alone the sign of lordliness; and in the teaching of the Greek sovereignty was displayed in strength. But for the Christian meekness is the badge of mightiness" (H. D. McDonald).

Meekness is a virtue that Jesus commended when he pronounced "blessed" those who exercise it (Matt. 5:5) and that he manifested in his own life and teaching. We should not misunderstand the term as though it were synonymous with weakness. R. Gutzwiller says of the meek, "These are not the weak in character, the meekly submissive or the fearful compromisers. Christianity is not a crutch for the sick or a parapet for the dizzy, a substitute for those who have missed something else. Therefore the gospel is not a hymn in praise of people without stuffing or strength" (Gutzwiller, *Day by Day with Saint Matthew's Gospel* [London: Darton, Longman, and Todd, 1964], p. 27). We should be clear that meekness is a virtue of the strong, those who *could* exert force to get their own way but choose not to.

To this Paul adds, "with long-suffering" (another Pauline word; Paul has it in ten of its fourteen New Testament occurrences). We have the word "short-tempered"; we do not usually speak of the opposite virtue as "long-tempered," but this is the literal meaning of the word Paul uses here. It points to the virtue that resists provocation. When a wrong is done to us our natural tendency is to resist strongly, perhaps even to pay back the wrongdoer for the wrong that has been done. The Christian, however, is not self-assertive in that sense. The Christian is one who is considerate of others even under provocation, one who resists the temptation to strike back. God is long-suffering even toward the impenitent (Rom. 2:4), and God's people must follow in God's ways. Long-suffering is part of the fruit of the Spirit (Gal. 5:22; meekness is also found in this list), and believers must always look to the Holy Spirit for help to achieve this quality.

Next on Paul's list is "bearing with one another in love." Paul is realistic. Christians are not always easy to get on with, and fellow Christians sometimes have irritating faults, so the temptation comes to be short with one another. But this, Paul says, is not the Christian way. Rather, Christians should always bear in mind that they have been forgiven at great cost and that a most important part of the new life they enjoy in Christ is that they live it in love. And love, as Christians know it, is not an affection for the kind of people we like naturally. It is a response to the love that God has shown us in Christ, a love that dies to redeem the unworthy. Christians love, but not because it has been their good fortune to come across attractive people. They love because of what they have become, not because of the qualities they admire in other people. God loves the unworthy and so do the people of God. Redeemed in Christ, they have become loving people, and because they are loving people they bear with one another. They know that people are not always as considerate as they should be, but that is not the point. The point is that believers have been died for, and part of their response to that atoning death is love—love for God, who saved them, and love for the people whom God loves, trying though they may be at times.

Paul now turns to the importance of Christian unity (v. 3). This is not the achievement of believers; it is something that is done for them by Christ. They are not commanded to bring this unity about, for Christ has done this. They are to "keep" it, that is, to ensure that it continues. That believers are to bear with one another surely implies that sometimes they will not see eye to eye and that one believer will think that another is in error. Though among other groups that might be thought cause for quarrels, that is not the way Christians should behave. When we consider the grievous quarrels believers have had with one another through the centuries, it is clear that some of us have given insufficient attention to the apostle's injunction. But whatever mistakes believers have made, that is no cause for us to forsake the command Paul gives. Unity among believers is of first importance and we are to show diligence in maintaining it. There may be occasions when we cannot succeed, but that should never be our fault. We should all put forth our best effort and be diligent to maintain unity.

I am not denying that sometimes the differences between believers have been so strong that schism was the necessary result. Nor am I denying that in the modern church it is sometimes necessary for a strong stand to be made in the face of firm opposition from other believers. But I am saying that nothing gives us license to ignore the apostle's directions. Whatever be the case with other people, and no matter how necessary it may be to stand firm in some matter where there are divergent opinions, nothing gives us license to cease to act in love or to let unity slip away. Those who love the Lord are called upon to be loving people and to see the importance of unity with others who likewise love the Lord, even when they take action that seems to us to be less than desirable. E. K. Simpson points out that "not a few genuine, but crotchety, believers have no sense of proportion or perspective. To their distorted vision molehills and mountains are much alike; either of them presents a fatal barrier in their cantankerous judgments to co-operation." We

115

must be on our guard against making such errors ourselves and must also treat those who do make them as our brothers and sisters in Christ.

Whatever the situation, believers are to be "diligent to keep the unity of the Spirit in the bond of peace" (v. 3). The verb for "be diligent" has about it the idea of being quick to do something. From that we get the idea of keenness to do it and thus of diligence. What follows is a duty not to be neglected. The King James Version reads "endeavouring," but it has been pointed out that this translation implies the possibility of failure. Paul's word, however, does not have this implication: it simply points to the importance of diligent application.

Notice again that the verb "to keep" does not mean "to produce" or the like. Paul is saying there is *already* a unity, not that his readers should bring unity about. And "the unity of the Spirit" of course does not mean that there is only one Spirit—that is a truth quite independent of anything that believers may say or do. Rather, it signifies the unity the Spirit gives, so that all believers are in some sense one. Some expositors have suggested that Paul is here referring to ecclesiastical unity, while others have thought that the human spirit is in mind, so that something like inner harmony is meant. But such views are inadequate. It is surely the unity the Holy Spirit gives that is in mind. Earlier Paul has said that Christ himself "is our peace" and that Christ has made "the two" (i.e., Jew and Gentile) one (2:14). Clearly both there and here he is speaking of a supernatural unity, a unity brought about from one point of view by Christ, from another by the Holy Spirit. Though this is not a unity that believers create, it is a unity they are responsible to keep.

The command "to keep the unity," then, means that we must promote this unity rather than hinder it. The command must jolt us all with the reflection that we have failed in this respect. The multiplicity of denominations and of parties within those denominations witnesses to anything but unity. That there is an underlying unity is surely true. And that we must not pursue organizational unity at the expense of treating great Christian doctrines lightly is also true. God has brought us into salvation through what Christ did at Calvary, and this must remain a bond between all true Christians. But our organizational disunity cannot but leave us convinced that somewhere along the line we have come short of our responsibility to "keep the unity of the Spirit."

Believers are to keep this unity of the Spirit "in the bond of peace." The word for "bond" is cognate with that for "prisoner" in verse 1, a link that is difficult to bring out in English. Perhaps Paul is hinting that the believer is the prisoner of peace. We should also notice that the Greek word is a compound, which we could render literally as "the with-bond." There was no need for the "with" to be inserted, and we find it difficult to insert it in English. But it strengthens the idea of unity: believers are

116

"with" one another, united by a bond that includes the thought of withness. As we have seen elsewhere, "with" is a frequent word in this letter—Paul hammers home the truth that believers belong "with" one another.

Christian Unities

This launches Paul into a listing of an interesting group combining divine persons and important aspects of the Christian faith (vv. 4–6). The style is staccato; there is a scarcity of verbs (we can insert "There is" at the beginning but Paul actually starts right in with "One body"). Paul simply has a series of nouns, each preceded by "one." The word "one" runs through the whole section; seven times Paul uses this word. Clearly it is important for him that believers are one.

He begins with "one body" (v. 4). To make a reasonable sentence in English we must insert "There is" (or some equivalent). The "one body" clearly refers to the church. Already in this letter Paul has spoken of "the church, which is his body" (1:22–23), and he has referred to the work of Christ as that of reconciling both Jew and Gentile to God "in one body" (2:16). When we look at the fragmented modern church we cannot but think that believers have failed to obey the Pauline command. But at this point it is important to notice that Paul thought of but *one church*. In his day it would have been easy to think of a Jewish church and a separate Gentile church, but nobody seems to have thought of such a solution to a number of difficult problems. For Paul, the unity of believers was very important.

He links "one body" with "one Spirit." There is, of course, no question of any other spirit than the Holy Spirit, nor is there any question of division within that Spirit. Paul's listing of the Spirit alongside the church, and his use of "one" before each, underlines his insistence on a unity of believers that clearly means so much to him. Elsewhere Paul writes, "In one Spirit we were all baptized into one body, whether Jew or Greeks, whether slaves or free" (1 Cor. 12:13). The linking of one body with one Spirit was important to him. And to us.

"Just as you were also called" moves the argument along to the divine call that God has given to his people, and to which Paul has made recent reference (v. 1). The church is not made up of some people who were called by God and some who were not. Paul sees all believers as "called" into the one body.

It is important not to have a shortsighted attitude toward life. Many years ago I first heard a story about a visitor to the site where Saint Paul's Cathedral was being built in London. The visitor asked one workman what he was doing. "I'm shaping this piece of stone," the man replied fully. The same question put to another elicited the reply, "I'm earning my pay." A third man responded with "I'm helping Sir Christopher Wren build a cathedral." All the answers were true, but the third showed that the man worked with a vision, with the realization that there was more in his job than appeared at first sight. Christians must always be like that. Whatever our job, we are helping our Lord do his work in the world. To see it as anything less is to rob ourselves as well as him.

Paul speaks of "one hope of your calling," which brings out the importance the apostle attaches to hope. In the New Testament hope contains an element of expectancy that is lacking in much modern hope. The New Testament believers *expected* what they hoped for. It is no gain but a grievous loss that the modern church has to a large extent lost that New Testament idea of hope. For most Christians these days, hope means much the same as it means to the non-Christians among whom they dwell—a kind of lukewarm optimism. This is a long way from the blazing certainty the word held for Paul, the certainty that there awaited believers the fulfillment of God's promises, with all the blessing that this implies. Here Paul is making the point that there is but one hope among believers. It was not that there were many hopes among believers, such that some, for example, hoped that Jesus would return and establish God's rule on earth, while others hoped no more than that Christians would live out the implications of their faith. Paul saw in the church "one hope of your calling" and that unitary hope meant a great deal to him. He can speak of "the hope of the gospel" (Col. 1:23) and of "the hope of glory" (Col. 1:27), but these are not two hopes; they are two aspects of the *one* great hope that results from the divine call to all believers.

From this Paul moves to "one Lord" (v. 5). The term "Lord" was used in a variety of ways in the first century. It could be a polite form of address much like our "sir," and we find this sometimes in the Gospels (e.g., Matt. 21:30). But since it was also the word used to translate the divine name when the Hebrew Old Testament was translated into Greek, it could be used in a very exalted sense. Throughout the Roman Empire it was in common use when people spoke of the deity they worshiped. For Christians, there was but one Lord. Jesus was not to be thought of as a petty deity, like the gods and goddesses so many people worshiped throughout the Roman world. He was the only Lord, the one whom Christians delighted to honor.

To the lordship of Christ Paul adds "one faith." This draws attention to the trust in Christ that was fundamental to the Christian way. Paul does not agree that there are many ways to salvation. There is only one way, the way of faith in Jesus Christ. We sometimes today talk about "the Christian faith," where "faith" refers to a whole system of beliefs and practices, but this is not what Paul is speaking of here. The use of the term for a body of belief is not common in the New Testament, and some students hold that it is never found there. This is probably going too far (cf. Jude 3), but certainly it is not a system of beliefs and practices that Paul has in mind here. He emphasizes the place of faith in the sense of trust in Christ and uses the concept again and again. He is here saying emphatically that Christianity does not know a variety of ways of being saved. There is one faith, faith in Jesus Christ who alone brings salvation.

So is it with baptism. Through the centuries Christians have had their arguments about baptism, but for Paul there was just one baptism. The baptism that took people out of whatever previous religious allegiances they had had and marked them as Christians. Those who have been baptized into Christ have put on Christ (Gal. 3:27). It is possible to argue about whether the apostle has primarily in mind baptism in water or baptism in the Spirit, but Paul is surely not making such distinctions at this point. We must bear in mind that on the day of Pentecost, when people who had been impressed by what had happened asked Peter what they should do, he told them to be baptized in the name of Jesus for the forgiveness of sins and they would receive the gift of the Holy Spirit (Acts 2:37–38). Paul is surely talking about such an experience. Baptism, the forgiveness of sins, and the coming of the Holy Spirit on the believer all went together. This does not, of course, mean that the outward rite of baptism automatically brings spiritual benefits. Baptism must be the outward mark of an inward faith if it is to be effective. But Paul is not stopping to go into detail and list every qualification. He is quickly laying down some Christian certainties, and that there was one baptism was obvious to him.

One God

Having made it clear that there is but one Spirit and one Lord, Paul goes on to say that thee is "one God and Father of all" (v. 6). In the world of his day that was an outrageous claim. For most people there were "gods many and lords many." Though an individual might worship only one God, he was conscious that there were many other deities who were worshiped and he did not deny their reality. He just did not worship them, but that did not mean for him that they did not exist. Yet Jews and Christians held firmly to the truth that there is one God and one God only. Paul is affirming this as he comes to the end of his little list of unities.

And this one God is "Father of all." That God is to be understood as Father means that he loves and cares for his worshipers. All that is best in human fatherhood and much more may be ascribed to God. This means that we may put our complete trust in him, knowing that as our

Father he will care for us without ceasing and will provide for our every need. That he is Father "of all" meant a good deal in a day when there was a sharp division between Jew and Gentile. Even though Jewish Christians seemed sometimes to have been convinced that Gentiles were no more than second-class Christians and had to be circumcised and thus admitted to Judaism before they were acceptable to God, Paul would have none of this nonsense. For him, it was clear that in God's sight divisions like that between Jew and Gentile meant nothing. God is the Father "of all."

Paul brings this little creedal statement to an end by telling us that the Father "is over all and through all and in all." There is an ambiguity here in that the Greek term "all" may be either masculine or neuter. Paul may be saying that God is over and through and in all *things* or in all *people*. And if "all" means all people there is a further problem as to whether he means all believers or all the human race. While there is no way of proving beyond any doubt that any one of these ways of taking the words is the right one, it seems that all believers is probably the best suggestion. While it is true that God is to be found throughout the entire creation (cf. Acts 17:28), it is more likely that as the climax of this little creed Paul would be speaking of God's indwelling of his people. And the same reasoning means that it is his presence in believers rather than in the whole race of which Paul is writing. Some manuscripts read "in us all" and a few "in you all" (so KJV) rather than "in all" and, while there is no real doubt that these insertions are not what Paul wrote, they are clear indications of how some early scribes understood the passage.

That God is "over all" points to his supremacy; he has the highest place of all and is sovereign over all his people. He is also "through all," which seems to mean that he works out his purposes "through" his people. And that he is "in all" points us back to the truth Paul expressed earlier when he spoke of believers as a "dwelling-place for God in the Spirit" (2:22). God lives in his people.

When we speak of the Trinity we usually employ the order Father, Son, and Holy Spirit, so it is worth asking why Paul reverses the order here. It may be that this is because he referred to the Spirit in verse 3 and this led him to speak of the Spirit first when he moved to the Godhead. It has also been pointed out that this is the order in which people are usually led to know God. There is first the evidence of the Holy Spirit at work in believers, which leads to the work of Christ that made possible this activity of the Spirit. And this in turn leads to the Father, the Creator of all.

12

The Perfecting of the Saints

Now to each one of us grace was given according to the measure of Christ's free gift. Therefore it says,

> *When he went up on high*
> *he took captive a host of captives*
> *he gave gifts to men.*

Now what does "he went up" mean if not that he also came down to the lower parts of the earth? He who came down is also he who went up high above the heavens so that he might fill all things (Eph. 4:7–10).

From the great realities of the Christian faith, centering on the Spirit, the Son, and the Father, Paul turns to the individual. Three times in 4:6 he has used the word "all" as he spoke of what is common to believers generally, but now he turns to what is characteristic of individuals. We all differ from one another, of course, in respect to our natural endowments, but Paul is not speaking of such variations. Rather, he is concerned with the different spiritual gifts that God has given to his people. He starts with the fact that it is all a matter of grace. To "each one of us," the apostle says, "grace was given" (v. 7). If the aorist tense is significant, it probably points to the time when we became Christian; from the beginning of our Christian life we were the recipients of grace. We are not to think of grace as a gift reserved for the great ones in the Christian church. Grace is the rightful possession of the lowliest of believers. There is no believer who lacks grace, which means that none of us is left to his or her personal devices as we seek to live the Christian life. God's grace is freely given to us all.

And that makes all the difference! I was recently reading about a comment made by one of our knowledgeable experts on the situation in which we all find ourselves these days. He started by saying, "Whenever I read that the world is going to pot, the government is threatened, the fabric of society is in danger, humanity is on the down grade, drunkards, gamblers, drug addicts are on the increase and the future of the race is bleak, one thought comforts me." The friend to whom this man was speaking asked, "What is that?" The expert replied elegantly, "It ain't so!"—to which I am tempted to retort, equally elegantly, "Ain't it?" While I am not prepared to endorse everything said in that gloomy assessment, I am not happy with people who gloss over our modern predicament as though there is nothing seriously wrong. There *is* much that is wrong in today's world, and unless we take vigorous action against the evil that flourishes in our communities our future is bleak. However, the wrong that evil people are perpetrating is not the whole story. The whole story includes the wonder of grace. God is at work in our world, and the grace he gives to those who trust him makes all the difference.

We might have expected Paul to say something like "according to our need," but instead we read, "according to the measure of Christ's free gift." The definite article precedes "Christ" in the Greek, so that Paul is saying, "according to the measure of the free gift of *the* Christ" or ". . . of the Messiah." But as he usually says "the Christ" rather than "Christ," perhaps we should not press the point. With the thought of this verse we might compare Romans 8:32: "He who did not spare his own Son, but delivered him up for us all, how will he not together with him freely give us all things?"

According to F. Büchsel, the word used here for "free gift" is "more legal" than the other word often used for "gift," and this one "denotes formal endowment" (*Theological Dictionary of the New Testament*, 2, p. 167). Paul is viewing grace as a regal gift made to us from the highest authority there is. The force of it all is that grace is a wonderful gift coming from the supreme power in the universe and given bountifully to each and every one who comes to Christ in faith. Paul used this word for "free gift" earlier in another passage that spoke of grace (3:7). Indeed he uses the word in all five times, and on every occasion the thought of grace is found in the context. That grace is a magnificent gift from the supreme authority is clear and is important.

God's Good Gifts

Paul cites Psalm 68:18 in support of his position (v. 8) and introduces his quotation with a verb that may mean, "it says" (i.e. "scripture says," as REB), or "he says" (i.e., "God says," as NIV mg.). Paul would not have put much difference between the two meanings. He is quoting from the authoritative Scripture and that carries conviction.

A problem arises here because the psalm speaks of God as receiving gifts, and Paul of God as giving gifts. But Bruce points out that Paul's reading is attested in the Syriac Old Testament and in the Targum of the Psalter. It may well be that Paul's Bible has one reading and the manuscripts behind our Bible have another. In any case, conquerors in antiquity characteristically distributed some of the spoils of war to their loyal supporters. And, as D. Kidner points out in his commentary on the Psalms, the psalm goes on immediately to the thought that God shares the benefits of his victory with his people, and Kidner cites E. E. Ellis: "God . . . shares with them the booty of His victory; Paul applies the Psalm . . . to the gifts Christ gives to the Church after His victory over the 'captivity' of death."

Abbott does not notice that the psalm goes on to speak of God's gifts to his people and holds that Paul is not quoting, but is using the language of the psalm to bring out his own point. Another view is that Paul is quoting from some previous writer who has adapted the language of the psalm; the suggestion is that this is why Paul uses "it says" rather than "Scripture says" or the like. The position of Ellis seems preferable—the psalm goes on to speak of the distribution of gifts to those the conqueror chooses, and Paul cites it for this reason. This psalm is a song of triumph, though scholars are not in agreement as to which particular triumph is being commemorated. It may be that the psalmist is not thinking of any one victory, but is singing exultingly of God as the victorious God who brings about victory after victory.

The King James Version reads, he "led captivity captive," but the expression refers to captives rather than to the abstract idea of "captivity." We should understand it as "a host of captives." And "he took captive a host of captives" is a striking way of emphasizing the greatness of the victory. God has overwhelmingly defeated the enemy. Paul does not explain who the captives were; evidently he was more interested in the victory than in the identity of the defeated.

Christians have often made attempts to identify the enemy, and Chrysostom, for example, thought that Paul is here referring to the devil, death, and sin. That it is proper to see Christ as overthrowing such enemies as these is no doubt true, but that Paul had such specific foes in mind at this point is more than doubtful. If he did, there is no reason why he should not have listed them. Another view is that the captives are those whom Christ came to save. But the taking of captives seems to be distinguished from the giving of gifts to men, so that the two groups are not the same. The apostle is saying simply that whoever and whatever Christ's enemies were, he overthrew them completely when he came to earth. It is the note of victory that is important, not the identity of the foes that were so signally defeated.

When Paul follows this with "he gave gifts to men" he turns to the thought of God's goodness to his people. It is true that God is far mightier than any person or thing or force in this mighty universe. But it is also true that God is interested in the well-being of his people and that he has given them gifts that will help them on their way, specifically in this context, the gift of grace. Though here Paul's word for "gifts" is not the one he used in verse 7, there seems to be no significant difference of meaning. A conqueror in ancient times would, of course, at times make gifts to his supporters, but normally he regarded his conquest as a means of enriching himself and would demand (and get) gifts from the conquered. So Paul is speaking of a God who does the reverse of what would be expected. He won a mighty triumph but used it to give gifts to people, not to extract gifts from them.

In verse 9 Paul proceeds to focus attention on the first part of his quotation, "he went up." He reminds his readers that "went up" demands that the person of whom the expression is used must be down; if he were on high there would be no place to which he could go "up." He is, of course, referring to Christ, who first "came down to the lower parts of the earth." This may mean either "the lower parts" (i.e., the earth), or "the grave," (which is lower than the surface of the earth) and thus is a reference to Jesus' death, or the region of Hades held to be lower than the earth (cf. 1 Peter 3:19). Though each of these possibilities has strong defenders, there is nothing that proves conclusively that any one of them is right, to the exclusion of the others. Perhaps there is most to be said for the first view, in which case Paul is referring to the incarnation.

The quotation in verse 8 refers to one who "went up"; Paul now says that this is the one "who came down" (v. 10). He brings out the magnitude of the victory the Savior won by saying not simply that he returned to where he was before, but that he "went up high above the heavens." This is a way of saying that he ascended to the place of highest honor. There was an idea among the Jews that there were seven heavens (cf. Paul's reference to "the third heaven" in 2 Cor. 12:2). However many "heavens" there may be, Christ went "high above" them all. It cannot be imagined that there is any place of honor higher than the one to which he ascended.

It is not easy to see why Paul has appended "so that he might fill all things." It looks as though he is saying that Christ fills the universe (cf.

Jer. 23:24), but it is not easy to see why occupying a place "high above the heavens" leads to filling the universe. It seems that Paul is repeating the thought of 1:23, which sees Christ as present throughout all things. H. D. McDonald says, "By His ascension Christ went from the here to the everywhere," and this may be the thought. Christ's departure from life on this earth, with its limitation to being in one place, meant his entering a different mode of being, one in which he is active in all places.

Gifts for the Work of Ministry

And he gave some to be apostles, some prophets, some evangelists, some pastors and teachers, with a view to the equipment of the saints for the work of ministering, for the building up of the body of Christ until we all come to the unity of the faith and of the knowledge of the Son of God, to mature manhood, to the measure of the stature of the fullness of Christ, so that we should no longer be infants, tossed to and fro and carried about with every wind of teaching, by the trickery of men, by craftiness with ingenuity in devising error, but speaking the truth in love let us grow up in all things into him who is the head, Christ, from whom the whole body fitly joined together and knit together through every supporting ligament according to the working in due measure of each separate part makes the increase of the body for the building of itself up in love (Eph. 4:11–16).

In this next section of the letter Paul has one of his very lengthy sentences (4:11–16 form one sentence in the Greek). In it he brings out the truth that it is important that every believer does his or her work well in the service of Christ. Likening the church to a body, he points to the importance of every part performing its function properly. If this does not happen, the whole body is impaired, but if all the parts are working together as they should, the body is effective. It *does* things. Paul also brings out the way the sinfulness of wicked people hinders the operation of the church and the importance of growth in Christ.

Some translations agree with the New Revised Standard Version in beginning this passage with "the" gifts he gave or the like. But since this gives the impression that the following list covers all the gifts Christ gave the church, there is a problem in that other passages mention other gifts. It seems better to understand the Greek in verse 11 as "It was he who 'gave gifts to mankind'" (GNB). Paul is telling his readers that the divine gifts in the church came from Christ; he is not giving an exhaustive list of those gifts.

He, the subject of the first verb, is emphatic; Paul emphasizes that those who exercise ministry in the church are Christ's gift to the church. Nobody can simply take it into his head to be an apostle, for example, and thus become one. If God calls someone to be an apostle, then that person is an apostle and he must be an apostle. If God does not so call him, nothing can make him an apostle. Elsewhere Paul speaks of false apostles (2 Cor. 11:13), evidently people who claimed the office but who were not the gift of Christ to the church. True apostles were always given by Christ. They were of high importance and come first in the list of God's gifts to the church (1 Cor. 12:28). It is not known how many apostles there were. The Twelve whom Jesus called were, of course, included in the number (though Judas Iscariot fell away), and we know also of James, Paul, and Barnabas. There were evidently others. (See comments on Eph. 2:20.) Though it is not known who they were nor how they were authenticated to the church, clearly they were regarded as the most important among the church's ministers.

Very important also were the "prophets." They apparently were ranked second to the apostles (1 Cor. 12:28), and some passages shed light on what they did (e.g., 1 Cor. 14:26–33). Though exactly what they did is nowhere spelled out for us, clearly they were at any rate people who uttered inspired words; a prophet could say, "Thus saith the Lord—." Just as there were false apostles, so there were false prophets (1 John 4:1). Care had to be exercised, but Paul is not concerned here to tell his readers how to recognize the genuine prophet. Rather, he is making it plain that Christ had given the gift of prophecy to some people in the church.

"Evangelists" were evidently people who proclaimed the evangel, that is, the good news, the gospel. The word for "evangelist" is used again in the New Testament only in Acts 21:8; 2 Tim. 4:5. Though the noun is not used often in the New Testament, the corresponding verb, "to evangelize," "to preach the gospel," is much more frequent, occurring 54 times (25 of which are in Luke-Acts and 21 in the letters of Paul). Evangelists were clearly important in the small but growing church of the first century. It mattered immensely that Christ had given to the church people who had the special gift of commending the gospel.

"Pastors and teachers" are here joined under one article, which may signify that both functions were performed by the one person. But teachers are not elsewhere linked with pastors and seem to have an importance of their own (cf. Acts 13:1; Rom. 12:7; 1 Cor. 12:28). The word translated "pastors" is used elsewhere in the New Testament of a shepherd looking after sheep (e.g., Matt. 25:32) or of Christ, the Good Shepherd (e.g., John 10:11). This is the only place where it is used of a group of persons in the Christian church, but there seems no doubt that we should understand the meaning as "pastors." Then, as now, pastors appear to have been people who could act towards the local congregation in the way a shepherd acted towards his sheep. They had the special gift of providing for the spiritual welfare of those to whom they ministered. We assume that their functions were much the same as pastors in the modern church, while recognizing that in their different circumstances some things about them were necessarily different.

Although "teachers" also represent an office with which we are familiar, we must recognize that they were even more important in the early church than they are today. We take it for granted that every member of the church, at least in western countries, can read and thus become familiar with the Scriptures and make use of the many books that give instruction in the faith. In the first century, however, most people could not read, so the place of the teacher was critically important. All that we look for in a teacher was necessary in the ancient church, but the teacher was also the person who made the content of the Bible available to the ordinary believer. And the teacher conveyed to people whatever else had been committed to writing and was seen as important for church members. There would also have been teaching carried on orally (cf. "the tradition," 2 Thess. 3:6), which the teachers would have committed to memory and passed on. People who could do this sort of thing were God's gift to the church.

Paul then moves to the purpose of these gifts to the church (v. 12). "Equipment" is the translation of a noun with a meaning like "a making fit or complete" (the corresponding verb is used of mending nets, Matt. 4:21). Many of the church's members must have been very imperfect in those days (as, alas, in these!), and the various gifts of ministry that Christ had given the church were directed towards completing the spiritual development of the members. The word translated "ministering" was used originally for waiting at table (cf. John 2:5, 9) and later for service of various kinds, mostly humble service. The early Christians used it for service to the members of the church, and it is the word that came to denote the deacon in the church.

We should notice two further points. The first is that it is "the saints"—that is, the whole congregation—who are equipped for ministering. Every member of the church has a ministering function, and we should never confine this work to a small paid segment. Ministry is the function of the whole church. The second point is that the aim of the great gifts Christ has given the church is that the saints should be equipped to do "ministering," or lowly service. It does not come naturally for us to do what is lowly; instead it is natural for us to want to be seen in some exalted place. The grace of God is evident when we do lowly service well.

The church has all too often tended to confine ministry to those who have been ordained. (In reaction to this, some in modern times have all but ruled out any ministerial function for the ordained.) Stott has a useful comment as he points to the ministries of both pastor and people: "The New Testament concept of the pastor is not of a person who jealously guards all ministry in his own hands, and successfully squashes all lay initiatives, but of one who helps and encourages all God's people to discover, develop and exercise their gifts." This is surely what Paul is teaching in this passage.

"For the building up of the body of Christ" is parallel to "for the work of ministering"; the equipping of the saints is for this double purpose. Paul does not object to mixing his metaphors and here uses the word "building," a metaphor from constructing edifices, to refer to "the body" where we might have expected something about growing. Earlier he has spoken of the building as growing (2:21). Both ways of putting it look for the prosperity of the church.

The apostle turns to the ultimate aim of all this labor (v. 13). "We all" means "all Christians" (not "all people"; he has just referred to the same people as "the saints"), and Paul sees the ultimate aim as "the unity of the faith." A few verses earlier he has spoken of being diligent "to keep the unity of the Spirit" (v. 3); now he speaks of unity as a goal to be pursued. Unfortunately, believers do not always preserve the unity that the Spirit gives, and Paul now says that they are to put forward their best effort to maintain that Spirit-given unity. The apostle proceeds to connect unity with faith. He may mean that we are to be united in believing in Christ (Gal. 2:20 speaks of faith "of the Son of God"). Then the passage would be speaking of saving faith and the knowledge of Christ. But it is perhaps more likely that here "the faith" stands for the whole body of Christian teaching. The Pauline correspondence reveals that many false teachings had made their appearance in the churches with which the apostle was connected, and this exhortation makes it clear that he looked for his readers to be at one in the essentials of the faith. (In verse 14 he contrasts "infants" driven by any "wind of teaching.")

With "the faith" he links "the knowledge of the Son of God." The object of all Paul's teaching was not simply the promotion of orthodoxy, but the bringing of people to know Christ. There is, of course, a sense in which all believers know Christ, but in another sense there is still further knowledge of him to be pursued. Paul can profess his own desire "to know him (i.e., Christ) and the power of his resurrection" (Phil. 3:10). So here he is looking for the Ephesians to increase in their knowledge of their Savior. The linking of "the faith" and "the knowledge of the Son of God" indicates that it is the relationship of believers to the Son of God that is at the heart of it all.

Maturity in the Faith

Paul moves on to the result of all this in the life of the believer. He looks to the Ephesians to attain "mature manhood." We could translate "to a perfect man," but in English this seems to mean "a man without fault" whereas the Greek term translated "perfect" signifies "having reached its aim or end." In the case of a person's growth it means "adulthood," "maturity." The "aim" of babyhood is adulthood, and Paul is looking for believers to have reached that end; they must be mature in their faith. If we understand the word as "perfect," we must bear in mind that Christ is the perfect man and we would then see Paul as urging us to Christ-likeness. We should notice that he speaks of a perfect "man," not perfect "men," a way of putting it that places some emphasis on unity. Christians are not simply so many isolated units; they belong together.

Maturity is also in mind when the apostle goes on to speak of "the measure of the stature of the fullness of Christ." "Stature" translates a term that may signify "age" (as it does in John 9:21; it is often used of mature age) or "height" (as in Luke 19:3). The use of "measure" here makes it seem as though we are to understand "stature" as referring to those who have reached their full height, but if we take it to mean "age" (those who are fully adult), it points to the attainment of maturity. "The fullness of Christ" points to the superabundance that is in Christ; it carries to its conclusion the expressions that indicate maturity. It points us to the perfection of Christ and to the maturity that should characterize those who are the followers of such a Christ.

Paul proceeds to develop his thought with what J. G. Strelan calls "a wonderful set of mixed metaphors" as he cites G. B. Caird's summary: "Christians are warned not to be babies, in an open boat at the mercy of wind and wave, driven off course by the roll of the dice"! Paul has no objection to mixing his metaphors, and he can come out with some striking and forceful expressions, as he does here.

The apostle brings out the truth he has enunciated in the previous verses by drawing attention to its opposite (v. 14). All this, he says, should be done "so that we should no longer be infants," where his word for "infants" denotes very young children (in Heb. 5:13 the word means someone who is fed with milk). Paul uses it of the Corinthians who were "babies in Christ" (1 Cor. 3:1). He is referring to what is childish rather than to what is childlike. Immaturity is inevitable when people first become Christians, but it is a state that should not continue, as all Paul's letters show. He is concerned that his correspondents should develop into mature believers.

So here he goes on to explain "infants" by speaking of being "tossed to and fro and carried about with every wind of teaching." The noun corresponding to "tossed to and fro" is used of the waves in a stormy sea (Luke 8:24); it seems always to have the connotation of rough water rather than gentle waves. It is a graphic metaphor to bring out the instability of immature Christians. This is continued with a reference to their being "carried about," where the verb conveys the idea of being carried here and there rather than making any significant progress to a destination. "Every wind of teaching" carries on the thought as it points to nothing more substantial than the blowing of the wind, which can alter its direction very quickly. This whole expression underlines the idea of instability, and Paul is warning the Ephesians against having such an uncertain Christian life.

The failure to attain stable Christianity may be due not to chance forces encountered along the way of life, but to "the trickery of men." The word rendered "trickery" really means "dice-playing," a practice we would not naturally link with converts to Christianity. But since everybody in Paul's day knew that those who threw dice had learned how to manipulate the dice to their own advantage, the term came to mean "cheating" or "trickery." It includes a certain plausibility, but the ultimate aim of the dice-player was not fairness. It was profit by deceiving the unwary.

The word translated "craftiness" conveys the idea of a readiness to do anything; like dice-playing, it is mostly used in a bad sense. This term was not used of a readiness to take infinite pains in order to get a good result. Rather, it signified a readiness to do anything, honest or dishonest, in order to further one's own aims.

This is further brought out with an expression difficult to translate. The first word is *methodeia* (from which we get our word "method"). Theoretically this word ought to be used in a good sense as well as a bad one, but the good sense does not seem to be attested. Paul uses it again in 6:11, where it refers to the devil's methodical approach. So here it is "devising," "scheming," rather than planning for what is good that is in mind. The word rendered "error" is a noun with a meaning like "roaming" but is another word often used in a bad sense, that of roaming away from truth. A standard lexicon gives its meaning as "error, delusion, deceit, deception," so it denotes what is far from desirable. (Moffatt's translation runs, "men who are dexterous in devising error.") Clearly Paul was well aware that there were crafty people who were ready to take advantage of gullibility that might be found among simple Christians. He warns his correspondents to be careful.

The word "but" introduces a very different course of action (v. 15). We are almost compelled to translate the verb into English with "speaking the truth," because "truth" is a noun for which we do not have a corresponding verb. However, what Paul is saying is literally, "but truthing in love." He can do this because in Greek the verb covers action as well as speech (cf. John 3:21, where we read, "he who does the truth . . ."). Paul is urging the Ephesians to manifest the quality of truth in all that they do. He adds "in love," for this is a most important feature of Christian living. Somewhere I have read that it is possible to be morally upright repulsively, and it can scarcely be denied that some Christians have put this into practice. But it is not *this* way of life that Paul is advocating. Though he certainly wants Christians to be morally upright, and his "truthing" brings this out, he does not want them to do this in a repulsive manner. Their truth-commending lives are to be characterized by love.

This forms the introduction to an exhortation, "let us grow up into him," where Paul again makes use of the imagery of the church as the body and Christ as the head. The church is not static; it is to "grow up." But Paul is not speaking of growth of any sort and growth at any price. He is speaking of growth in love and growth that accords with Christ, the head. It is growth "into him." "In all things" indicates that this is to be wholehearted; the believer does not have some areas of life that are not subject to growth into Christ in love. The whole of life is involved.

He goes on to speak of Christ as "the head." Growing up into the head is not an easy concept. Bruce draws attention to R. A. Knox's point that a baby's head is much larger in proportion to its body than is that of a grown-up person. Growing up may thus be seen as bringing the body into the right proportion with the head. Whether this is the apostle's thought at this point or not, the important of the body's growing up into the head is clear.

There is a good deal of debate on the meaning of headship in the New Testament, some holding that it affirms the superiority of the head, others that it points to the head as the source (as the source of a river was called its "head"). This passage seems clearly to support the "source" view, for immediately after speaking of Christ as "the head" Paul goes on "from whom. . . ." Paul is speaking of Christ as the one "into" whom we grow and "from whom" we grow.

"From whom" (v. 16) makes it clear that the Christian life is not one lived by the unrestrained use of human resources. It depends on Christ, who supplies what his people need for their spiritual growth. This is true of "the whole body"; we are not to think that some parts of the body do not need this divine assistance. All the members draw their sustenance from the head. They are "fitly joined together" which employs a verb found elsewhere in the New Testament only in Ephesians 2:21 and not cited anywhere before Paul used it (he may have coined it himself). It indicates that the parts of the body whose head is Christ are to fit in with one another. This and the following "knit together" are present participles, which shows that the process is still taking place.

"Knit together" is another verb that brings out the harmonious fitting together of all the parts of the body (it is used of the fitting together of a convincing argument in Acts 9:22). "Every supporting ligament" is more literally "every ligament of supply," and the word for "supply" goes back to the idea of supplying what was needed for the chorus of a theater. It thus points to a liberal supply, perhaps also hinting at the harmony and beauty of the Christian life. The word I have translated "ligament" is not a common word, and there is evidence that it can mean "contact." Some scholars take it in this way here, in which case we must understand it as "every supporting contact." Another possibility is to see it as meaning "joint" (as GNB), and this may be supported by its use in Colossians 2:19 and by the translation *junctura* in the Latin Vulgate. But "ligament" is more likely for a part of the body that "knits together."

The whole body must fit in with all its parts if it is to work properly together. Paul speaks of "the working in due measure of each separate part," which brings out the variety of functions that are exercised by the parts of the body and the importance of balance. If one part of the body overperforms, there is a malfunction; the same is true if it underperforms. There is a proper balance in every fit and healthy body. And what is true of the physical human body is true also of the church, the body of Christ. Each of us is to fulfill his or her proper function, neither slacking on it so that our work is left undone, nor taking over functions that properly belong to someone else.

The body will never reach its proper development without this balance, but when all the parts—the variety of its members—are working properly together in this way, this "makes the increase of the body." All this, says Paul, is "for the building of itself up in love" (he has already used "building up" in 2:21; 4:12). And when he goes on to add "in love," it is clear that he has in mind relationships in the church and is no longer working with the "body" metaphor. Once again we see the centrality of love in the apostle's thinking. There cannot be a church as he understands a church without love between the members.

13

Renewal

Therefore I say and testify this in the Lord, that you should no longer walk as the Gentiles walk in the emptiness of their mind, being darkened in their understanding, alienated from the life of God on account of the ignorance that is in them on account of the hardening of their heart, who, lacking sensitivity, have handed themselves over to licentiousness to work all kinds of uncleanness in greediness (Eph. 4:17–19).

Paul has drawn attention to the bountiful provision that God has made for his people in sending his Son. He has reminded his readers of the free gift of grace that liberates them and of the wonderful variety of gifts of ministry that God has given them to build them up in the faith. In the light of all this, he now argues that the Ephesians should go on to become mature and reliable Christians. His "therefore" at this point is important. He is going to call on them to have nothing to do with the evils so manifest in the lives of worldly people in the community in which they lived. But he makes this call in the light of all that God has done for believers. *Because* of the work of God in Christ, *because* of the wide range of ministries that God has provided in the church, and *because* the church, the body of Christ, has before it the prospect of growing up into Christ and of being a perfectly harmonious body of Christ, *therefore* certain things follow.

Paul further emphasizes the importance of the words he is about to write by introducing them with *"and testify this in the Lord"* (4:17). Although he could have simply gone straight on to say that his readers should not live like the Gentiles, his *"therefore"* links this up with the basis set forth in the previous section of the letter. His *"I say and testify"* is a solemn and unusual introduction (REB renders, "I urge it on you"). And his *"in the Lord"* makes it plain that this is not simply a sample of the wisdom of Saul of Tarsus, but an injunction that has the backing of Christ behind it. What follows is the utterance of a man who is "in Christ" and who is speaking as a man "in Christ" to people who are "in Christ." There is to be no doubt about the importance of what Paul is about to say.

We might wonder a little at the solemnity of this introduction to a command that the converts should not live like the Gentile community of which they were members. We might think that this should go before some marvelous and positive section, perhaps one that brings out the wonder of the Christ and the provision he has made for salvation. Or it might well befit a passage dwelling on the nature of the Christian life with its love and its peace and its joy. Why does it come in a section that simply draws attention to the shortcomings of the life his readers had left to become Christians?

Perhaps the answer is that Paul recognized the pull exerted on the new Christians by their former habits. When they became Christians they left a way of life they had followed all their days up to that point. The influence of the past must have been strong, and there would have been a constant temptation to revert to the old and familiar ways. They would recall companions and pastimes that had given them pleasure and be tempted to go back to them, even though they now knew that the service of the one true God ruled out returning to their old way of life and their old habits.

With that we must take the fact that there is always a tendency for people to fit in with the ways of the culture in which they live. We feel this today just as strongly as any first-century community. Indeed, in view of the constant bombardment of ideas from television, radio, and newspapers, and the examples of people idolized by the masses, the temptation may even be greater for us. Whether or not that is so, it is just as true for us modern Christians as for the believers to whom Paul was writing that we must not take our standards from the communities in which we live. We have been died for—and it is a great thing to have been died for by the Son of God. People for whom such a price has been paid must never take their standards from those whose minds are set on this world.

Paul uses his favorite idea of walking as he tells the Ephesians that they "should no longer walk as the Gentiles walk." "No longer" reminds them that this is the way in which they have habitually walked. It may even indicate that to some extent they are still walking in the way of which he is speaking. The expression indicates that, whatever their past, they should no longer live in the manner characteristic of those who do not know Christ. Paul mostly uses the idea of walking when he is bringing out the importance of making progress in the Christian way, but it is important to realize that some people may "walk" in a different direction. The apostle is not suggesting that the Gentile way of life is one that makes significant progress, but his verb does indicate that the Gentiles do not stay in the same place. Their "walking" means they are going farther and farther along the road that leads away from God. "The Gentiles" here will stand for all those people who do not acknowledge and worship the one true God. There is no profit in walking in their "way."

The apostle proceeds to make some unflattering references to the way of the Gentiles. He first speaks of "the emptiness" or perhaps "the futility" that characterized their thinking. J. A. Robinson holds that this "suggests either absence of purpose or failure to attain any true purpose," and Lock suggests "aimlessness." The Greeks in particular prided themselves on their mental excellence (and Christians today are well aware of a mental snobbery exercised toward them by some of our "intellectuals"!). We should not miss the emphasis Paul places on the use of the intellect in this passage. He refers to the "mind" and the "understanding" of the Gentiles but also to their "ignorance," and he will go on to speak of believers as those who "learn" Christ, who have been "taught" in him and have been renewed in the spirit of their "mind." There is far more to being a Christian than intellectual achievement, but we should be clear that being a follower of Christ means using the brains God has given us to their fullest capacity. Says Stott, "Scripture bears an unwavering testimony to the power of ignorance and error to corrupt, and the power of truth to liberate, ennoble and refine."

For Paul, it is abundantly plain that, however acute the mind that rejects God in all his love and mercy, the person who bases his or her whole life on a thought process that leaves God out confines himself or herself to an empty and ultimately futile way of life. "Thou hast made us, O God, for thyself," prayed a sage in antiquity, "and the heart of man is restless till it finds its rest in thee." It is a prayer that we do well to keep in mind.

Darkness

The Gentiles, Paul proceeds, are "darkened in their understanding" (v. 18; by contrast the Ephesian Christians are "enlightened," 1:18). "Darkened" is a perfect participle, conveying the force of permanence. The apostle is not referring to an occasional dark passage. The mind without God (who made that mind) is permanently in darkness. Moulton and Milligan cite from the papyri an example of the verb used where a complaint is made about some people who were drunk in these terms: "I think that the new wine has already blinded them." The word is clearly used of those whose thinking is far from reliable. "Understanding" is, of course, much the same as "mind" in the previous expression; Paul is still dealing with the mental processes of those who live without God. He is contemptuous of the attempt to make sense of life while leaving God out of account.

Such people, Paul says further, are "alienated from the life of God," and "alienated" means belonging to the camp of the enemy. These outsiders are not simply neutral; they are quite separate from those who have cast in their lot with the people of God. We are here reminded that in some aspects of life it is impossible to be neutral. If we do not oppose evil, we are condoning it. If we do not stand with God, we are opposing him. So Paul characterizes the Gentile thinkers as "alienated." Interestingly, he does not say they are alienated "from God" but "from the life of God." That will, of course, include alienation from God, but the reference to "life" draws attention to the whole way of life that is involved in acknowledging God. God lives in his people, so that to be alienated from them is to be alienated from him. The Christian life is not some more or less interesting but trifling intellectual pursuit for those who have a taste for this sort of thing. It is a whole way of life.

And this alienation, Paul says, takes place "on account of the ignorance that is in them." Sometimes ignorance is quite innocent. There are many things of which we are ignorant because they are not relevant to our lives or are too difficult for us to understand, or for some other good reason. But there is some ignorance that *is* blameworthy: ignorance of things we ought to know, things we could well know but have not chosen to know. There is a willful ignorance that is not far away from sin, and the ignorance of God is one such ignorance. It is an ignorance that cuts people off from what is most worthwhile in life—not because God is punishing those who refuse this knowledge, but because the people in question decline to know God, "whom to know is life eternal." Of their own free will they cut themselves off from the greatest good.

Paul traces this ignorance to "the hardening of their heart." The word for "hardening" was used of the formation of a callus, a thickening of the skin or a stonelike formation in the joints or other parts of the body. Since such a formation, of course, meant a loss of sensitivity, the word is used metaphorically for hardness of heart, insensitivity in general. (Barclay translates "because of the petrifying of their hearts" and explains that the word "describes something which has become so hardened, so petrified that it has no power to feel at all. That is what Paul says the heathen life is like.") Hardness of heart leads to insensitive actions, which Paul sees as inevitable when people harden themselves against God and the way in which God would have them walk. Perhaps we should notice that petrification in the body does not take place all at once; the hard layer is built up gradually. So in life. Nobody becomes thoroughly evil all at once. There is one small step into evil, then another. And another. Paul is referring to the inevitable end result of embarking on this downward path.

Paul moves on from the kind of people they were to the kind of actions they did (v. 19)—"lacking sensitivity" is the inevitable result of the "hardening" of which he has just spoken. His "who" is the relative of quality: "who were of such a kind that. . . ." He speaks of them as "lacking sensitivity," where the word means originally a ceasing to feel pain (H. C. G. Moule comments, "as when mortification sets in; a deeply suggestive metaphor"). This passes over to the general concept of insensitivity. When we no longer feel pain at the plight of the world's unfortunates, we have hardened our heart and are alienated from the life of God. Paul is attacking the self-centered life, the life of the person who is insensitive to the pain of other people.

The result of this lack of sensitivity is that the people in question "have handed themselves over to licentiousness." In Romans Paul speaks of God as handing people over (the same verb as here) to their sinful lives (Rom. 1:24, 26, 28). Part of the punishment of sin is simply that we become sinners, with all the sin-centeredness that this implies. The word I have translated "licentiousness" could be understood as "wanton violence." Whichever way we take it, the term points to the unrestrained exercise of the bodily appetites. Paul is speaking of the person who is concerned only with the gratification of his or her own desires.

Some sinners retain a sense of the fitness of things and, although they do wrong, they make no parade of their evildoing. But the sinners being castigated here have no sense of shame. Trench says the word denotes the sinner "who acknowledges no restraints, who dares whatsoever his caprice and wanton petulance may suggest." He sums up the meaning as "lawless insolence and wanton caprice." The apostle sees this as the inevitable result of rejecting God. When people refuse to acknowledge God they are themselves the supreme arbiters of what they do. And, while some exercise that freedom to do what they want with a due regard for other people, all too many do not. Modern society, with its prevalence of such evils as violence and rape (in the most "civilized" countries as well as in those that are considered backward), is just as guilty of this as was the ancient world. Yet such conduct is incompatible with an understanding of Christ. Mitton quotes the French writer, C. Masson: "The Sermon on the Mount and the cross for ever excluded the union of faith and immorality."

Hand in hand with the surrender to licentiousness goes the working of "all kinds of uncleanness in greediness." "Uncleanness" may be literal, as when it is used of a sepulcher: "full of bones of dead people and all uncleanness" (Matt. 23:27). But it is also used of moral failure, as it is here. It is possible to take "in greediness" with the preceding word and see the meaning as "greedy to work all kinds of uncleanness," but it is better to see greediness as a separate item in Paul's list. The person who rejects God is apt to give free rein to greed. The word in Greek is made up of two other words with the meaning "have" and "more"; basically it signifies the desire to have more. This may take the form of greed in the bodily appetites or greed in a more intellectual form. But, however it is understood, it points to an emphasis on one's own desire for "more" that places this desire above all other considerations.

The Life of the Christian

But you did not so learn Christ, if indeed you heard him and were taught in him, as truth is in Jesus, that you should put away as concerning your former way of life the old man that is corrupt according to the deceitful desires, but that you be renewed in the spirit of your mind and put on the new man who has been created according to God in righteousness and true holiness (Eph. 4:20–24).

From this catalogue of evils, Paul turns to the Christian way (v. 20). His introductory "but" marks the contrast, and his "you" is emphatic. Paul is here setting the Ephesian Christians in strong contrast to the worldly, sensual people of whom he has just been speaking, and his "not so" immediately follows, again with some emphasis. Paul is saying quite emphatically that the Christian way is nothing like the way he has just been outlining.

To "learn Christ" is not a very common expression. It is possible that it means something like "learn in the school of Christ" or "learn the ways of Christ." It might also be understood in the light of Paul's following statement that "truth is in Jesus." Hodge holds that the phrase does not mean merely "to learn his doctrines, but to attain the knowledge of Christ as the Son of God, God in our nature, the Holy one of God of God, the Saviour from sin, whom to know is holiness and life." It points to the learning experience of coming to know Christ.

This certainly includes the thought that the kind of evil living on which the apostle focuses throughout the preceding section is not what should be found in the lives of those who follow Christ. When Paul says, "if indeed you heard him" (v. 21), his "if" does not imply any doubt but emphasizes that the teachers who taught the Ephesians had themselves been taught by Christ. They passed on what Christ had said. That the Ephesians had "heard" Christ means that the teaching of Christ had been faithfully passed on to them. The Ephesians "were taught in him," and the "in" reminds us again of the importance of being "in Christ," a truth that comes out again and again in the Pauline correspondence. Even though the new Christians still had a lot to learn about the Christian way, they could rely on what they had already learned.

The following words—"as truth is in Jesus"—are sometimes rendered "the truth as it is in Jesus," which draws attention to that aspect of truth that we find in Jesus. But it seems that Paul is saying more than that. He is saying that truth, real truth, is to be found in Jesus and, by implication, in him alone. Jesus could say, "I am . . . the truth" (John 14:6), and there is something of this in the present passage. The truth of God, saving truth, is in Jesus in a way that it is in no one else. Paul usually links "Christ" or "Lord" with "Jesus"; this is the only place in this letter where the simple name occurs by itself.

Paul expands the meaning of this (v. 22). The result of making contact with Jesus, the truth, is that we "put away . . . the old man" (for this expression, cf. Rom. 6:6; Col. 3:9) Before we make the acquaintance of the truth in Jesus and learn what that means, every one of us is self-centered in some way. We may be blatantly selfish, seeking only our own profit. Or we may aspire to academic excellence or to sporting prowess or to philanthropic kindness or to any other of a multitude of human choices. But, whichever way we follow, we do so because we ourselves have chosen it. This is the way we want to live. Our "self" dictates the way we live, and all too often this means that our way is a "self"-ish way.

Paul turns the thoughts of his readers to their "former way of life" and instructs them to "put away . . . the old man." This means that being a Christian means entering a wholly new way of life. It does not mean to carry on with the old way with perhaps a few of our worst habits dusted off. It means to start something radically new, and the newness includes a wholehearted repudiation of all that was wrong in the old way. Interestingly, Paul also can say elsewhere that his converts have put off the old man (Col. 3:9), and both the indicative and the imperative are important. F. F. Bruce comments, "The tension between the indicative and the imperative, between the 'already' and the 'not yet,' is common in the Pauline letters; it is summed up in the admonition: 'Be what you are!'—Be in practice what the calling of God has made you."

Paul says that "the old man" is "corrupt according to the deceitful desires" ("rotting in deceitful desires," M. Barth) which, of course, gives a reason why it should be "put away." The Greek verb translated "corrupt" may be used in a variety of ways; a standard lexicon says it means "destroy, ruin, corrupt, spoil" and gives examples of its use for

139

financial ruin, and for the seduction of a virgin as well as for corruption in the realm of morals and religion (as here). Paul spells this out with "deceitful desires," where "desires" is a neutral term that may refer to good desires (like Paul's desire to depart and be with Christ, Phil. 1:23) or to those that are evil (like "the lust of the flesh," Gal. 5:16). Here, of course, the desires are evil ones, desires that in a person's pre-Christian days may well have seemed quite normal but are now seen to be quite wrong. "Deceitful" is more literally "of the deceit," where the noun is used as it is, for example, of "the deceit of riches" (Matt. 13:22), that which is apparently attractive but may well lead people astray. Paul is warning that the pull of the old way of life must be resisted, whatever superficial attractiveness it may have.

In contrast with this ("but" has adversative force), Paul urges "that you be renewed in the spirit of your mind" (v. 23). The verb "renewed" points to a thoroughgoing process. Becoming a Christian means more than eliminating a few minor bad habits; it means a complete overhaul, the remaking of all of life. "If anyone is in Christ, he is a new creature; the old things have passed away, look, they have become new" (2 Cor. 5:17).

This is further brought out by the direction that the renewal be "in the spirit of your mind," where both "spirit" and "mind" point to the inward and the important. Perhaps we should understand the expression to mean "in mind and spirit." The Christian must be thoroughly remade. Jesus spoke of the necessity of being "born again" ("reborn from above," John 3:3–7). We should notice a change of tense. The verb "put away" (v. 22) is in the aorist, which points to a once-for-all decisive action, but "be renewed" is present, which indicates an ongoing process. Paul is speaking of a decisive renunciation of the old way of life and the entrance into a new life where the believer is constantly being renewed.

The process of renewal is now described as putting on "the new man" (v. 24). There is a return here to the aorist tense; putting on the new man is also a decisive, once-for-all action. Elsewhere Paul can say, "Put on the Lord Jesus Christ" (Rom. 13:14; REB translates, "Let Christ Jesus himself be the armour that you wear"). "The new man" is not to be seen as the result of a strong moral effort put forth by the old man. It is the result of a remaking of the person by the power of the Lord Jesus Christ, by the indwelling of the Holy Spirit.

Perhaps we should notice that Greek has two words for "new," one of which means "young" or "recent," the other (which is used here) "fresh," "unworn." We see the difference in Matthew 9:17, where both words are used. There we read that new wine (i.e., wine recently made) must be put into new wineskins (i.e., unused, unworn wineskins). There is a freshness, a new quality about "the new man." Perhaps we should not press this too hard, for the other word is applied to the new man in

Colossians 3:10. Furthermore, the verb for "renew" here is cognate with the word for "recent," and the verb in Colossians with that for "fresh." We see therefore that what is meant by both words is applied to the new man in both passages! Paul speaks of the new man as one "who has been created," and we should not minimize the force of "created." The apostle is speaking of the creative divine power that is at work when anyone becomes a Christian. This means a remaking of the whole person, and it can be done only by the power of God.

The result is "righteousness and true holiness." This is more literally "in righteousness and holiness of the truth," and it is possible to see "of the truth" as referring to both nouns: "True righteousness and true holiness." It does not matter greatly which way we take the words, for in either case Paul is pointing out that genuine righteousness and genuine holiness characterize the Christian life. "Righteousness" signifies the performance of upright actions that accord with the new life and "holiness" the personal piety that characterizes that life (Foulkes points out that in Philo and Plato the two words are used for the fulfillment of our duty to other people and our duty to God). In English we use the adjective "true" rather than the noun that Paul prefers here—literally, "of the truth"—but Paul's use of the noun may be meant to direct attention to the truth of God, which is so important for New Testament Christians and which should characterize all their actions.

14

Don't Grieve the Spirit

Therefore put away the lie and speak truth, each one with his neighbor, because we are members of one another. Be angry and do not sin; do not let the sun go down on your anger, nor give a place to the devil. Let him that steals steal no longer, but rather let him labor, working what is good with his own hands so that he will have something to give to someone who has a need. Let no rotten word go out from your mouth, but only what is good for building (people) up as there is need, so that it may give grace to them that hear. And do not grieve the Holy Spirit of God in whom you were sealed for the day of redemption. Let all bitterness and anger and wrath and clamor and slander be put away from you together with all malice. And be kind to one another, compassionate, forgiving each other even as God in Christ has forgiven you (Eph. 4:25–32).

"Therefore" (4:25) introduces an exhortation based on the truths that have just been enunciated. Because the Ephesians have "put on the new man," certain consequences follow. "Put away the lie," Paul says, using a verb that may be employed literally of putting off clothing and then comes to be used of putting away almost anything. Here the use of the singular preceded by the definite article seems to indicate lying in general ("falsehood in all its forms," Westcott; Stott thinks of "the great lie of idolatry," as in Rom. 1:25, but the passage does not seem to be as specific as that). Lying may be an accepted weapon in the warfare waged by the worldly, but it has no place in the life of the Christian.

For Christians there is the command, "speak truth," and we are probably correct in seeing the present imperative as signifying "speak truth habitually." Christians are habitual truth-speakers. Paul proceeds, "each one with his neighbor." This is a quotation from Zechariah 8:16, where it heads a list of "the things that you shall do"; clearly it was regarded as important. It may be that Paul is concerned here primarily with relationships among Christians, for he goes on, "we are members of one another." However, while it is true that Christians must be very careful not to mishandle the truth when they are talking to one another, it is impossible to hold that Paul meant that they should keep truth for their dealings within the fellowship and that they were free to lie to unbelievers. He expected believers to be truthful at all times, but here he is emphasizing the special importance of truth within the church. He says, "we are members of one another." A lie told by a Christian hurts not only the believer who told it but the church as a whole. The spiritual health of the whole body is hindered when one member is defective.

The apostle has a similar expression in Romans 12:5, where he speaks of the many members that make one body in Christ. But in this Ephesians passage it is not so much the unity of the members in the one body that is stressed, as the fact that the members of a body belong with one another. A member of the physical body does not function if it is cut off from the other members. So in the body of Christ the members belong together. They have a special relationship to one another. And one consequence of that relationship is that they can trust one another. Members of Christ's body do not lie.

Paul moves on to deal with anger with another quotation, this time from Psalm 4:5, "Be angry and do not sin" (v. 26). The older English translations from the Hebrew run like the King James (which has it as v. 4 as do many modern translations), "Stand in awe, and sin not," but Paul is clearly using the Greek version, which has "Be angry and do not sin" (Kidner understands the Psalm to show that anger "need not and should not be sinful"). It is possible that Paul is taking these words in the sense of "be angry but in such a way that you do not sin." It is plain enough that there is such a thing as righteous anger; we should remember that Jesus himself could be angry (Mark 3:5). If this is the sense of it, Paul is saying that believers should be angry only in this righteous way. Simpson takes it in this sense and comments: "A man totally destitute of indignation is a maimed sample of humanity. In such a world as this the truest peacemaker may have to assume the role of a peacebreaker as a sacred obligation." Righteous indignation is an important part of right living.

William Barclay tells of an incident when Dr. Samuel Johnson was asked to mitigate some of the asperities in a piece of vigorous writing he had composed. The great man declined, saying that he "would not cut off his claws, nor make his tiger a cat, to please anybody." Barclay goes on, "There is a place for the tiger in life; and when the tiger becomes a tabby cat, something goes lost." He rounds off this section of his discussion with: "The anger which is selfish, passionate, undisciplined, uncontrolled is a sinful, a useless and a hurtful thing, which must be banished from the Christian life. But the anger which is disciplined into the service of Christ and of our fellow men, and which is utterly pure and utterly selfless, is one of the great dynamic forces in this world." In the face of such things as oppression, cruelty, depriving people of their rights and so on, it is right to be angry. Indeed, to lack the ability to feel "righteous indignation" is to live an impoverished life.

But it is also possible that Paul is recognizing that anger is a very human emotion and instructing his readers that when they are angry they must not let their anger take control and cause them to sin (GNB translates, "If you become angry, do not let your anger lead you into sin"). We should bear in mind Jesus' warning that anger can be a breach of the commandment not to kill (Matt. 5:21–22).

What Jesus was saying when he spoke of anger as breaking God's commandment, and what Paul is saying about anger here, is that anger is an all-too-common human failing. We so easily give way to anger when our purposes are frustrated and, as F. F. Bruce reminds us, "there is a subtle temptation to regard my anger as righteous indignation and other people's anger as sheer bad temper." We must be on our guard against making a special case of ourselves. Paul is saying that when the human emotion of anger assails us we are not to give way to it. We are not to let the sun go down on our "anger" (strictly the word means what provokes anger; ASV mg. reads "provocation"; we must not dwell on what causes the anger). In other words, we must not nurse it up, letting it become a continuing part of us. We must see to it that anger is speedily controlled. When the sun went down, of course, a new day began for the Jews. Paul is saying that we should not let anger spill over into another day.

"Nor" (v. 27) translates a little word regularly used to carry on a preceding negation. Not only should we not let the sun go down on our wrath, but we should not "give a place to the devil" (Paul mostly speaks of Satan when he refers to the evil one, but in Ephesians and in the Pastoral Epistles we have references to "the devil"; cf. Acts 13:10). The word translated "place" is used in a variety of ways, one of them being for "possibility, opportunity," which seems to be the meaning here. The word is used of the Roman practice of allowing anyone who is accused of a crime "a place to defend himself" (Acts 25:16) and of Esau's finding "no place of repentance" (Heb. 12:17). Paul is urging his readers not to let their anger give the devil a "place" and thus become the means of helping him do his evil work.

Paul moves on to the dishonest (v. 28). It is tempting to go along with translations like "The man who used to rob must stop robbing" (GNB), but this overlooks the force of the present tense. Though we like to think of the early church as full of upright and decent people, this may be an exaggeration. Certainly some of the first Christians came from the lowest strata of society, and they may well have had many unpleasant habits that would not drop off immediately when they were admitted to the Christian assemblies or even when they were accepted for baptism. In any case there is a problem with translations like the one cited, for if the man in question only "used to rob" he cannot now "stop robbing." That he is to "stop" indicates that he is now engaging in the practice. The Revised English Bible renders, "The thief must give up stealing," and it seems that this is what Paul is saying. The probability is that the early Christians in their outreach made effective contact with people whose practices were far from honest. When such people became Christians they must cease their dishonesty. Paul is pointing out that the follower of Jesus Christ does not engage in dishonest practices.

Such practices seem to have been widespread. Slaves, for example, apparently regarded the picking up of unconsidered trifles as part of the natural way of life. They had so little and other people had so much. Even poor people normally had much more than slaves had. And, of course, others than slaves also regarded stealing as a normal practice. Paul insists that Christians are different. They do not do things just because other people do them, and stealing, even on a small scale, is wrong.

In fact Paul looks for a complete reversal of the thief's practices. The comparative adverb "more, rather" is used here, following a negative, in the sense "instead of." Not only is the thief not to steal anymore, but he is to replace his stealing with hard work. When writing to the Thessalonians Paul said, "If anyone will not work, neither let him eat" (2 Thess. 3:10). He saw it as very important that everyone should work to earn a living.

But here the apostle says more than that. Whereas the thief uses the labor of other people to supply his own needs, the Christian is to use his own labor to supply the needs of others. The verb I have translated "labor" means literally "to become weary" and from that it comes to denote the toil that makes one weary. In other words Paul is pointing to hard work as the future role of the erstwhile thief. And he is to labor in this way not in order to obtain a multitude of riches for himself, but so that he will be able to help other people. The thief had probably been busy using dishonest hands to rob people, but he is exhorted to use those hands, now honest, to do something good for other people.

Paul does not explain what this "something" good should be and is probably leaving the new course of action wide open. There were many things a man could do with his hands, and Paul does not specify in detail, but he expects that in the new life the convert will engage in manual labor. There is a tendency these days to move away from the older view that most of the converts in the early church were from the lower classes, as it now is pointed out that there were quite a number of people of more exalted station among these believers. We must accept this, but Paul's almost incidental reference to manual labor reminds us that there were many from the lower strata of society among the early believers.

The apostle advises the thief to "give to someone who has a need." This is usually understood in some such way as "to help the poor" (GNB), and in general this would be what would happen. But Paul's expression is wider than that translation, and there is nothing in what Paul says to rule out the former thief's doing something to fill a need in any of the membership (or for that matter outside it) who had a particular need, whether they were poor or not. The point is that the thief-become-Christian is no longer concerned to make dishonest gains for himself. He will now do some hard work and use the proceeds to help wherever help is needed.

Next, Paul turns his attention to speech and urges his readers that they "let no rotten word go out from [their] mouth" (v. 29). The word for "rotten" is used of rotten fruit (Matt. 7:17–18; Luke 6:43), rotten trees (Matt. 7:17–18; Luke 6:43), and rotten (i.e., unsuitable) fish (Matt. 13:48). This is the one place in the New Testament where it is used of anything other than material things mostly in a state of decomposition. It is a very expressive term for the kind of speech that Christians are to avoid. In this context O. Bauernfeind sees "rotten word" as related to "good word" in the same way "as stealing is to helping people in need." It is easy for us to take the expression here to signify what we call "bad language," and, of course, it covers this. But it also covers any form of speech that works to the harm of other people. Christians are to remember that their words can be powerful and are to make sure that they use them in the right way.

It is said that a man once came to Mohammed and asked how he could make amends for falsely accusing a friend. Mohammed told him to put a feather on every doorstep in the village. Next day he told the man to collect them. "But that is impossible," said the man, "the wind has scattered them beyond recall!" The prophet replied, "So is it with your reckless words." It would seem that Mohammed was not a great help to his questioner, but at least he said something that is important for us all to bear in mind. We must guard our words, because it is impossible to recall them.

The right way to use our words is indicated in the expression "what is good for building (people) up." It is easy to engage in harsh criticism and to use what we say as a means of pulling other people down, a practice for which there is plenty of evidence in contemporary society. But that is not the way in which the followers of Christ speak (cf. Luke 4:22). For them, words are the means of helping others. F. F. Bruce cites J. A. Findlay for the view that Paul is using the expression in the sense of "pointed saying" or "good story" and for seeing the meaning of the verse as "Let no unclean speech issue from your lips, but such witty talk as is useful for edification, that a pleasant impression may be left on those who listen to it." Though this may be reading into the passage a mite more than Paul intended, we should be in no doubt but that the apostle wants his readers to be careful that they speak in such a manner that they will help other people, not bring the Christian way into disrepute. Paul keeps his language general; he does not say who is to be built up (we have to supply "people" or perhaps "the church"), nor does he define "need." But the general language covers a multitude of situations and means that believers have guidance that will be of use in a variety of places.

The overruling principle is "so that it may give grace to them that hear." We noticed earlier that "grace" is a word that Paul uses very frequently and which clearly means a great deal to him. It means especially the great and good gift we receive when we are saved by Christ and also denotes the great and good gift that enables us to go forward on our Christian way. But it may also mean a gracious deed that one person may do for another, an unmerited favor, a benefit. It may well be that this is what Paul has in mind here, though we cannot rule out the possibility that he is thinking of the fact that a good deed done by a Christian may point an unbeliever to that "grace of our Lord Jesus Christ" whereby the unbeliever may be saved.

That leads on to the command, "And do not grieve the Holy Spirit of God" (v. 30). The verb is in the present tense and if it is used strictly, the expression means, "Stop grieving the Holy Spirit." But more probably Paul is simply urging a continuing course of conduct: "Habitually, don't grieve the Spirit." The words may apply to either the speaker or the hearer—Paul may be saying that the use of uncouth speech grieves the Spirit within the speaker who utters such speech, or he may mean that when such words are heard the Spirit within the hearer of the words is grieved.

Paul has spoken earlier of the Holy Spirit as having "sealed" the Ephesians at the time they became believers (1:13); the Spirit is the sign that they are Christians. The seal is a mark of ownership, so that the presence of the Spirit showed that people belonged to God. Without that

147

sign they have no reason to call themselves Christians. Now again we have the thought of sealing, this time with the addition of "for the day of redemption." This means that the apostle is looking for that day at the end of this world system when our redemption will be brought to its consummation in the kingdom of God. Redemption, of course, means the freeing of captives on payment of ransom, and the figure looks at Calvary as Christ's paying of the price that sets sinners free from their captivity to evil. But linked with "day" in the expression "day of redemption," it looks forward to the fulfillment of all that redemption means in the climax of all things at the end of the age.

Paul concludes this section of his letter with a direction that his readers avoid a series of evils, followed by a further direction that they hold fast to a number of good qualities. The first of the evils is "bitterness" (v. 31). The word is used of things with a bitter taste, sometimes of what is inedible, but comes to signify a wider range of unpleasant behavior. The lexicon refers to its use, for example, of "the inhuman cruelty of a slaveholder" and of "animosity, anger, harshness." Here "bitterness" seems a suitable equivalent.

There are two Greek words for anger or wrath, and Paul proceeds to use them both. They are often indistinguishable in meaning but in some contexts a difference may be discerned. The word I have translated as "anger" *(thumos)* is connected with the idea of boiling up and accordingly is the right word to use of an overwhelming passion of anger. "Wrath" *(Orge)* may be linked to the idea of swelling, like the swelling of a bud when the sap rises, and it may thus indicate the anger that takes its origin in what one is. It is this second word that is normally used in the New Testament for the wrath of God. Here, where both words are used of human anger, there is probably no great difference of meaning (though Strelan suggests "passionate outbursts" for the first word and "seething rage" for the other). Paul is simply denouncing all human readiness to give way to temper. It is a loss of self-control that brings a great deal of unhappiness into many human situations.

"Clamor" denotes "shouting," "outcry." It can be used in a good sense, such as loud crying in prayer (Heb. 5:7), and it is interesting that it may be employed to signify fervent prayer. But it is more common in a bad sense, like that of raised voices in a quarrel (Acts 23:9). Because it is so often used in ways like this, it is not surprising that Paul employs it here as something Christians must avoid. With it he links "slander" *(blasphemia)*, a word that denotes insulting speech of all kinds, abusive speech. It comes to be used especially of impious speech against God (which gives us our word "blasphemy"), but here Paul seems to have in mind offenses against people, so the meaning will be something like "slander." All these things, Paul says, are to be "put away from you." The

Christian is totally opposed to all forms of evil. There is no place for any of them in the life of the believer. Having said all that, Paul pops in one last reference to evil when he adds "malice" to the list of things to be repudiated. This word in Greek *(kakia)* is a general term for badness and is used for evil of many kinds, but the lexicon can say, "a special kind of moral inferiority . . . something like *malice, ill-will, malignity.*"

All this makes a formidable catalogue of wickedness as the apostle leaves no room for doubting that the Christian way involves a thoroughgoing repudiation of every form of evil. It is worth reflecting that this list is not likely to be one sent to a modern church (except perhaps to a new church in the developing world). It is not that we lack sinfulness, but rather that we prefer other sins; for example, we tend to be smug, self-satisfied, perhaps hypocritical. But Paul's converts were fresh from heathenism and all the customary faults of first-century life, and once again we see that the early church made converts whose whole way of life had been distinctly unfavorable for the development of the qualities looked for in Christian living. Nevertheless, from such unpromising material there came the saints of God. We are not to miss the point that *our* different sins are to be repudiated as decisively as Paul looked for the first-century believers to repudiate theirs. And, like them, we are to become the saints of God.

Paul turns from the qualities to be repudiated to the qualities to be sought after (v. 31) and begins with "be kind to one another." This is perhaps not a heroic virtue, but in the ordinary day-by-day life surely nothing is more important. Kindness smooths the path of life and makes for helpful social intercourse. It should always characterize Christians, whoever and wherever they may be. I like the story of a lecturer who pinned to a board a large sheet of white paper with a black dot in the middle of it and then asked his class what they saw. With variations in the way they put it, they all told him that they could see a black dot. In the end he asked plaintively, "Doesn't anybody see a large white square?" It is a curious feature of human nature that we mostly are better at seeing black dots in our neighbors than large white areas. Paul is counseling kindness, not criticism.

"Compassionate" carries on much the same theme. We should notice that the word Paul uses is a compound of the adverb for "well" and the word for "entrails." The compound denotes that the person is deeply moved, and in Christian circles this means "compassionate." Here we might notice a change of meaning that the Christians made in the word for "entrails." The ancients in general regarded the entrails as the seat of the emotions, and a lexicon of classical Greek can say of this word, *"the seat of the feelings, affections,* esp. of anger." When the ancients were deeply moved they were very angry, but when the Christians were deeply moved they were very compassionate. The change in the way the term was understood is very revealing.

Forgiveness is important, of course, and Paul proceeds to remind the Ephesians that the forgiveness they have received imposes on them the obligation to be forgiving in their turn. They are to forgive "each other." Once again we see that Paul had no illusions about the converts. They had come from a background where people did many things that required forgiveness. They were learning that they ought not to do these things, and their conduct was beginning to show what their new allegiance meant. But they could not lose all their bad habits in a moment, so offenses occurred. When this happened, Paul urges, they were to be forgiving. Perhaps we should notice that the verb is from the root that gives us "grace." While surely no one will quarrel with the translation "forgive," Paul is using a verb that may have the added nuance of "deal graciously with."

And he gives them a good reason for "forgiving each other," and with it a high standard: "even as God in Christ has forgiven you." "Even as" signifies that Christians must not make do with a halfhearted forgiveness grudgingly given. And Paul points to God's forgiveness "in Christ"—it is the cross of Christ that brought forgiveness, and the Ephesians must never forget the price that was paid for them. Their forgiveness must accordingly be wholehearted. Quite a number of good manuscripts read "us" instead of "you," and that may possibly be the correct reading. If so, Paul is including himself and other believers with the Ephesians as the recipients of forgiveness.

15

Imitators of God

Therefore be imitators of God as beloved children, and walk in love just as Christ loved us and gave himself for us, an offering and sacrifice to God for a fragrant odor. But let not fornication nor all uncleanness or greediness be even named among you as it is fitting for saints, and wickedness and silly talk or coarse jesting, which are not proper, but rather the giving of thanks. For be assured of this, that no fornicator or unclean person or greedy person, who is an idolater, has inheritance in the kingdom of the Christ and of God. Let no one deceive you with empty words; for on account of these things the wrath of God comes upon the sons of disobedience. Therefore do not be partners with them (Eph. 5:1–7).

Again we have Paul's "therefore" (5:1). The apostle is no academic theologian. He is fond of proceeding from the things we know about God, Christ, and the Christian way, to the practical consequences our theology has for the way we live (REB has "in a word" here, but Paul is not summing up what he has just said; he is giving a reason for the paragraph he is now beginning). He has said something about the kind of lives that evil people live and has pointed out that his readers have been delivered from all this. "Therefore" they should now live lives different from those of the unbelievers round about them.

"Be imitators of God," he writes (*Moffatt*, "Copy God"), or perhaps "become imitators" (as Lock, McDonald, and others suggest). This is perhaps not quite what we would have expected, since mostly the New

Testament writers, Paul included, call on believers to imitate other followers of God. Paul once indeed calls on people to imitate him as he
imitates Christ (1 Cor. 11:1), but more often he simply urges them to
imitate him (1 Cor. 4:16) or him and his colleagues (2 Thess. 3:7, 9), or
he says that people did this (1 Thess. 1:6) or that they imitated the
churches (1 Thess. 2:14). Other writers also refer to the importance of
imitation (Heb. 6:12; 13:7; 3 John 11; etc.). Clearly the early church set
a high value on following good examples.

These days, people are not very much inclined to speak of setting an
example or of following one, but the force of example must have been
of the utmost importance in the early church. Until that time, people
had never seen what Christian living means. The general standard of
morality was low, and they would never have encountered a group that
asked them to live lives wholly given over to the service of God and of
other people. They would not even know what that kind of life looked
like, so seeing it in the examples of Paul and of other believers would
have been of the utmost importance. But this passage goes beyond that.
The Ephesians are told not simply to live like Paul or other outstanding
Christians, but to be "imitators of God." Paul is not urging them to aim
at living the best lives that humans can live. He is telling them to set
their sights as high as they could possibly be set.

"The imitation of Christ" is a concept with which Christians have
become somewhat familiar through the centuries, and this has its roots
in the New Testament, as we have seen (1 Cor. 11:1). Paul can even speak
of the Thessalonians as having become imitators "of us and of the Lord"
(1 Thess. 1:6). He sees Christ as having set the pattern for his followers
(Phil. 2:5).

But this is the only passage in which a New Testament writer calls on
his readers to imitate God. It is understandable, however, for it turns
our thoughts to the Most High as the One on whom we should model
our living. And we should never overlook the fact that Jesus himself
called on his followers to model themselves on what God does. They are
to be perfect as their heavenly Father is perfect (Matt. 5:48). Jesus told
them they are to love their enemies and pray for their persecutors so
that they might become sons of the heavenly Father, and he went on to
remind them that God sends his sunshine on evil and good people alike
and that he makes it rain on both just and unjust (Matt. 5:44–45). God
is kind to the ungrateful and to the evil (Luke 6:35). Jesus saw the Father
as our model, and Paul is but following in his Savior's footsteps at this
point.

Paul ended his previous paragraph by urging his readers to be kind
and compassionate and to forgive one another "even as God in Christ
has forgiven you" (4:32). The imitation of God for which the apostle was

looking is thus likely to have been along the lines of forgiving one another. "Getting your own back" has always been a favorite device of sinners. It flourishes in modern communities, and we need not think it was lacking in the Ephesian community of Paul's day. The call to forgive other people just as God has forgiven the Ephesian believers must have come home to them with considerable force. It still requires us to do some hard thinking. And clean living.

Although "as beloved children" does not specify the family in which they are children, there can be no doubt that Paul means that his readers belonged in the heavenly family. He is reminding them that they are members of God's family. As we read elsewhere, believers are "partakers of the divine nature" (2 Peter 1:4). In any family it is right that children should look up to and respect their father, but this is especially important in the heavenly family. We become members of this family only because the heavenly Father in his great love sent his only Son to die on a cross for us and thus bring us salvation. With love like that as the basis of our membership, it is incumbent on us that we imitate God and live as loving people. John puts it this way: "Beloved, if God so loved us we too ought to love one another" (1 John 4:11).

Love

The same thought continues with "walk in love" (v. 2). As we have seen in earlier passages, Paul is fond of the idea of "walking" as a symbol of making progress in the Christian way (2:10; 4:1; etc.). Here his addition "in love" makes it clear that the Christian life of service that he is advocating brings something of the love of God before this world's sinful and restless souls. There are many things God does in which it is impossible for his people to imitate him—for example, creation and the outworkings of providence. But Paul sees love as one thing in which we *can* imitate our heavenly Father. And because of what God in Christ has done for us, we must imitate him.

It does not come naturally to us to love as Christians should. In general people like to take advantage of one another wherever they can. Somewhere I picked up a story about a blind golfer who played the game very well. After winning a tournament for blind golfers, he challenged a golf pro to a match for charity and emphasized that he did not want any advantages to compensate for his blindness. "Okay," said the pro. "When would you like to play?" "Any night you like," replied the blind man. We do like to make sure that we have the advantage over other people, however correct our words. But that, of course, is not the way of love.

And it is to real love and not a pretense that Christians are called. Paul does not choose some uncertain human love as our model, for he goes on, "just as Christ loved us and give himself for us." The New Testament writers consistently see the love so strikingly demonstrated at Calvary as showing us what love really is. "In this is love," wrote John, "not that we loved God but that he loved us and sent his Son, the propitiation for our sins" (1 John 4:10). Similarly, Paul points out to the Romans that Christ died "for ungodly people" (Rom. 5:6). A person would scarcely lay down his life even for a righteous man, he points out, then adds, "on behalf of the good man perhaps someone would dare to die" (v. 7). He is not suggesting that this is likely; it is an outside possibility. Then he goes on, "But God commends his own love to us in that while we were still sinners Christ died for us" (v. 8).

It is love like this that is held out as our model. Believers are not to love as the world loves. The world loves only attractive people, those who have appealing qualities (by the world's standards). There is, of course, no reason why believers, too, should not love people they find attractive, for that is part of life on this earth. But what Paul is calling on his converts to do is to love other people as God loved them. We are to love others not because of their merits, not because of their natural attractiveness, not because of anything they are or do. We are to love them because of what *we* are now that we have become Christians, people transformed into loving people by what Christ has done for us. We will have our close friends, of course, people bound to us by ties of natural affection and the like. But our love will not be confined to those we find naturally attractive.

A Sacrifice to God

Paul goes on to assure us that Christ "gave himself for us." The Greek verb is used of a variety of ways of looking at Christ's saving work. Sometimes we read that evil people "gave Jesus up" (Matt. 26:15; 27:2–3; John 18:35; 19:16; Acts 3:13), where, of course, it is a sinful betrayal of a good man that is in mind. But we also read that the Father gave him up (Rom. 8:32) and that Jesus gave himself for us (Gal. 2:20). The saving work of Christ may be viewed from any one of a number of perspectives. Here Paul brings before us the very moving truth that because of Christ's love for sinners, he gave himself up for their salvation.

This giving-up of Christ was as "an offering and sacrifice to God." "Offering" is a word with a number of meanings in the secular Greek of the day, but in the New Testament it is confined to the offerings made in sacrifice to God. So Paul's use of it here is quite in character. He adds "and sacrifice," which underlines his meaning and makes it quite plain that he is concerned with the familiar religious offering. M. Barth distinguishes between the two terms: "The first term could denote, e.g., products from the fields and trees, which, after deposition at the sanctuary, contributed to sustaining the priests; the second term described animals from the flock or stable which were killed at the holy place and portions of which were burnt upon the altar. In addition, the first could signify a life of obedience, the second a reference to atoning death." Barth thinks, however, that in this passage the distinction may perhaps be no longer in mind. This is the more likely in that the linking of the two terms is common and may have become a way of referring to all sacrifice, however offered. In other words, while the two terms may be distinguished in meaning, it is likely that in this passage they simply underline the idea of sacrifice.

In our day, the offering of an animal sacrifice is no longer the central religious rite (at least for most religions), but when Paul wrote, people everywhere knew the thrill of approaching their altar with the prescribed animal, going through the appropriate ritual, and watching while their sacrifice ascended in the smoke of the altar fires. All over the Roman world (and beyond), the imagery of sacrifice had its appeal. And Christians found the fulfillment of all that sacrifice meant in Christ's offering of himself to save sinners.

Christ's offering was made "to God." Paul is not concerned with the multiplicity of little deities that the Roman world knew. For him there was but one God; if a sacrifice was offered to deity, it was offered to that one great God. The apostle goes on to speak of Christ's offering as "for a fragrant odor." His "for" indicates the purpose—the sacrifice was intended to please the Father. "A fragrant odor" is more literally "a fragrance of sweet odor," where the combination of "fragrance" and "odor" underlines the attractiveness of the offering's fragrance. It is a way of saying that the sacrifice that Christ offered in dying for sinners was completely acceptable to the Father. It accomplished perfectly the salvation for which it was offered. Chrysostom brings out the point that the death of Jesus for enemies is important in understanding this passage: "To suffer for one's enemies is 'a sweet-smelling savor,' and an 'acceptable sacrifice.'"

What Is Fitting for Saints

Paul has made it clear that the recipients of this letter are imitators of God and beloved children of the Father, children who are the recipients of the love of Christ and the beneficiaries of his sacrifice of himself. The apostle now turns to the kind of conduct from which they must distance themselves. His "But" in verse 3 introduces a contrast. He has been speaking of the "fragrant odor" of Christ's sacrifice and now turns from that to what is diametrically opposite, from the self-giving of Christ's death to the self-indulgence of fornication.

Paul uses the term "fornication" only here in this letter. The word strictly denotes the use of a prostitute, but it comes to be used of almost any form of sexual immorality. It, says C. L. Mitton, "covers a wide range of sexual evils, and in a Christian context would mean any sexual indulgence outside the permanent relationship of marriage, in circumstances where the sexual appetites are used merely as a means of pleasure without any sense of responsibility and care for the partner." For the people of Paul's day, some sexual sins were recognized as such; for example, incest was seen as a very great evil. For other sexual practices there was a gender difference in the way they were treated. All sexual intercourse outside marriage was forbidden to a wife, though not to a husband. Adultery was seen as clearly wrong for a married woman and also for the man if he was engaging in intercourse with another man's wife. His sin lay in the fact that he was infringing on the rights of another male, yet it was seen as quite natural if he had sexual relations with a single woman. It was held to be acceptable for a man to indulge in sexual adventures as long as he steered clear of other men's wives. Not so for the married woman. Any woman who engaged in such practices was despised and punished.

The Christian classification of all fornication as a sin was something new. Barclay cites Cicero for the accepted viewpoint when he says of anyone who denies that men should have intercourse with courtesans: "he is at variance not only with the license of what our own age allows, but also from the customs and concessions of our ancestors. When indeed was this not done? When did anyone ever find fault with it? When was such permission denied? When was it that that which is now lawful was not lawful?" Cicero was in no doubt as to the antiquity and universality of fornication.

But the Christians totally rejected this common point of view. For them, all extramarital sexual intercourse was seen as wrong, and this resulted in a new attitude toward women. The early Christians regarded a woman as not simply a source of sexual satisfaction for a male, but a person in her own right, "a partner of equal dignity before both man and God" (F. Hauck/S. Schulz, *TDNT*, VI, p. 590). The firm prohibition of fornication was an important step in bringing this about.

Paul says that such activities should not even be talked about. Mitton points out, "There is a danger that by talking about evil activities, even though disapprovingly, one can come to enjoy a perverted pleasure in them, even while ostensibly condemning them." This is something Christians must avoid.

Paul links "all uncleanness" with fornication. The word may refer to physical uncleanness; for example, it is used of decomposed matter inside a grave (Matt. 23:27). It is used also of moral impurity and may be employed in this way as the opposite of sanctification (1 Thess. 4:7). In his letter to the Romans Paul uses it of unnatural vices (Rom. 1:24). He also links it with sexual sins in a number of places besides this one (2 Cor. 12:21; Gal. 5:19; Col. 3:5). His use of "all" makes the case comprehensive. The apostle is not leaving the door open for some minor uncleanness, as though a little evil did not matter. For Paul, "all uncleanness" was wrong, and the whole thing had to be repudiated with decision.

With "uncleanness" he links "greediness" (as he did in 4:19), and evidently the combination made sense to Paul. The Revised English Bible renders the term as "ruthless greed," which at least brings out the truth that there is always a certain lack of compassion when greediness is given full rein. The greedy person is concerned with his or her own personal satisfaction and advantage; the Christian is concerned with the service of God and of people. There is a profound change of emphasis.

These evil qualities, Paul says, should not "be even named among you." There is, of course, nothing wrong in mentioning the evils as Paul himself is here doing by way of denunciation. (Bruce complains about "a mealy-mouthed refusal to call a spade a spade," which he finds in some modern translations that use vague terms like "immorality" or "unchastity" where Paul is "quite explicit" with "fornication.") What the apostle is warning against is the tendency to discuss evils that one is not at present committing, but in such a way that the door of possibility may be pushed ajar. Foulkes sees it as "incongruous for those who are called to be *saints* . . . to take any pleasure in talking about such things, by their conversation to approve or condone, or by gossip to make light of the sins of others, or to excite sexual passion in the unwary." It is better not even to mention these sins, so that our repudiation of them can be seen to be wholehearted and permanent. That, Paul says, "is fitting for saints."

Sometimes this is pressed as though the meaning were that believers should talk only about "spiritual" things, but this is probably to misunderstand the apostle. Elsewhere he can talk about the duty that Christians owe to the state (Rom. 13:1–6) or about marriage and divorce (1 Cor. 7); a wide variety of topics finds a place in his letters. So here he is not saying that believers must have only one topic of conversation, but rather that there are some subjects that do not help the spiritual life. Since they hinder spiritual growth, to dwell on them is to make life more difficult for the people of God. The only wise thing in such circumstances is to avoid such topics. Let them not even be mentioned. Saints are to bear in mind their whole range of duties in life, and that range will indicate the things that should dominate their conversation. And they should not be raising barriers to their spiritual advance by exercising their tongues (and their minds) on evil things.

This leads on to other topics that are better avoided by believers. "Wickedness" (v. 4) might have been rendered "shamefulness." Whichever way we take the word, it points to evil, and Paul is strenuously advocating an abandonment of every such thing even as a topic of conversation. At the same time we should notice that his word means more than talk; he is counseling the abandonment of the evil thing itself as well as urging his readers not to talk about it.

With that he links "silly talk" (REB, "flippant talk") and "coarse jesting." The attempt to acquire a reputation for scintillating humor is all too often sidetracked into merely repeating what is foolish or coarse. Paul is not, of course, saying that Christians must not tell jokes; as Strelan puts it, "Paul is not talking about wittiness, or having fun with a pun; these things spice speech." There is certainly room for humor in Christian conversation, and many fine Christians have been noted humorists. But this is not something to be sought at any price. And it must certainly be abandoned if one's talk degenerates into silliness or offensiveness.

The word rendered "coarse jesting" is in fact often used in Greek writings in a good sense, to denote "facetiousness" or "wittiness," or as Calvin puts it, "for that sharp and salty pleasantry in which able and intelligent men may properly indulge." But it can easily slide into low buffoonery, which is what Paul is castigating here. R. C. Trench cites a passage from Plautus in which a man characterized by this quality urged that this was natural, because he was a native of Ephesus. Evidently the Ephesians were fond of this kind of jesting. It is the things that "are not proper," not the things that are amusing, that the apostle is repudiating (cf. J. R. W. Stott, "All three refer to a dirty mind expressing itself in dirty conversation"). The verb I have translated "are not proper" points to doing the right thing. It is used of doing one's duty (Philem. 8) and of doing what is "fitting in the Lord" (Col. 3:18).

While Paul is certainly not instructing the Christian to conform to a series of conventional straitjackets, he is certainly reminding the believer that there are some things that are accepted as right in the servant of God and some things that will turn people away from following Christ. The follower of Christ is to make the right choice in conversation.

What is right for Christians is "the giving of thanks." Curiously, this tends to form only a very small part of the conversation of Christian people, though its importance is obvious. Being a Christian means being the recipient of many, many blessings. We can never earn our salvation or merit a heavenly reward for service. Yet we daily receive a multitude of blessings, and these, Paul is saying, should occasion a multitude of thanksgivings. The continuing attitude of the believer should be one of thanksgiving (not one of persistent complaint!).

The next words in the Greek (v. 5) may be taken as an imperative, "know, knowing," which leads to the translation of "Be sure of this" (NRSV). Or they may be seen as a statement, "you know, knowing," which leads to the affirmation "For of this you can be sure" (NIV). Either way, Paul is drawing attention to a certainty. His correspondents are to be in no doubt but that persistent sinners make sure of their exclusion from God's kingdom. In verse 3 he has denounced three very earthy sins and now comes back to them, this time denouncing the perpetrators of those sins: "fornicator," "unclean person" ("the dirty-minded," *Phillips)*, and "greedy person." He is not, of course, singling out these sins as worse than any others; he is taking them as typical of the way careless sinners live, interested in their own pleasures rather than the service of God and their fellows.

Paul proceeds to castigate the "greedy person" as "an idolater." The making and worshiping of literal idols is not as common in our day as it was in Paul's, but it is just as true with us as with the early church that to put acquisition or personal pleasure in the first place in our lives is to turn ourselves into idol-worshipers. Nothing must be allowed to take priority over the worship of God. Paul is clear that greed is a certain way of displacing God from that first place.

The apostle here comes back to the idea of "inheritance" to which he alluded earlier (in 1:14, 18). As with us, the word basically refers to possessions that come to us as the result of the death of a previous owner or owners. But, as such possession gives a sure title, the term comes to be used of secure possession. It was used a good deal of Israel's "inheritance" of the land that God gave them in Old Testament times, where, of course, there is no thought of inheriting from the deceased. The thought is simply that of settled and sure possession. In the New Testament it is frequent in the sense of the good gift that comes to believers as the result of Christ's saving death. Believers may even be spoken of as "heirs of God" and "joint-heirs" with Christ (Rom. 8:17). God does not die, so the usual idea of inheritance cannot be read into the passage. Paul is referring there to the great privilege that God accords believers who are admitted to the heavenly family. "Joint-heirs with Christ" surely brings home to believers the truth that they have a place with Christ in heavenly family.

The inheritance of which Paul writes now is "in the kingdom of the Christ and of God," an expression found only here in the New Testament (though Rev. 11:15 is not dissimilar). The "kingdom of God" is, of course, the great topic in the teaching of Jesus (in Matthew it is usually "the kingdom of heaven"), but it must be understood carefully. Jesus was not speaking about a kingdom like earthly kingdoms, but about the rule of God at work in the lives of his people. The kingdom belongs not to the mighty but to the lowly and the childlike (Mark 10:14–15). Although Paul does not make as much use of the concept of "the kingdom" as do the Gospels, he speaks of it often enough to show that it is important for him. And he makes it clear that it is not a matter of human energy but of the power of God (1 Cor. 4:20). He sees both a present and a future aspect to the kingdom, and both may well be involved here. Greedy people show by their greed that they are not in God's kingdom now, and, of course, as long as they continue in their selfish ways they never will be.

The kingdom is more usually called "the kingdom of God" than it is "of Christ," and the designation here is unusual. There is an article before "Christ" but none before "God," which leads some to suggest that we should take the words to refer to one person and understand the meaning as "the kingdom of one who is Christ and God" (Hodge finds this "the most natural interpretation," though he does not deal with the point that the article is not needed before "God"). However, this would be very unusual, and we have no reason for thinking that it is Paul's meaning. He may, of course, mean the article to give the sense "the Christ" (i.e., "the Messiah"), but perhaps it is more likely that he is simply referring to "Christ" (as he does, for example, in 5:1); he often uses the article with this term without making reference to a title. We should probably understand the apostle to be referring to the greatness of the coming kingdom by linking it both with the Savior and the Father, perhaps also indicating that there is one kingdom, not separate kingdoms for the Savior and the Father.

But Paul is not concerned here with unfolding the glories of the coming kingdom or dwelling on the Savior and the God who will bring it about. His concern is to warn sinners lest they be tempted to take their place in the kingdom for granted. There is danger in presuming that our place is so safe that we may spend our remaining time on earth in laxity and sin.

The Disobedient

Sinners usually seem convinced that the consequences of their sins will not really be very serious. They know there are warnings, but they apparently hold that these are meant for other people. Few sinners really believe they will suffer for their sins. Paul accordingly turns his attention to the problem they face. He first calls on his readers not to let anyone deceive them (v. 6). There is no indication of who he expected might do the deceiving. It has been suggested that he was thinking of worldly people from the unbelieving community, or again that he thought the temptation would come from some within the believing community who did not take sin seriously enough. Perhaps we are not wise in trying to trace the precise people the apostle had in mind. What matters is the importance of keeping away from evil, whatever the origin of the temptation. Clearly Paul thought there would be persuasion exercised to turn his readers from the right way, though such persuasion would be no more than "empty words" (or "shallow words," M. Barth). The adjective is used of a variety of things that lack content (such as empty jars), but here the reference is to words without a basis, without truth to sustain them. It is possible for people to give sinners the verbal assurance that in the end they will be all right. But such words have no power, no sustaining truth. They are "empty."

In the previous verse Paul has listed some sins he finds heinous. Now he says that those sins have consequences. On account of "these things," the very sins he has been denouncing, "the wrath of God comes upon" the disobedient. This is the only time in Ephesians that he uses the expression "the wrath of God," but he has spoken of certain sinners as "children of wrath" (2:3), an expression that makes it clear that they could look forward in the end to nothing less than the divine anger.

Although Paul always writes of a God who is ready to forgive, he is equally insistent that that God is totally opposed to evil. Those who persist in wrongdoing must expect in the end to find themselves exposed to that dreadful thing that the apostle calls "the wrath of God." The present tense may be meant to indicate that even now such sinners experience something of the divine wrath, though, of course, its full manifestation will not be seen till the end of the age.

Paul goes on to speak of the sinners he is denouncing as "the sons of disobedience." As in 2:2, this forceful expression points not to people who, as it happens, commit the occasional act of disobedience, but to people for whom disobedience is characteristic. In the last resort we either submit to God or we do not. If we do, then we are the children of God. If we do not, then we go our own way—and "sons of disobedience" is the biblical description of our state. And if this is the case, we must look forward to nothing less than "the wrath of God."

Having made clear the situation that sinners face, Paul rounds off this section of his letter with an appeal to his readers to make sure they escape the fate he has been outlining (v. 7). "Therefore" carries on the argument with sweet reasonableness. Because these things are so, a certain course of conduct is highly desirable. The verb might mean "do not be" or "do not become"; either meaning is possible. "Partners" translates a compound word with a meaning like "fellow-partners"; it emphasizes the fellowship with sinners that the apostle is deprecating. Some argue that Paul is saying, "Do not be partners in their sin"; others see

"Do not be partners in their punishment." But surely this is a foolish dispute. Paul is urging his readers to have nothing to do with the whole course of sinful conduct he has outlined. The sin and the punishment go together. It is not possible to experience the one without the other. In other words, "Do not experience their sin and you will not experience their punishment."

16

Wake Up, Sleeper!

For formerly you were darkness, but now, light in the Lord; walk as children of light—for the fruit of the light is in all goodness and righteousness and truth—approving what is acceptable to the Lord, and have no share in the unfruitful works of darkness, but rather reprove them. For it is shameful even to speak of the things done by them secretly, but all things are reproved when they are made manifest by the light, for all that is made manifest is light, therefore it says, Get up, sleeper, and rise from the dead, and Christ will shine on you (Eph. 5:8–14).

P aul now turns from the fate of the disobedient to the position of believers (5:8). He reminds his readers that "formerly" they had been in no good state themselves. "Formerly" is a very general word and does not pin down the time with any exactness, but clearly Paul is referring to the time before the recipients of his letter became Christians.

Darkness

During that period, he says, "you were darkness." We might have expected him to say, "you were *in* darkness," but the apostle is concerned with what they were themselves rather than what their environment was like. Before they became Christians they shared in the world's darkness, and Paul uses the stronger expression to describe their condition (all told, Paul has this word for "darkness" eleven times, three in this letter being the most in any one of his letters). The lexicon classes this use of the word under the heading, "In several places . . . has the sense *bearer* or *victim* or *instrument of darkness*" (as in Matt. 6:23a; Luke 11:35).

Some translations read "in the darkness" (as GNB) but, while this expresses a truth, it does not appear to be what Paul is saying here. Rather, his point is that at the time of which he is writing the people to whom he is addressing his letter had been part of the forces of darkness. They extended the darkness wherever they were. Jesus once spoke of the light within people as darkness (Luke 11:35), on which I have commented, "That is the ultimate disaster. Then what is good in the person is wholly corrupted." Apart from Christ, that is a person's state, and it is that of which Paul is speaking here. By contrast Jesus says that his followers "are the light of the world" (Matt. 5:14).

"But now" introduces the contrast. Paul is writing to people who have put their trust in Christ and who therefore have been transformed. They are no longer darkness. They are in fact "light in the Lord" (cf. Matt. 5:14), not merely "enlightened." The addition "in the Lord" is important, for as Calvin points out, "While we are outside Christ, all is under the dominion of Satan." Paul is exulting in the fact that in Christ they are free. "Light in the Lord" signifies that they are illuminated by the light that Jesus brings, perhaps that they are filled with the light that comes from the Savior. The Good News Bible has "you are in the light," but Paul is saying something more forceful—"you are light." To be "in the Lord" means such a transformation that they are now light-givers as well as light-receivers. The person who is illuminated by Jesus will be "full of light" (Luke 11:34–36), and it is this kind of illumination of which Paul is speaking.

The addition "in the Lord" makes it clear that the apostle is not writing about people who merely make their very best effort to pull themselves up by their bootstraps. He is referring to people who have come to salvation in Jesus Christ and who find as a result that their whole life is different. Whereas before it was fair to characterize them in terms of darkness, now they are rightly known as "children of light." "Children" is not used as often in the figurative sense as is "sons," but there is no difficulty about the expression: Paul is talking about people who are characterized by light. "Light" dominates Paul's thoughts at this point; he uses the word three times in verses 8–9 and twice more in verses 13–14. The expression unmistakably links Paul's readers with God, for God is light (1 John 1:5), as is Jesus (John 8:12; 9:5). To say that the Ephesians are "light in the Lord" is to place them firmly with God over against all that is evil.

Once more Paul urges his readers to "walk." We have seen this manner of speech before; Paul likes to describe the Christian life in terms of slow but steady progress. Here he is referring to the believer's whole way of life. He is saying that the Christian life must be characterized by light. Just as "walk" stands for the whole way of life in terms of progress towards some goal, so "children of" refers to the characteristic of that life. Believers, Paul is saying, will be known by the light that has come to them, the light that illuminates their whole way and is their guide as they live out their faith day by day. Light is in them (and not in their pagan contemporaries). Cassirer translates, "Rule your lives, then, as men native to the light." They belong with light. They live in light. They radiate light.

In a little aside Paul draws attention to three characteristics of the Christian life (v. 9). He has no objection to mixing his metaphors, as "the fruit of the light" shows. Some manuscripts, including the Chester Beatty papyrus (the oldest manuscript we have for this letter), read "the fruit of the Spirit" at this point, and this is the reading accepted by the King James translators. But modern scholars generally agree that this is an early alteration made by scribes who had Galatians 5:22 in mind. The context as well as the bulk of the manuscripts favors "light" as, of course, does the mixed metaphor.

This is the only place in this letter where Paul uses the term "fruit." He can use the term in the literal sense of produce borne by a tree or a plant (1 Cor. 9:7) or use it metaphorically of the good results he looked for from his ministry (Rom. 1:13). He uses it of the bad living of the unconverted Romans and of the good living he expected from them when converted (Rom. 6:21, 22). Mostly he uses the term in a good sense; for example, he writes to the Galatians of the "fruit" of the Spirit, but of "the works" of the flesh (Gal. 5:22, 19). So here he speaks of "the fruit of the light" but goes on to "the unfruitful works of darkness" (v. 11). The apostle can leave the term undefined, as in the passages cited, or he may define it as "the fruit of righteousness" (Phil. 1:11). Here he is clearly referring to the result of having "the light" within one. When the light is received it has marked effects on the receiver; it brings forth "fruit."

It is worth reflecting that light is necessary if there is to be fruit. A tree in darkness cannot bring forth any fruit at all. And Paul is saying that a life lived in the darkness he is opposing can never bring forth spiritual fruit. Fruitful lives are lives illuminated by the light of the gospel of Christ.

Goodness

The first thing to notice about the fruit mentioned here is that it is "in all goodness." Abbott points out that the word translated "goodness" is not found in classical Greek. But it is important for Paul. He could have said that the fruit of the light is all goodness, but when he says it is "in" all goodness he indicates that the fruit is not so much to be equated with goodness as that it manifests itself in goodness. There is not a great deal of difference between "goodness" and "righteousness." In some contexts the latter word will be concerned with the fulfillment of the law (e.g., Phil. 3:6), but Paul uses it often for the righteousness that believers have before God, a righteousness he explicitly says is not due to their keeping of the law (Rom. 3:21–22; Gal. 3:21; etc.). It is the righteousness that is imputed to the believer (Rom. 1:16–17). Although in this context there will be no particular emphasis on this, the word will reinforce "goodness" as pointing to the way in which believers must live.

Paul adds "and truth." As we have seen in earlier passages in this letter, truth may be seen as a quality of action as well as of speech, and it will be action that is in mind here. The apostle is emphasizing that believers live their lives on a higher level than do unbelievers. "Truth" is made manifest in both what they do and what they say.

Testing the Teaching

The apostle returns to his main theme with "approving what is acceptable to the Lord" (v. 10). Although some translations have "try to learn" or the like (as GNB, NRSV), the idea of an attempt—which may or may not be successful—is not what Paul is discussing here. The verb, used here only in this epistle, means "to put to the test" but may also point to the result of the test, when it means "to approve." (M. Barth gives lists of passages in which these two meanings are found [p. 569, n. 62].) Thus Paul may be commending the Ephesians because they did not accept uncritically everything they were told. They put the teaching to the test to ascertain what is true. More probably he means that when they tested teachings they held fast to what is right. Either way, he is saying that they were not gullible; they tested the teachings and thus arrived at the truth. Westcott points out that "We cannot divest ourselves of the responsibility of judgment. An important part of the discipline of life lies in the exercise of that power of discrimination which God quickens and strengthens."

The right teaching, Paul says, is "what is acceptable to the Lord." The word "acceptable" is used in the New Testament almost exclusively by this apostle; when he uses it, with only one exception, it refers to what is pleasing to God. He is now commending the Ephesians because, when they applied tests to teachings, they came up with the right answers. They approved what is acceptable to the Lord. This is a way of saying that they had spiritual insight; they did not simply approve what is obvious to human wisdom. "The Lord" may refer to God the Father or to God the Son. In the Greek Old Testament, the Bible of the early Christians, the word is used frequently of the Father, but in their own writings the Christians often used it also of Jesus Christ. In many passages (such as this one) there is no clear indication as to which is meant, and this brings out the high place they assigned to Jesus.

Avoid Darkness

In verse 8 Paul has given a positive command, "walk as children of light," and he now links a negative command with that one: "have no share in the unfruitful works of darkness" (v. 11). In Greek his verb "have no share" is a compound employing the preposition "with," which is a notable feature of this letter. We cannot in English say "be not with-partners," but that is the force of it. Paul is thinking in terms of partnership as he commands his readers not to align themselves with the wickedness in question. A. Skevington Wood remarks, "Notice that it is the 'deeds'" *(ergoi)* "that have to be shunned, not the doers. Paul is not advocating pharisaical separatism. The follower of Christ will go where his master went and meet those his master met. But though he does not withdraw from the world, he refuses to adopt its standards or fall in with its ways."

If the present imperative ("have no share") is used strictly, Paul means that they have been doing this and he commands them to desist, though this may be pressing the construction unduly. But the apostle is certainly commanding his readers to have nothing to do with the evil in question. They are to be partners with those who do good; they are not to be partners with those who do evil. The verb translated "share" may be used of having a sympathetic understanding of the plight in which Paul stood (Phil. 4:14), but here it is the actual taking part in the dark deeds that is meant.

The Ephesians are to keep themselves from "the unfruitful works of darkness." Paul does not say that they are not to do such deeds but rather that they are not to have fellowship with them. He pictures other people as doing the deeds of which he complains and urges his readers not to have fellowship with those deeds—that is, not to countenance them.

Unfruitfulness

The word "unfruitful" is always used metaphorically in the New Testament; it may refer to people who are likened to trees that lack fruit (Jude 12) or, as here, to deeds that produce nothing good. Paul frequently speaks of "works" (he has the noun 68 times) and has the expression "works of darkness" again in Romans 13:12. It denotes evil deeds, "darkness" being a suitable way of referring to what is evil ("the armor of light" in the Romans passage by contrast points to what is good). There is no need to spell out what is in mind; "darkness" is sufficient to point the readers to deeds that are the opposite of light. Paul is making it clear that there are terrible results when people take the action he is opposing, but no "fruit." *Phillips* translates "let your lives show by contrast how dreary and futile these things are," and, while this is far from being a literal translation, it shows us something of Paul's meaning.

"Rather" introduces the preferred conduct (as in 5:4, etc.). Far from sharing in the unfruitful things, believers are to take the opposite side. They are to "reprove" the deeds of darkness. In the New Testament there are two words for "reprove," and Abbott-Smith says that, whereas one word indicates no more than rebuke that may be "undeserved or ineffectual," the word Paul uses here "implies rebuke which brings conviction." In the context the rebuke is delivered not so much by words as by deeds. By living in a Christian way, the Ephesians will deliver a telling rebuke to those whose lives are evil. Just as light is silent but yet shows up darkness, so must the lives of Christians show up evil works for what they are. Paul is not advocating a rebuke to evil that is merely conventional and thus ineffective, but rather one that effectively marks off the believer from those who are committing the sin. The lines are to be clearly drawn. Evil is to be shown up for what it is.

"For" in verse 12 introduces the reason, but we must not confine this to the first clause; instead, we should take it as introducing the whole sentence. Paul is making his exhortation not so much because it is "shameful" to speak of these things as because of the shamefulness plus the rebuke plus the light's making all things manifest. "The things done by them secretly" are not to be identified with "the unfruitful works of darkness." Paul may be referring to the same deeds, but if he is it is because of their character as "done . . . secretly" rather than from the fact that they are "darkness." "Works of darkness" may be done quite openly; it is their evil character—the fact that they belong to the realm of darkness—not their obscurity, to which that expression draws attention. But "secretly," which is Paul's word here, indicates that there is an intention to keep these deeds from people's notice.

Paul utterly repudiates these dark deeds. He says that it is "shameful even to speak" of them (much less to do them!), and perhaps we should say that he demonstrates this by not even mentioning what these deeds were. He knew, and the Ephesians knew, and he will not dignify those deeds by so much as naming them. They are done secretly—those who perpetrate them recognize that they are not to be brought to the light.

"All things" (v. 13) in this context will mean "all those secret things," the sins of which Paul has been speaking. Paul is contending that in

Christ light has come into this world and that this has repercussions in all sorts of ways. The particular way on which he is putting emphasis at this point is that the light associated with Christ shows up the shameful things for what they are. Before the message of Christ came, the Ephesians could engage in such activities without being aware of how sinful those acts were. But now that the light of the gospel has come, evil things are shown up for what they are.

John's Gospel has a somewhat similar thought in that Jesus tells us that everyone who does base things hates the light and refuses to come to the light "lest his deeds be reproved," and he goes on to say that "he who does the truth comes to the light so that his works may be made manifest that they have been wrought in God" (John 3:20–21). Both passages connect light with the reproving of evil. Büchsel points out that, whereas in Greek generally the verb has a wide range of meaning, in the New Testament it means "to show someone his sin and to summon him to repentance." This may be done by a prophet's confronting him, by the working of conscience, and in other ways, here "by the self-revelation of light." Büchsel sees the meaning of the verb as not only "blame," "reprove," or the like, but "'to set right,' namely, 'to point away from sin to repentance.' It implies educative discipline."

There is a slight problem with Paul's statement that what is made manifest "is light" (v. 14). When light falls on an object that object is illuminated and can be seen for what it is, but this does not mean that it becomes a source of light for other objects. Perhaps there is a hint that in the Christian life there is something at work that we do not see in physical objects, namely that the person who receives light becomes in turn a source of light for other people. At the very least the passage from John 3 shows that when people come to the light not only do other people perceive their work, but the divine origin of that work becomes clear.

J. B. Phillips has an interesting translation: "For light is capable of 'showing up' everything for what it really is. It is even possible (after all, it happened with you!) for light to turn the thing it shines upon into light also." Although the Greek is obscure, this may be the thrust of what Paul is saying. Whatever his exact meaning, the words express an important truth and one that arises naturally enough from what the apostle has written.

Rise, Sleeper . . .

Paul's next statement is supported by a quotation ("it says"), but the source is unknown. Although there are some resemblances to Old Testament passages, they are hardly close enough to say that Paul is quoting or even referring to a specific text. It seems more likely that the reference is to an early Christian hymn that has perished and can no longer be identified. If so, we are reading a few lines from one of the oldest of Christian writings.

These final words of verse 14 are an exhortation to be busy in Christian service. They are addressed to one who is called "sleeper," a designation that points to the person's pre-Christian life. This sleeper is called to "rise from the dead," and the addition "Christ will shine on you" makes it clear that the death in question is the death in sin, which is the lot of all those who do not put their trust in the Savior. As often in Scripture, life and light go together. Light is associated with the whole ministry of Jesus (Matt. 4:15–16), and his followers are "the light of the world" (Matt. 5:14). When those who are in the darkness of sin receive illumination, they rise from the death of sin into the life of service of God. And in that new life the wonderful thing is that "Christ will shine on" them.

In this little quotation from a hymn (if that is what it really is) the Christian life is looked at from three angles. It is an awakening from sleep, a rising from the dead, and a going from darkness into light. Once again there is emphasis on the fundamental newness of the Christian life. We should notice, of course, that although the sinner is called on to rise and get up, the light is seen as the gift of Christ, not the reward of human merit.

17

Redeeming the Time

Therefore be very careful how you walk, not as unwise people but as wise, redeeming the time because the days are evil. For this reason do not be fools but understand what the will of the Lord is. And do not get drunk with wine, in which is debauchery, but be filled with the Spirit, speaking to one another in psalms and hymns and spiritual songs, singing and making melody to the Lord in your heart, giving thanks to God the Father always for all things in the name of our Lord Jesus Christ (Eph. 5:15–20).

For the third time in this chapter of Ephesians we have the word "therefore" (5:15; cf. vv. 1, 7) as Paul carries on his chain of reasoning. This is how he makes it very clear to his readers that *because* certain great Christian truths are so, *therefore* they must live in a certain way. Calvin begins his discussion of this verse by asking the question, "If believers should drive away the darkness of others by their own brightness, how much less ought they to be blind as to their own plan of life?" He adds, "What darkness shall conceal those on whom Christ, the Sun of righteousness, has arisen?" In other words, there is no point in accepting Christian doctrine if we refuse to let it shape our lives.

Christian Wisdom

Paul has been using the contrast between light and darkness to bring out the implications of Christian faith; now he uses the contrast between wisdom and folly. His emphasis on logic should not be overlooked. For him it was important that in Christ certain great truths have been brought to light. And because these truths have now been made known, it is important that believers live in the light of those great truths. Paul is not interested in logic purely as an intellectual discipline, nor in doctrine as an impressive gathering together of great truths that people could never have discovered for themselves. There is a measure of truth in both these pursuits, but Paul's great interest is in the salvation that God has made possible for believers and made actual for them when they put their trust in Christ. He looks for the Ephesians to live in the light that Christ has brought to a dark world. It is imperative that they live out their faith.

In bringing out this truth, the apostle makes use of an adverb that means "accurately," "carefully." It might be thought that Paul would use the word of the teachings he had given that the Ephesians had understood correctly, with his point then being that they should be making those truths clear in the way they understood Christianity. But Paul is referring to the way Ephesian Christians *lived*, not to the way they understood Christian teachings. He looks for them to be accurate, "careful" copies of the Christian model (for the use of the term as applied to a clear understanding of the Christian way, cf. Acts 18:25–26; 23:15, 20; 24:22; 1 Thess. 5:2).

What Paul writes means literally "See (or 'Take heed') therefore accurately how you walk. . . ." He is asking his converts to take notice of the way the Christian faith they had professed affects (or should affect) the way they live. "Walk," of course, refers to one's whole manner of living. As we have seen, "walking" is an important concept in this epistle. (Paul uses it no less than eight times: three by way of warning against a bad way of living [2:2; 4:17, twice] and five times to stress the importance of living rightly [2:10; 4:1; 5:2, 8, and here]). There is no point in professing to be followers of Christ if we do not live Christ-like lives.

Here Paul is urging his readers to be diligent about applying their faith to their whole manner of life ("act sensibly," REB). Paul is fond of the word "wise" (he uses it all told 16 times, but only here in this letter; "unwise" occurs only here in the New Testament). He makes more use of the noun "wisdom," reminding his readers that God has given them the wisdom they need (1:8) and telling them that he himself prays that God will give them "a spirit of wisdom and revelation" (1:17). And he looks for "the multi-colored wisdom of God" to be made known through them (3:10). Clearly, wisdom means a lot to Paul, and he wants his friends to be in no doubt about that. We are not to think of wisdom as something we apply only to our worldly affairs while we live our religion on some ethereal plane. Wisdom applies to the spiritual life just as it does to other areas of living. A good deal of nonsense has been written about the spiritual life, but, while we should always bear in mind that there is much more to serving God than the intellect can yield, we should certainly serve him with nothing less than our whole mind.

Our Use of Time

Paul carries on the thought with an unusual piece of imagery: "redeeming the time" (v. 16). The lexicon gives the meaning of the verb as *"buy, buy up . . . or redeem* (lit. 'buy back')." Moulton and Milligan see much this meaning when they say that in the passage we are considering "the meaning is not so much 'buying up,' 'making market to the full of' the opportunity, as 'buying back (at the expense of personal watchfulness and self-denial)' the present time, which is now being used for evil and godless purposes." Believers are to make the most of the opportunity while it is there.

The concept of redemption seems to have had its origin in the practices of warfare in antiquity, when it referred to paying a sum of money for the release of captives (as we noted in examining 1:7). It brings out the truth that sinners are slaves to their sin and that if they are to be saved, a great price must be paid for them. It is not within any sinner's power to provide such a price, but the wonderful truth at the heart of the gospel is that God in Christ has provided the ransom so that sinners are now free. That the sinner is quite unable to provide the ransom and that Christ's death is that price are the truths to which the metaphor of redemption draws attention.

Here Paul speaks of "redeeming the time," which is a difficult concept. M. Barth notices a number of ways of taking the expression. He sees Calvin as understanding it to mean being redeemed from the devil, Bengel from evil men, Aquinas from the depravity deriving from Adam's sin, and Robinson from loss and misuse. With such a variety of opinion, it is difficult to be certain of the apostle's exact meaning, but clearly he is speaking of freedom from some form of evil.

Part of our problem with this phrase lies in the precise meaning of the word translated "time." It may mean "opportunity" (so REB) or "time" in the usual meaning of that term. Is Paul saying that the Ephesians should make the most of every opportunity? Or that they should use all their time wisely? Surely he means at least that the Ephesians should take advantage of every opportunity of doing good that presents itself. That they are to "buy up" the opportunity seems to signify that the opportunity will not last forever; they must seize it eagerly at whatever cost and make the best possible use of it. "Buy up" is not often associated with time, but it brings out the point that the opportunity to do good is valuable. It reinforces the thought that any opportunity is available for no more than a limited time, so it is important that the servant of God make good use of each opportunity while it is there.

Christians in the Midst of Trouble

We might have expected Paul to say "although the days are evil," rather than "because" this is so. But Christians are not to expect that they can live in a holy huddle, with no contacts other than those with fellow believers. We are all members of a society that is basically secular and does not accept Christian values. Precisely there, in a society scornful of our values, it is imperative that we use time wisely.

Mitton makes the point that Paul's expression underlines the truth that Christians must be outward-looking. He says, "If one is pre-occupied with one's own spiritual excellence to the extent of becoming indifferent to down-to-earth actions of simple Christian goodness (such as helping to relieve the distresses of others, carefully avoiding evil talk, ill-will, and hostility), that will mean wasting God-given opportunities of serving him." It is easy for Christians to be so taken up with their own spiritual development that they let slide opportunities for doing good to others. We are warned that time is relentless. It moves on. If we do not take advantage of the opportunity to do good when it presents itself, we lose it forever. Of course, our ever-merciful God may present us with other opportunities later, but the one we neglect will not come back. That is not the way we should observe time. Rather, we should do whatever good we can as soon as an opportunity appears.

The expression also reminds us that all of life is God's. It is said that William Temple was fond of saying, "God is not primarily interested in religion." This was his way of drawing attention to the fact that God does not command us to withdraw from society and set up a little holy enclave. We are to live for him in a godless society. It is there that the reality of our Christian profession is to be seen.

I like the story of the traffic cop who pulled up a clergyman for speeding. The man of the cloth tried to argue his way out of it. "Please excuse my hurry," he said, "After all, I am here on earth to do God's work."

"So am I," replied the cop.

"How is that?" asked the minister.

"It says in the good book, 'Go out into the highways and compel them to come in!'"

We may well feel that the policeman's exegesis was suspect, but on the main point he was right. Each of us is called to live for God, whatever our occupation. Part of being a traffic cop is to book speeding motorists, whoever they may be. And so with all other occupations.

"Redeeming the time" means seeking the will of God in all we do and obeying that will in every situation.

Just as the metaphor of "redeeming the time" is curious, so is the reason for doing this: "because the days are evil" (unless Paul means that his readers are to redeem the time because they are to live as wise people). The presence of evil may readily be seen as an incentive to do good and overcome evil, but it is not immediately obvious why the fact that there is so much evil should be an incentive to Christ's followers to "buy up" the opportunity. Perhaps the thought is that the people of God should never acquiesce in the presence of evil. Wrongdoing abounds, but for the servant of God this is always a challenge to put things right, not a reason for acquiescing in the wrong. Probably every servant of God has felt at some time the pressure of the mass of evil that is in the world, and the temptation comes to think that what any one servant of God can do is so little that we might as well not bother to combat the evil. But Paul will have none of this. The servant of God must never cease in his or her warfare against evil. "Because the days are evil" means that there is always a challenge to do something more; it is never a justification for ceasing to fight against wrong.

There is also probably the thought that since the opportunities for sowing on good soil are so few, they must not be neglected when they come. The multiplicity of evils in which our lot is cast is itself a reason for making good use of every opportunity for doing good.

"For this reason" (v. 17) carries on the logical sequence. "Do not be fools" is a forthright expression, and Wood says it alludes to "stupid imprudence or senseless folly in action." Paul is calling on his readers to act according to the best they know and not to give way to the forces of evil; believers are expected to act wisely as well as in a holy manner. Again, precisely because there is much evil in the world, those who have heard the call of Christ must respond and not allow the evil free rein. To do that would be foolish as well as defeatist. Those who have heard God's call have aligned themselves with him in the strife against evil. Let them then press onwards in that strife.

The Service of God

We should notice Paul's emphasis on acting wisely. He has called on his readers to be "wise," not unwise, and told them not to be "fools." Now he says they are to understand what God's will is in the situations in which they find themselves. The Christian way is not to be understood as a mindless conformity, as obedience to a set of rules that are only partially understood. It is the service of God with one's whole person, a service in which our minds as well as our wills are active and in which to some extent at least we enter into an understanding of what God is doing in this world and of what our part is to be in setting forward the divine purpose. Paul is calling on his readers to put their whole being at the service of Christ.

The word he used for "unwise" in verse 15 may be differentiated from that for "fools" in that the word used here (v. 17) refers "rather to imprudence or folly in action" (Abbott; the other word denotes a lack of wisdom). Paul sees it as important that the followers of Christ recognize something of the divine purpose that is being worked out in human life. It is not without interest that, although he sees God as so high and holy—far removed from the sinful lives that are the best that we can bring—he still takes it for granted that people like the Ephesians can understand what the divine will for them is.

Paul moves from a direction to understand the divine will to a command: "do not get drunk" (v. 18). If that seems quite a big step, we should bear in mind that people in Paul's day did not have the great variety of beverages that we take for granted. If they did not drink water, the chances were that they would drink an alcoholic beverage of some kind. So it is not out of place, even in a letter to a church, that Paul should remind his readers of the danger of drunkenness. We may recall also that when the gospel was first preached in Jerusalem, some of the hearers said that the Christians were full of new wine (Acts 2:13). There is an exhilaration in the Christian way, but we must make sure that our exhilaration is that which comes from God, not from the world's tawdry substitutes.

The word Paul uses here for "debauchery" is not found often, and W. Foerster sees it as essentially referring to "one who by his manner of life, exp. by dissipation, destroys himself." Paul is reminding his readers that there is danger in drinking wine, for it can so easily lead the drinkers into a way of life that is self-destructive. And that is no way for people who have been saved by Christ's death on Calvary to live.

It is natural that we should all seek the best in life, and there is nothing wrong with this desire. What is wrong is the way many people pursue the quest. Paul is reminding his readers that they should not seek exhilaration from the wrong kind of sources. That way can lead only to disaster.

It is uncertain whether we should take the next exhortation (which means literally "be filled in spirit") as "be filled with the Spirit" or "be filled in your spirit." The New Testament speaks a number of times of Christians being filled with the Spirit, and this would suit the present context very well. Against it is the fact that the construction used here is not the usual one for being filled with the Spirit, though we should notice that "in spirit" occurs in three other places in this letter and in all three the Holy Spirit is meant (2:22; 3:5; 6:18). In any case, "be filled in your spirit" is such an unusual expression that we are justified in accepting the view of J. A. Robinson that, while "Be filled with the Spirit" is "not strictly accurate," it "suffices to bring out the general sense of the passage." Westcott sees a reference to the human spirit with "let your utmost capacities be rightly satisfied: find the completest fulfillment of your nature." Lock gets the best of both ways of taking the passage with "reach the fulness of your personality, in feeling and in utterance, under the influence of God's Spirit."

Christian Song

Paul goes on to say that the Ephesians should speak to one another joyfully (v. 19). It is possible to take "speaking to one another in psalms . . ." as an exhortation to engage in responsive chanting or the like, but it is more likely that the apostle is speaking more generally. Since God has given the Ephesians such a wonderful salvation and since this has brought them into such a wonderful family of believers, they should be joyful, and their communications to one another should reflect this.

The word translated "psalms" originally referred to playing on a stringed instrument, from which it came to signify the song that was thus accompanied. There will be no emphasis here on the accompaniment; the word simply signifies something that is sung joyfully. The "hymn" was a song of praise, often of praise to a god. The "song" was a sacred song. If we are to understand Paul to be speaking of three different kinds of song, the first will be the psalms of the Old Testament, the second will be songs composed by Christians and in use generally, while the third may well signify spontaneous outpourings of praise under the leading of the Holy Spirit.

We have taken all three words over into English, the first giving us our word "psalm," the second "hymn," and the third "ode." But in this place there is probably not a great deal of difference between them; they are simply different ways of expressing the truth that a lively Christian faith will always express itself in appropriate music. "Spiritual" could grammatically be taken with "songs," but more probably we should understand it as qualifying all three of the musical modes of which Paul is speaking. The apostle is urging his Ephesian friends to get into the joy of being Christ's and to give expression to this in singing appropriate songs. Calvin points out that in the wider community "the songs most frequently used are almost always on trifling subjects, and are far from being chaste." The songs that believers sing should befit their Christian profession.

Paul underlines the importance of cheerful music with "singing and making melody to the Lord in your heart." It is possible to take this as referring to something different from the singing he has just mentioned. He will then mean that in addition to the songs of which he has spoken, the Ephesians should be joyful in their hearts. But it is more likely that the two verbs emphasize the meaning of the three nouns he has just used. We should not think that Paul is picking out two of them as specially significant; he is simply pointing to the importance of cheerful music in the lives of Christians (something that should give us cause for some hard thinking about the way Christians so often sing anything but cheerfully; all too often we make our hymns into dirges!).

"In your heart" does not imply that this cheerfulness should find no outward expression. Rather, it signifies that Paul wants the songs of believers to be heartfelt: to reflect their inward feelings. Singing cheerfully does not mean putting on a brave show when we are anything but cheerful. Paul means that the singing of believers is to be the outward expression of a joy that is rooted in the innermost depths of their being. Perhaps we should reflect that these words come from a man who, while in the jail at Philippi with his feet fastened in the stocks, could sing the praises of God (Acts 16:24–25). Paul practiced what he preached.

So here the apostle is amplifying the thought of joyful song by saying that this is to be "in your heart." Believers do not live on the edges of life with a mindless repetition of joyful-sounding words that correspond to nothing in their innermost being. No. Their joy goes into the very depths of their being.

Thanksgiving

This leads on to the thought that believers are to give thanks "to God the Father always for all things" (v. 20). Although this presents us with no problem when things are going well, it raises problems when we encounter evil. Stott reminds us that we cannot thank God for "blatant evil." He further points out that God abominates evil, "and we cannot praise or thank him for what he abominates." But in whatever situation we find ourselves, God will always supply our need (Phil. 4:19). Paul is saying that there is never a time when we are without something for which we should give God thanks. Chrysostom long ago pointed out that believers can give thanks in all sorts of situations. He thought we should be thankful for such things as disease and poverty and should give thanks when "in afflictions, in anguish, in discouragements." He even held that we should give thanks for hell because of its deterrent effect on our behavior as we contemplate the possibility of ending up there! We may not be prepared to go along with Chrysostom completely, but at least we may profitably reflect that in even our worst difficulties there is always something for which we can give thanks. We must not let ourselves be so overwhelmed by a difficulty that we do not perceive what God is saying to us.

Paul says our thanks are to be given to "God the Father" and "in the name of our Lord Jesus Christ." As our prayers are addressed to a God we know as "Father" and uttered in the name of the Christ who died for us, there can be no surer guarantee that our thanks are heard where it matters.

18

Wives and Husbands

*Be in subjection to one another in the fear of Christ, wives to
their own husbands as to the Lord, for a husband is head of his
wife as also Christ is head of the church, being himself the Savior
of the body; but as the church is subject to Christ so also are
wives to their husbands in everything. Husbands, love your wives
as also Christ loved the church and gave himself for it, so that he
might sanctify it, having cleansed it by the washing of water with
the word, so that he might present the church to himself a glorious church, not having spot or wrinkle or any such thing, but so
that it might be holy and blameless. Men ought so to love their
own wives as their own bodies. He who loves his own wife loves
himself. For no one ever hated his own flesh, but nourishes and
warms it, even as Christ does the church, for we are members of
his body. For this reason a man will forsake his father and
mother and be closely united to his wife and the two will be come
one flesh. This mystery is a great one, but I am speaking with reference to Christ and the church. Nevertheless this also applies to
each one of you: let each man so love his wife as himself and let
the wife see that she reverences her husband (Eph. 5:21–33).*

After centuries of Christian teaching, we scarcely appreciate the revolutionary nature of Paul's views on family life set forth in
this passage. Among the Jews of his day, as also among the Romans and
the Greeks, women were seen as secondary citizens with few or no rights.
The pious male Jew daily said a prayer in which he thanked God for not
making him a woman. And he could divorce his wife by simply writing

"a bill of divorcement" (which must include the provision that she was then free to marry whomever she wanted). The wife had no such right. Barclay points out that at this time "the very institution of marriage was threatened, because Jewish girls were refusing to marry at all because the position of the wife was so uncertain." If anything, the woman's position in Roman and Greek society was even worse.

It was definitely a man's world, and teaching like that which Paul gives at this point cut across what was the norm in the societies of that period. In our day people sometimes focus on Paul's statement that the husband is "head of his wife," and they therefore see the apostle as teaching an aggressive masculinity. But we should take his words in their context and bear in mind that at the same time, Paul demanded that the husband should love his wife with a sacrificial love that is to be like that of Christ for the church. When we reflect that Christ went to the cross out of his love for the church, we see that in Paul's view a man takes on a great responsibility when he enters the state of matrimony.

In this section of his letter (which extends through 6:9) Paul deals with some important relationships in life: wife and husband, children and parents, slaves and slaveowners. A Christian regards all these relationships as important, and Paul sheds new light on the way they are to be understood by emphasizing love and cooperation. As McDonald points out, "This was a totally revolutionary concept. There was nothing like it abroad in the society of the apostle's day." It is natural to the human race to be zealous of its rights, but Paul here addresses himself to the duties of believers, not their rights.

Love and Subjection

The command to "be in subjection to one another" (5:21) draws attention to a Christian distinctive. Calvin points out that "where love reigns, there is a mutual servitude." He goes on, "I do not except even kings and governors, for they rule that they may serve." It is a natural human trait to try to secure the top place for oneself. If that goal seems beyond our reach, we aim for the highest possible places. Such an attitude runs through every society. A great American coach is reported to have said, "Winning is not the most important thing; it is the *only* thing," and the philosophy that produced this saying is widely accepted in modern communities. But it is a rather silly way of looking at competition. In the nature of the case there can be only one winner of the grand final, so it is stupid to take up the attitude that all the other teams finish as losers. It is far better to put forth one's best effort and to enjoy that, wherever one may finish in a competition.

Be that as it may, the Christian way is not that of competing with one another in an endeavor to show oneself to be superior. We are followers of the Christ who left the glory of heaven for the lowliness of Nazareth. His whole life was lived in a lowly station, and on a cross he died the death of a felon. Jesus called on his followers to take up their cross and again and again told them to pursue lives of humble service. This attitude is frequently urged upon believers in the letters of the New Testament (cf. Rom. 12:9–21; Phil. 2:3–4; Col. 3:18–4:1; Paul uses the verb I have translated "be in subjection" 23 times), so his call to lowliness in this passage is typical. Instead of thrusting ourselves forward and claiming high places for ourselves, we are called on to "be in subjection." As Bruce puts it, "reciprocal submission is a basic element in Christian ethical tradition."

The subjection is to be done "in the fear of Christ." This is the only place in the New Testament where we read of "the fear of Christ," though it is possible that it means the same as "the fear of the Lord" (Acts 9:31; 2 Cor. 5:11). But it is also possible that those passages mean "the fear of God." "The fear of the Lord" is found frequently in the Old Testament, where it means "the fear of God." Some manuscripts have "the fear of the Lord" or "the fear of God" here (and the KJV translators accepted the reading "the fear of God"). But most translators agree that the correct reading here is "the fear of Christ" and that some early scribes had altered this to the more familiar "the fear of God" or "the fear of the Lord."

Paul does not, of course, mean that his readers are to be afraid of Christ. He is saying, rather, that they must have a deep respect for Christ, a respect like that which the writers of the Old Testament Scriptures repeatedly said was the right attitude of created people to the God who created them. We should bear this in mind when we go on to the examples of "subjection" that Paul adduces. He is not saying that the people he orders to be subject "to one another" should obey unthinkingly every command given to them. Their obedience is to be such as accords with the fact that they live in the fear of the Lord.

Wives

As Paul moves to directions for a number of groups among the Christians, he begins with wives. They, he says, must have the same kind of reverence for their own husbands as the church has for Christ (v. 22). Notice that Paul speaks of their "own" husbands, so he is not saying that all women should be subject to all men. This verse is sometimes quoted as though Paul was insisting that wives were the only believers to be "in subjection." But we should notice that there is no verb in this clause. Paul is citing the attitude of wives to their husbands as a particular exam-

ple of a universal Christian duty. Strelan comments, "The call to wifely
subjection comes within the framework of the call to mutual subjection;
hence the deference shown by the wife to her husband is a specific example of the deference which all Christians are to show to one another."

Barth comments, "Though the very use of the term 'subordinate'
reflects the esteem in which women in general were held, actually Paul
announces a drastic restriction of women's subordination: it is due only
to her husband, just as the husband 'owes' marital love only to his wife
(vv. 25, 28, 33). This corresponds to his subordination to her (v. 21) which
consists of a love measured after Christ's self-giving love for the church
(vv. 25–27, 32–33)." It is *love* rather than trying to be boss that should
characterize a Christian's relationships.

In first-century society it was considered important for wives to be
submissive to their husbands; to abandon this idea would have been to
mark Christianity out as a wild new religion. Mitton says of Paul, "As a
wise pastor he had to try to see to it that the new freedom and status of
the Christian woman within her own home and marriage relationship
was not so practised as to create dangerous misunderstandings and
resentments among pagan neighbours, especially if these misunderstandings would militate against these neighbours feeling able to listen
to the gospel and to respond to it." Paul's "as to the Lord" indicates that
this submission is not to be some shallow thing, but a very real subjection—while at the same time the reminder of the relationship of both
to the Lord prevents the submission in question from being a menial
servanthood. It is a partnership of which Paul is speaking, and McDonald says of it, "Here indeed is a new charter for wives. No longer are they
to be drudges and drones; but persons and partners."

We should also bear in mind the fact that, although Paul says that the
husband is the head of the wife (v. 23), he does not say that the wife is
the body of the husband, as he says that the church is the body of Christ
(1:22–23; 4:12, 15–16; etc.). There are differences in the two relationships as well as similarities. We see this in the last part of the verse,
where Paul reminds his readers that Christ is "himself the Savior of the
body." The word "himself" is emphatic; it is Christ, not the husband,
who is in mind. We can see that that husband is the protector of the
body, but he is certainly not the Savior of the wife in the same sense that
Christ is the Savior of the church.

Westcott sums up the teaching given here: "The Church offers to Christ
the devotion of subjection, as the wife to the husband. Christ offers to
the Church the devotion of love, as the husband to the wife. Both are
equal in self-surrender." Stott says of the wife's submission, "There is
nothing demeaning about this, for her submission is not to be an
unthinking obedience to his rule but rather a grateful acceptance of his

183

care," and he goes on to point out that Barth says that Paul "is thinking of a voluntary, free, joyful and thankful partnership, as the analogy of the relationship of the church to Christ shows." Stott also holds that the courses of conduct laid down for the two partners are not so very different: "What does it mean to 'submit'? It is to give oneself up to somebody. What does it mean to 'love'? It is to give oneself up for somebody, as Christ 'gave himself up' for the church."

"But" in verse 24 is the strong adversative, which may mean, as many commentators think, that Paul maintains that the headship of Christ over his body is more significant than that of the husband over his wife. Or it may signify that Paul is declining to go into detail about the headship of the husband and, instead, sums it all up by drawing attention to Christ's headship as the pattern. We should interpret the word "everything" with care, for clearly Paul does not hold, for example, that a wife should go into apostasy if her husband were to command it.

Husbands

When Paul turns to the corresponding duty of husbands, he expresses it in terms of love (v. 25; "each party is reminded not of rights, but of duties," says Moule). Love is an important topic for Paul (he has the noun 75 times, the verb 33 times, and the adjective "beloved" 27 times). That he has in mind a thoroughgoing love is seen in his statement that the husband's love is to be "as" the love of Christ for the church. This love is seen in the fact that Christ died for the church. Interestingly, he does not say that Christ "loves" the church (though this, of course, is true), but that he "loved" it and "gave himself for it." Clearly the apostle is referring to the love we see at the cross; the very highest standard is being held before the readers. Chrysostom has a good deal to say about this. Among other things, he asks his male readers, "Wouldest thou have thy wife obedient unto thee, as the Church is to Christ?" and answers, "Take then thyself the same provident care for her, as Christ takes for the Church. Yea, even if it shall be needful for thee to give thy life for her, yea, and to be cut into pieces ten thousand times, yea, and to endure and undergo any suffering whatever,—refuse it not. Though thou shouldest undergo all this, yet wilt thou not, no, not even then, have done anything like Christ."

The purpose of Christ's death was "that he might sanctify it" (v. 26). The idea in sanctification is that of being set apart for God. This, of course, will result in better conduct, but it is not the higher standard of behavior that is primarily in mind when the term "sanctification" is used. The truly sanctified person will, of course, live on a higher level and seek to conform to higher standard, but this is the result of sanctification, not its cause.

Sanctification, says Paul, is preceded by "the washing of water with the word" (cf. Ezek. 16:8–9). Clearly "the washing of water" here refers to baptism, while "the word" may be the baptismal formula ("washing her in water with a form of words," JB), the confession of the baptized ("baptism as she utters her confession," *Moffatt*), or the teaching that accompanied it ("with the word being spoken," Cassirer). Perhaps the last mentioned is the most probable. Baptism is not enough of itself. It must be accompanied by "the word," which here surely signifies the word of teaching. There are basic Christian doctrines that must be accepted. Paul is not a ritualist saying that baptism is enough of itself. Baptism is important, but it must be accompanied by instruction in the Christian faith. The importance of Christian teaching is clear throughout the Pauline correspondence. It was very important for the apostle that believers be informed about the faith, as is evident from the kind of letter that he wrote to the churches.

The imagery is that of marriage, with the church being depicted as a bride for whom Christ, the Bridegroom, gave his life. There is the thought of the great love that brought Christ to the cross in order to bring salvation and also that of the church as loving Christ in the manner of a bride for whom her bridegroom has sacrificed much. The word "bride" is not used here as it is elsewhere, but the language Paul uses is such that there can be no doubt that he has in mind what happens at weddings. The bride would be given a cleansing bath, then arrayed in her bridal dress before being brought to the bridegroom. So Paul speaks of the church as "cleansed" with "water" and "presented" to Christ. The imagery breaks down in that Christ is seen as doing the cleansing and the presenting of the bride, whereas in an ordinary wedding the bridegroom would do nothing in the way of preparing the bride; his function began only when the bride was brought to him. But Paul is writing about a marriage that is unique, one in which all the preparation is done by Christ.

The Church

The cleansing is so that Christ "might present the church to himself" (v. 27). In the Greek "he" is emphatic; the apostle is emphasizing that this is a divine work. He does not say when this will happen, but it seems likely that he has in mind the *parousia*, the coming of Christ at the end of the world. It is then that the glorified church will be with Christ forevermore, and then that the church will be seen to be "glorious." This word is used of the clothing one would find in the courts of kings (Luke

7:25), of the glorious things Jesus did (Luke 13:17), and of the opinion the Corinthians had of themselves, where in contrast to the lowly apostle they saw themselves as "glorious" (1 Cor. 4:10). Clearly it points to a wonderful consummation for the followers of Jesus.

Paul proceeds to bring out some aspects of the "glorious church." Negatively, it will not have "spot or wrinkle or any such thing," where "spot" signifies the smallest blemish or stain, and "wrinkle" a pucker that spoils the smoothness of skin. The latter is often associated with age and thus points to a diminishing of powers. Westcott brings out the meaning with "without one trace of defilement or one mark of age." In this context "any such thing" is a general term for all other blemishes. At present the church may rightly be accused of many shortcomings, but Paul looks for a time when all its blemishes will be removed. We might also reflect that although a church made up of people like ourselves makes a sorry sight, yet, despite all our shortcomings, God has been pleased to use this church to bring about some wonderful changes.

On the positive side, the church will be "holy and blameless." The fundamental idea in holiness is, of course, attachment to a deity. A holy place is a place where the deity is supposed to have manifested himself, a holy man is one who belongs to the god he worships, holy vessels are those used in the worship of the deity. When Jesus completes his work on the church, it will be wholeheartedly given over to the service of God. "Blameless" points us to uprightness, to actions that are such that no criticism can be lodged against it. Paul is saying that in the end the church will be completely given over to the service of God and that her deeds will be what they *should* be.

Love in Marriage

Paul makes the point that a man should love his wife by saying that he should love her as he loves his own body (v. 28). This is a particular application of the commandment "You shall love your neighbor as yourself" (Lev. 19:18). We do not usually employ this terminology, but our bodies are very important to us, and we do all we can to secure their comfort. Of course, if we are Christians, we bear in mind that selfishness is sinful and seek God's help in enabling us to do all we can for the needs of other people. But Paul is dealing with the fact that after we have given ourselves over to doing all we can to help others, we still have a strong concern for our own bodies. As long as we live in this mortal life, that self-concern is inevitable. Except for a few abnormal souls, we all try to secure the best we can for ourselves. Christian men, Paul is saying, are to extend that attitude to their wives. So close is the unity between a man and his wife that the apostle can say, "He who loves his own wife loves himself."

He develops the theme by pointing out that no man "ever hated his own flesh" (v. 29). It is common to all people that the body is important, and although a few eccentrics sometimes engage in self-mutilation, what Paul says is still true of the human race as a whole. Each one "nourishes and warms" his flesh, which we must understand as indicating that every one of us looks after all the normal bodily needs. Even though from time to time ascetics have appeared and some of them have seen a merit in making their bodies uncomfortable, Paul's generalization about human beings holds true. This is not all of Paul's teaching on the body, and elsewhere he can say, "I keep my body under [his verb means literally "give a black eye to"] and make a slave of it" (1 Cor. 9:27). Both there and here he is saying that we are not compelled to be either self-mutilators or self-indulgent. But whereas in writing to the Corinthians Paul was warning against self-indulgence, here he is reminding his readers that their bodies are important to them.

That a man "nourishes and warms" his own flesh means that he takes care to see that his body has whatever it needs to remain healthy and comfortable. This is the most natural thing in the world for all of us, but Paul goes on, "Even as Christ does the church." He sees Christ's care for the church as the model for the husband's care for his wife. In other words, the husband must be wholehearted in this care.

Paul follows this up with the reminder that "we are members of his body" (v. 30). Elsewhere he enlarges on this theme (e.g., 1 Cor. 12), but here it is sufficient to draw attention to the fact that Christians belong to one another as well as belonging to Christ. That means they have obligations to one another, just as the members of our physical bodies depend on one another. If we have strong pain in one member, our whole body is affected. The failure of one member has inhibiting effects on all the others.

Paul proceeds to bring out the closeness of the union of husband and wife with a quotation from the Old Testament, namely Genesis 2:24 (v. 31; cf. Matt. 19:5; Rom. 12:5). It is accepted throughout Scripture that marriage is the closest link whereby humans are joined to one another. The passage quoted centers on the truth that in marriage such a strong link is formed that a man will leave his parents and go off with his wife to form a new household. When we consider the respect afforded parents throughout the first-century world, and specifically among the Jews, this indicates that marriage is a very close tie indeed. The verb translated "closely united" means literally "be glued to." No halfhearted commitment is in mind here, and this is further emphasized with "the two will become one flesh." Paul leaves his readers in no doubt but that marriage is an extremely close bonding.

The Mystery

For the meaning of "mystery" (v. 32), refer to our study of 1:9. Here the word signifies that the relationship between man and wife is something we could not have worked out for ourselves. But God has revealed it. Expositors differ, with some putting their emphasis on the hiddenness (cf. REB, "There is hidden here a great truth"), others on the fact that it is made known (cf. GNB, "There is a deep secret truth revealed in this scripture"). Whichever way we take it, Paul is speaking of this unity as a close one, as the Scripture he has just quoted makes plain. His "I" is emphatic. We do not know the reason for this, but perhaps there had been some false teaching about marriage, so Paul is leaving no doubt about his own deep conviction. We see the mystery in all its fullness, not in the unity between man and wife, but in that between Christ and the church. The oneness between man and wife is no more than a little picture of that between Christ and his church. It is *this* mystery of which Paul is speaking.

Although this mystical union cannot be completely understood, we can enter into it to some extent. For example, when a marriage takes place we know that the bride is removed from the family in which she was brought up and brought into the family into which she has married. Paul has made it clear that the heart of the mystery refers to "Christ and the church."

The lexicon tells us that the Greek word translated "nevertheless" (v. 33) can be used "in breaking off a discussion and emphasizing what is important." That is its significance here. There is some emphasis on "you," and Paul has an "also"—you Christian husbands as well as the heavenly Bridegroom! Paul's concern at this point is not to go deeply into the relationship between Christ and the church. Having said the most important thing, he reverts to the relationship between husband and wife, which is his main topic here. What he has to say applies to all his readers; this is not a piece of teaching referring only to church leaders or any other restricted group. Each man in the Ephesian church must "so love his wife as himself," and each wife must "see that she reverences her husband." The word I have translated "reverences" more literally means "fears," but we must take it here in the same sense as "the fear of Christ" (v. 21). In both places the thought is that of offering deep respect, not that of being scared. There are obligations as well as joys in the married state, and Paul leaves no doubt as to the depths of the obligation.

19

Christian Households

Children, obey your parents in the Lord, for this is right. Honor your father and mother, which is the first commandment with a promise, that it may be well with you and that you may live long upon the earth. And, fathers, do not make your children angry, but bring them up in the discipline and instruction of the Lord (Eph. 6:1–4).

Paul continues to discuss family life. He follows his words about wives and husbands with some directions to parents and children, and to slaves and masters. Because his remarks to children and to slaves are much longer than those to fathers and masters, some have drawn the conclusion that the apostle was simply trying to strengthen the positions of the authority figures of his day. But this is to miss a very important point, which M. Barth puts this way: "Unlike many Greek, Latin, and rabbinical teachers of ethics, Paul does not only or primarily address the free male members of the human society. He makes wives, children, and slaves as responsible for a good social order as those who wield, or presume to possess, superior power (cf. Rom. 13:1–7)." We should not miss the point that in this letter to a church ("the saints who are in Ephesus," 1:1), wives and children and slaves are specifically included. Their roles here on earth are very different (and different from that of adult males), but they are all included in the church. This cut clean across the accepted ideas of the day, so it is not surprising that Paul devotes more space to the sections of his letter that bring it out.

When he comes to children (6:1–3), Paul has two points of importance. The first is that of obedience: "obey your parents" (v. 1), a necessary part of family life. Parents have had a far wider experience of life in this world than their children have, and they are the people with the responsibility of bringing up those children. Surely their task will be even more difficult if the children refuse to obey their directions. So Paul urges the children to be obedient. Calvin evidently had some unhappy experiences with children, for he asks, "Do we find one among a thousand that is obedient to his parents?" Be that as it may, the duty of Christian children to be obedient to their parents is clear.

But Paul qualifies this with "in the Lord." He is writing to Christians and contemplating Christian families. There must, of course, have been many families in which one or more members had become Christian while the rest of the family did not believe. Paul is not saying that believing children are to obey non-believing parents in everything, for that might include instructions such parents might give that involved opposition to the Christian faith and harm to the Christian lives of the children. We do not know what the apostle would have said about this problem, but we should probably reason that the Christian child of non-Christian parents should obey those parents in all things in which the faith was not involved. Where it was, they would have to obey Christ rather than people; their obedience was to be "in the Lord." this would, of course, mean that obedience or the refusal to obey, whichever was right in a given situation, would be given in a spirit of love, not in defiance and self-assertion.

Hodge emphasizes the importance of these words when he says that the obedience of children is to be "religious; arising out of the conviction that such obedience is the will of the Lord. This makes it a higher service than if rendered from fear or from mere natural affection. It secures its being prompt, cordial and universal." And "this," Paul says, "is right." In all societies it is accepted that children should have proper attitude toward their parents, and this would include obedience. Paul, however, is not appealing to accepted social customs, but to the demands of Christian service.

Honoring Parents

The apostle makes his second point by moving on to the fifth of the Ten Commandments: "Honor your father and mother" (v. 2). When we cease to be children we still owe our parents respect. This virtue is recognized worldwide as a most significant part of family life; specifically for believers it is very important, and without it what remains is sub-Christian.

The meaning of Paul's comment on the commandment (v. 3) is not completely clear. He may mean, "This is the first commandment with a promise attached," or "This is a commandment of first importance and it is accompanied by a promise," or "For children this is the first commandment to be learned and a promise is attached to it." Any of these may be right, but there is no way of being certain which Paul had in mind.

Certainly there is a promise attached, namely that God's people are to do this so that they will live long in the land God gives them (cf. Exod. 20:12). It is often said that the second commandment also has a promise, but this is not really the case; it has a statement of what God will do (Exod. 20:4–6). Both the Old Testament passage and its citation here mention being in the land God has promised his people. This part of the promise, of course, could scarcely apply to Paul's Gentile addressees, but that does not diminish the importance of having a right attitude towards one's parents. We should bear in mind that Paul does not speak of Palestine, but says, "that you may live long upon the earth." For his Gentile readers, it is this rather than the Jewish connection that is significant. In any stable society, respect for parents has a significant place, and Paul does not want his Ephesian converts to be in any doubt as to its importance. Nor should we doubt that those who honor their parents receive the divine blessing.

Fathers

At this point Paul inserts a direction to "fathers" (v. 4). (It is possible that we should understand this word as "parents," and most take it in this way [e.g., in Heb. 11:23]; GNB translates it with "parents" here.) Christian fathers, Paul says, are not to act in such a way as to make their children angry (REB, "do not goad your children to resentment"). This idea would have been revolutionary in its day; in the first-century Roman Empire, fathers could do pretty much what they liked in their families. They could even sentence family members to death, as at an earlier time Judah did to his daughter-in-law (Gen. 38:24; cf. Deut. 21:18–21; see also the acceptance by both Abraham and Isaac of a father's right to kill his son, Gen. 22:1–14). There is a well-known papyrus, bearing a date equivalent to our 1 B.C., in which a man named Hilarion who was working in Alexandria wrote to his pregnant wife, Alis, letting her know that he would be in Alexandria for some time. The baby might well be born before he got back home, and he gives Alis the instruction that if it is a boy, she should keep it; if a girl, she should throw it away.

In the first century, then, a father was an august figure with absolute rights over members of his family. Yet Paul directs fathers not to make their children "angry," which would have seemed to most people of that day a most intolerable limitation of a father's activities. In a society with values like those we have noted, Paul's instruction was revolutionary!

We can see here that the apostle was not insisting on the status quo, merely pointing to something that decent citizens everywhere would accept. He was leading the Ephesians to recognize that the role of the father should not be that of indulging in an arbitrary rule over his household, as was commonly held. Rather a father's concern is for the well-being of each member of the family. Specifically, fathers are not to take the sort of action that will anger their children. This means that they must take care to understand what effect the things they say and do will have on their children. It is perhaps significant that Paul speaks of "children" not "boys." Christianity did not share the opinion of most people in antiquity that girls were inferior. Fathers must consider the effect of what they said and did on all their children.

On the positive side, fathers are directed to bring up their children "in the discipline and instruction of the Lord." G. Bertram can say of this expression: "Here the basic rule of all Christian education is stated." If there is any difference meant between the two nouns, "discipline" will refer to deeds, and "instruction" to words. Fathers are directed to use both to ensure a Christian upbringing for their children. The lives of fathers are to show the reality of their faith. They are to remember that their honorable place entails obligations as well as the freedom to order their offspring to do certain things or to refrain from doing other things. The word I have translated "instruction," according to J. Behm, "denotes the word of admonition which is designed to correct while not provoking or embittering." Simpson complains that "too many parents nowadays foster the latent mischief by a policy of *laissez faire,* pampering their pert urchins like pet monkeys whose escapades furnish a fund of amusement as irresponsible freaks of no serious import." Not so do Christian parents bring up their children.

Slaves

Slaves, be obedient to those who in the flesh are your owners with fear and trembling in singleness of your heart as if to Christ, not with eye-service as those who would please men, but as slaves of Christ doing the will of God from the heart, serving with good will as to the Lord and not to men, knowing that whatever good each one does, this he will receive from the Lord whether slave or free (Eph. 6:5–8).

Slavery was, of course, widespread in the ancient world, and Paul now turns his attention to slaves. We who live in the twentieth century find slavery abhorrent and sometimes wonder that the New

Testament writers did not denounce it forthrightly. But we must not try to impose today's ideas onto first-century people. In the ancient world slavery was a recognized feature of society. Slaves were universally seen as necessary for an ordered society; nobody seems to have envisaged the possibility of a society without slaves. It has been estimated that there were 60,000,000 slaves in the Roman Empire; slaves probably formed almost the entirety of the work force. Free men did not labor.

A slave was regarded as a tool. Barclay quotes from Aristotle, "A slave is a living tool, just as a tool is an inanimate slave." He also notes Varro's classification of agricultural instruments: the articulate (slaves), the inarticulate (cattle), and the mute (vehicles). Every nation had its slaves. The New Testament never protests against the practice, and we must see this as natural in view of the accepted ideas of the time. In due course this abominable practice would be abolished, with Christians in the vanguard of those who opposed slavery. But in the first century they could do no more than alleviate the lot of slaves as much as it lay in their power. The view that the New Testament writers should have opposed the whole system of slavery overlooks the fact that slavery was part of what was universally accepted. And we should bear in mind that we countenance other cultural evils. It is only recently that society in general has come to realize that its attitude to women and to people of color has often left a lot to be desired.

In light of the accepted ideas of the time, we should not take it as a matter of course that Paul includes in his letter some remarks addressed specifically to slaves. What other first-century group would receive a letter with such a section? This is a remarkable fact, and it is part of the revolutionary social ideas that were characteristic of the Christians. For them, owner and slave alike were the servants of Christ, brothers in the Lord. Paul could write to Philemon about his escaped slave Onesimus and tell him that he should receive Onesimus back, "no longer as a slave, but more than a slave, a brother beloved . . ." (Philem. 16). It is hard to think of any non-Christian in the first century calling a slave (let alone a runaway slave) "a brother beloved"!

In his letter Paul is insistent that both slaves and slaveowners should bear in mind their relationship to Christ the Lord. It is not without interest that he mentions Christ in every one of the verses in the section in which he speaks of slaves. They are to render their service "as if to Christ" (v. 5); they are to serve "not . . . as those who would please men, but as slaves of Christ" (v. 6); they are to serve "with good will as to the Lord" (v. 7); and "whatever good" anyone has done, "this he will receive from the Lord whether slave or free" (v. 8.).

First, Paul urges slaves to obey their masters. We should notice that he speaks of "those who in the flesh are your owners." The phrase "in the flesh" means that both writer and readers would know that slavery exists only in this life. The expression puts a limit to what ownership means in the case of slaves. Again, we should not miss the point that the word I have translated here with "owners" more literally means "lords." It is the word normally used in the New Testament for Christ as "Lord" of believers, as well as for a human "lord" who was supreme over his slaves. When Paul preached (and wrote), he was proclaiming what God had done to bring salvation to all who believe. He did not cease from pointing people to the glorious future that awaited believers beyond this life. So here he is telling slaves that their slavery is in this life only; entrance into the kingdom of God was open to them as freely as to the greatest in the land. Paul's short letter to Philemon lets us see something of the way believers had entered a way of life in which social distinctions matter little. The believing slave was a brother in the Lord to all who had a like precious faith.

But while slavery did not stop free Christians from exercising a brotherhood that went beyond earthly distinctions, it was important for Paul that slaves, like other people, should glorify God by the way they lived. As they were slaves, let them be the best slaves possible (just as Christian owners should be the best owners possible). So Paul calls on slaves to serve "with fear and trembling," an expression that was used of free people as well as of slaves (1 Cor. 2:3; 2 Cor. 7:15; Phil. 2:12). Paul wants Christian slaves to serve God as faithfully as slaves who are in constant fear of cruel masters serve their human overlords. Christian slaves are motivated by the fact that they are "slaves of Christ" and must serve in such a way that they will please him. They must accept their lowly status and serve God there as well as they can. That they are to serve their masters "as if to Christ" sets the highest standard before them. (Of course, it would be a thousand pities if they did not serve Christ as wholeheartedly as other slaves served their human masters.) McDonald sees the expression as one "which lifts all duty to the high plane of divine service and makes the factory as sacred as the church."

As Paul carries on with his exhortation to Christian slaves, he says they are to do their work "not with eye-service" (v. 6). This is an unusual word (found again in the New Testament only in Col. 3:22 and not cited in any earlier writing; Paul may have coined the word himself). It apparently denotes the kind of service that is done simply to attract attention. It is done to "please men" and not for the slave's own satisfaction in the knowledge that he has done the best he could. Nor, from the Christian point of view, was such service done in order to please God. Doing "eye-service" means that the slave will not do the work properly when he cannot be observed. Work like this is not Christian service, and it is Paul's view that everything the slave (or anyone else) does is to be done as service to God and therefore be the best that the person can do.

Paul's "but" (v. 6) is the strong adversative: far from pleasing men, Christian slaves live as "slaves of Christ." They have been redeemed by Christ, which means they have been purchased by him so that all that they have and all that they are belong to him. That should govern all that they do—and for that matter, all that *we* do, even though we are not slaves to men. Paul is asserting in strong terms the lordship of Christ over all his people.

Paul explains this a little more with "doing the will of God from the heart." Just like free people, Christian slaves are committed to doing God's will. That is foremost in Christian service. And it is to be done, not grudgingly as though we find it a grievous burden, but "from the heart." The word translated "heart" is frequently rendered "soul." However translated, it refers to the innermost part of our being, where our will is located. While in many places this noun must be translated "soul," here it seems preferable to say "from the heart." Paul is affirming strongly the importance of Christian slaves doing as much as slaves can do to set forward the purposes of God. They should not aim at doing merely as little as would be in accordance with their Christian profession. The same directive, of course, applies to free people, but Paul uses it of slaves because they must have often been tempted to do very little, telling themselves that they need do no more "because we are slaves and not free to do what we would like."

Paul goes on to speak of slaves as "serving with good will" (v. 7), where his verb means literally "slaving," "serving as a slave." This, of course, is a duty we all owe to God, whether we are free or not. But the word must have come with great force to Christian slaves, for every day they had the experience of serving as slaves to a visible earthly master. Paul is saying that this gives them a little picture of what it means to be servants of the living God. Nobody is to think that service to God is a shallow affair, as if easily complied with by engaging in a few religious exercises. Just as the slave of a human master is obliged to serve that master twenty-four hours a day, so the servants of God owe obedience to God every minute of their lives.

Paul has already said that what makes Christian slaves different from other slaves is that they are first and foremost "slaves of Christ." This means that whatever task their earthly master requires of them, they will see it as a task to be done in the sight of their heavenly Master and a task to be done *for* that heavenly Master. The highest standard is placed before them.

Service with Good Will

"Serving with good will" is literally "slaving with good will"; again we have the thought that Christian slaves are God's servants first of all and above all else. Both Paul and the readers to whom this letter was sent knew, of course, that the slaves in the church were slaves to men. But when people saw themselves primarily as servants of God, they would do whatever they were going as well as they possibly could do it. They were doing it for God.

Paul sees the service rendered by Christian slaves as done "with good will" (the term may mean "with enthusiasm") and "as to the Lord and not to men." They must not see what they were doing as nothing more than doing what their earthly owner wanted; it was work they were doing for God. The apostle is carrying on with the thought that the Christian slave is first and foremost the servant of God. Paul will not let the slaves in the congregation at Ephesus miss the point that while there was one sense in which they were slaves to men and one sense in which they were slaves to Christ, it was the latter slavery that mattered.

The apostle moves on to the further thought that the way we live now is important, for there are to be heavenly rewards and punishments (v. 8). The slave who serves well may not be rewarded here and now (slave-masters were not always kind to the people they owned). But God, who sees everything, will certainly reward the slave who has lived by faith and has discharged his duty. In due course the God who sees all and makes no distinction between slaves and free people will treat the faithful slave according to his desert. It is true that God's servants do not serve him for what they can get out of it; if they serve in the hope of a suitable reward they are not doing truly Christian service. But it is also true that God will reward faithful service—if not here and now, then in the life to come. And in that life there is no difference between slaves and free people.

Paul enlarges on the point when he speaks of Christian slaves as "knowing" that God acts justly. His "each one" refers to a universal rule; he is not speaking of what happens in the case of some people but not others. God is uniformly just, and the Ephesian slaves know that God will reward his people accordingly. Paul says that each one will receive from the Lord "whatever good" he has done. This, of course, means that the reward will be appropriate. The slave must not expect that the exact deed will be done to him as he has done to someone else, but he can rely on God to act justly. It is not without some interest that Paul speaks only of the "good" a person does, for in other places in the New Testament the fate of the wicked as well as the good is brought out (e.g., 2 Cor. 5:10; Col. 3:24–25).

We might illustrate this latter point from an incident at a girls' school, where one of the students was talking to a friend about the cookery class she attended. "Do they let you eat the things you cook?" asked the friend. "Let us?" asked the budding chef—"They *make* us." There is an inevitability about the consequences of wickedness staying with the wicked, a truth that we should all bear in mind.

The slave who does "good" will receive the reward "from the Lord," which may mean from God the Father or from God the Son. Elsewhere in the New Testament both are said to be active in the judgment, and Paul does not seem at this point to be differentiating between them. He concludes his advice to slaves by saying that "whether slave or free," all will be treated in this way. The differences between slaves and free people, which meant so much in first-century society, will have no place in the final judgment. In that judgment, earthly differences mean nothing at all.

Owners of Slaves

And masters, do the same to them, giving up threatening, knowing that the Lord of both them and you is in heaven and there is no respect of persons with him (Eph. 6:9).

Paul has a much shorter exhortation to slaveowners, but this is partly due to his opening words: "And masters, do the same to them" (v. 9). Much of what the apostle has written about slaves is just as applicable to masters, so they are to apply to themselves what he has just said. It must have come as a shock to some slaveowners to find that they should have the same attitude to their slaves as the slaves should have to them. The apostle has one specific direction: "giving up threatening." It must have been a constant temptation to owners of slaves to try to get the most out of their slaves by holding over their heads threats of punishments they would receive if their work was not satisfactory. Paul instructs Christian slaveowners to manage their affairs without the use of threats.

The apostle reinforces his rejection of threatening by reminding the owners that they, too, are subjects of "the Lord." Paul does not make it clear whether this refers to Christ or to God the Father. If he is differentiating here, he probably means Christ, for "the Lord" is so often used in this way in his writings. That "the Lord" is "in heaven" makes it plain that the apostle is speaking of a divine person, one far above this earthly life. It is interesting that Paul's plural, which I have translated "masters," is more literally "lords," and it is the plural of the word he uses for the divine Lord. This is perhaps a way of reminding slaveowners that while each could claim to be "lord" in his own domain, they were all lowly subjects of a far greater Lord.

Paul brings out this point further by reminding his readers that (literally) "of them and of you [a word order that puts emphasis on the fact that he is lord of all creation] the Lord is in heaven." He adds, "there is no respect of persons with him." This is a gentle reminder that earthly rank has no relevance in heaven. Here on earth the slave would be relegated to the lowest place, but that does not mean that the Lord is not mindful of slaves. Both owner and slave will in due course have to render account of what they have done. That the slaveowner is an important person here on earth does not mean that he is important in heaven. There he is no more than a sinner, saved by divine grace. He must give account of himself, just as is the case with his slaves. It is how we stand with Christ that matters, not how we stand with the society in which we live and move and have our being here on earth.

20

The Christian's Armor

For the rest, be strong in the Lord and in the strength of his power. Put on the full armor of God so that you will be able to stand against the stratagems of the devil; for our wrestling is not against blood and flesh, but against the sovereignties, against the authorities, against the world-rulers of this darkness, against the spiritual forces of wickedness in the heavenlies. For this reason take up the full armor of God, so that you may be able to withstand in the evil day and having accomplished everything to stand. Stand therefore, having girded your loins with truth and having put on the breastplate of righteousness and having shod your feet with the preparation of the gospel of peace, in all things having taken up the shield of faith with which you will be able to quench all the flaming arrows of the evil one, and receive the helmet of salvation and the sword of the Spirit, which is the word of God (Eph. 6:10–17).

While Paul knows that the Christian life is wonderful, he is also well aware that it is a conflict. He can take the example of a boxer at the athletic games and point out that he himself does not fight like someone who hits only the air (1 Cor. 9:26; in that passage he also likens himself to a runner at the games). He can exhort Timothy to "fight the good fight of faith" (1 Tim. 6:12), and he speaks of "conflict" as part of his own spiritual experience (Phil. 1:30; Col. 2:1). He reminds the Corinthians that though "we walk in the flesh, we do not war according to the flesh" (2 Cor. 10:3). He speaks of a "law" in the members of his body that "wars" against the law of his mind (Rom. 7:23). And, as he draws near to the end of his life, he can say, "I have fought the good fight" (2 Tim. 4:7).

Paul is clear, then, that the Christian is engaged in spiritual warfare, and he comes back again and again to the armor God has provided for his servants in that conflict (see Rom. 13:12; 2 Cor. 6:7; 10:4; 1 Thess. 5:8). In this passage he treats it more fully than elsewhere. We should not press the details of the imagery too far, for Paul is not consistent in his application of the figure. For example, in the Romans passage he speaks of "the armor of light" but does not mention individual pieces of this armor. Again, in Thessalonians he refers to "the breastplate of faith and love," whereas here the breastplate is "righteousness"; in Thessalonians the helmet is "the hope of salvation," but here it is "salvation." The differences are not vital, but we should be aware of them. Clearly what mattered to the apostle is that Christians are engaged in constant warfare, a conflict in which God has provided all the equipment they need to be victorious.

"For the rest" (6:10) is an expression that Paul uses occasionally and here has a meaning like "finally." The apostle has completed the bulk of his argument and it remains only to add a few important things. "Be strong in the Lord" may be a passive, as Foulkes takes it, to give the sense "be made powerful." Others take it to mean "be strong." Mitton thinks that this translation "is perhaps misleading, since it suggests the rallying of our own inward resources. What, however, the Greek actually urges is that Christians 'be made strong,' 'be empowered,' that is, by this new relationship with Christ and the resources he makes available to us." Mitton draws attention to the Phillips paraphrase: "In conclusion be strong—not in yourselves but in the Lord."

However we understand the verb, it reminds the readers that Christianity is no religion for weaklings. It is important that every Christian be made strong. Calvin emphasizes the importance of "in the Lord": "As if he [Paul] had said, 'You cannot reply that you lack the ability; for I only require you to be strong in the Lord.' And then in explanation he adds, *in the power of his might,* which greatly increases our confidence, particularly as it shows the help which God is accustomed to bestow upon believers." We are all called upon to resist evil and to fight against the devil. We can drift into sin, but we cannot drift into righteousness. Being righteous involves a conflict with evil, a conflict in which those who use the armor God supplies must emerge victorious. God has provided all that they need, and it only remains for them to use the weapons he has provided for them.

Christians, then, are to be made "strong," and Paul explicitly says that this be done "in the Lord." He is not referring to spiritual strength as something that originates in human endeavor. He is not saying that we are to put forward our best spiritual effort and in the process develop spiritual strength. He is saying that we should make the fullest use of the spiritual strength that is given to those who are "in the Lord." He proceeds to underline the importance of spiritual might by saying that this is to be "in the strength of his power." We should be quite clear that Paul is not urging his readers to develop their own resources so that they may become stronger and stronger. He is saying that God can and will make them stronger and stronger as they rely on him. "The strength of his power" is a striking use of two words for might. There is probably no great difference in meaning here, but the combination puts emphasis on the importance of the divine power at work in believers.

The Whole Armor of God

Paul proceeds to urge his readers to be fully equipped for the spiritual warfare in which all believers are involved (v. 11): "Put on all the armor that God gives you" (GNB). For the most part the apostle will speak of defensive armor, which accords with the fact that our strength is not our own, but is strength given by God. But first the apostle uses the term *panoplia* (which we have taken over into English as "panoply"). This word means the complete armor of the fully armed warrior, offensive as well as defensive. Apart from the use of the word twice in this passage, it is found in the New Testament only in Luke 11:22, where it refers to the strong man, Satan, who is overcome by someone stronger who takes away the "whole armor on which he put his trust." There the thought is of Satan in all his strength being unable to overcome Christ; here it is that the Christian, being fully armed by Christ, will be able to overcome all that Satan brings against him. The "panoply" will cover all the weapons Paul mentions in the verses that follow. There is perhaps the implication that living the Christian life is a varied affair, and we need to be armed at various points if we are to cope with it all.

The Christian's Opposition

That will be the point also of being "able to stand against the stratagems of the devil." It is important for the Christian to realize that the opposition is not the familiar flesh-and-blood type of foe, but spiritual forces of evil. Says Stott: "Our struggle is not with human beings but with cosmic intelligences; our enemies are not human but demonic." (Stott has a useful critique of the modern views that see the references to cosmic beings as applying to structures of society and the like.) In this situation Paul does not speak of the believer as taking the offensive, but of "standing," which is an idea on which he puts some emphasis in this passage (cf. vv. 13, 14; also "withstand" in v. 13). Believers may not be able to defeat the forces of evil on their own, for they are spirit beings of another order, and there is no reason for thinking that human might of any sort can defeat them. But when believers take up the armor that God supplies, they will remain standing on the battlefield when the conflict is done and the enemy is defeated.

Barth remarks that in this passage "far more emphasis is placed on readiness and firmness in the struggle than upon any actual human accomplishment during the battle." The armor is all provided by God; it is for us to take it up and use it. And the victory, when it comes, will always be seen to have been accomplished by God, not by his people. In other places in Scripture God himself is said to engage in warfare with the forces of evil and indeed sometimes to employ some of the same weapons as do believers (e.g., Isa. 59:16–17).

"The stratagems of the devil" is an interesting expression. (Strelan comments, "Paul knows that his adversary is a tricky devil.") "Stratagems" translates the word from which we derive "method" (see the comments on 4:14). This reminds us that one of the devil's approaches is to get believers so to trust in the methodical way in which they follow Christian precepts that they come to trust in their methods rather than in the Christ who saves. (I know of one believer who discovered that his besetting sin was pride and who then made strenuous attempts to become humble. It seemed that he was making progress until one day it dawned on him that he was becoming proud of his very humility!)

Paul is reminding his readers that evil does not always come to us plainly marked "This is wrong." While there are temptations to do what is obviously evil, we should not overlook the fact that the "stratagems" of the evil one include persuading the servants of God to do what is good from wrong motives. We should be in no doubt that the temptations we meet on our way through life may be subtle and confusing as well as blatant and obvious. Paul warns his readers against them all. Back of them is the evil one, who must not be dismissed with a wave of the hand as though he could be ignored. We ignore the tempter at our spiritual peril.

The apostle moves to a change of metaphors and speaks of "our wrestling" (v. 12; "wrestling" is used here only in the New Testament). This form of contest leaves the wrestler in no doubt as to the strength of his opponent, nor as to the skills that opponent has acquired through the years. Any wrestler is well aware that a variety of skills is necessary if victory is to be won. Paul puts emphasis on the power of the opposition. The Christian is not wrestling "against blood and flesh" (this order also in Heb. 2:14; the more usual order is "flesh and blood" but there appears to be no difference in meaning). This is a way of referring to what is human, part of the creation with which we are familiar. If our opposition were human, then—though we might be defeated now and then—we might expect a measure of success.

But, says Paul, we are confronted with a variety of oppositions, none of them human. He speaks first of "the sovereignties," an expression he has used in 1:21 and 3:10. The word points to those who are of first importance, and here this importance is in the realms of wickedness. "The authorities" are not significantly different, though we should notice that Paul uses the word more widely than that for "sovereignties" (see the comments on 1:21). "World-rulers" is a compound ("world" plus "ruler") found here only in the New Testament. Elsewhere it was used of gods that ruled the world, and also of the Roman emperor. It came to be used of the spirits that ruled this sinful world. "Darkness" is the ordinary word for the absence of light, but it is used also for the unseen forces of evil, as in "the powers of darkness." The expression "this darkness" is unusual; it points to this world as a sinful place where the dark powers exercise their sway.

"The spiritual forces of wickedness in the heavenlies" completes the muster of the evil powers. Paul does not use the word "forces"; more literally he speaks of "spiritual things," but in this context it is a way of summing up any other evil powers that the previous terms have not covered. Paul is in no doubt that in the spirit world the powers of evil are strong and varied. They will not be defied or defeated by any halfhearted effort that stems from a failure on the part of the people of God to realize the magnitude of the opposition they are facing.

This is the last of five references to "the heavenlies" in this epistle (for more on the expression, see the comments on 1:3). Paul usually employs the term in the sense of heaven as the place of blessing, but here it clearly means the abode of evil beings. Moule points out that the connection of this word "with anything evil is confined to this passage, and is confessedly startling." He sees the meaning as that "we have to deal, in the combat of the soul and of the Church, with spiritual agents of evil occupying a sphere of action invisible and practically boundless." Paul is saying that there are forces of evil beyond this world of ours, beings who are not in heaven itself, but in the realms proper to spirits. This underlines the difficulty of our spiritual task. We are to overcome not only the evil forces that are proper to this world, but those that can be characterized only by reference to "the heavenlies."

We should not misunderstand Paul's emphasis on the powers of evil, as though he were gloomily contemplating the inevitable defeat of the people of God. Far from that, he is simply telling his readers not to take the forces of evil lightly. It is important that they understand the serious nature of the conflict in which they are engaged. But it is also important that they understand the weapons with which God has endowed his faithful people. With God supplying their need, how can they fail?

"For this reason" (v. 13) carries us logically to the next point. It is *because* we are opposed by such powerful forces of evil that we must take full advantage of the weapons God supplies. The verb translated "take up" can be used in a variety of senses; it is used of Christ's ascension (Acts 1:11), of the taking up of a tent (Acts 7:43), and in other ways. The instruction that Christians "take up" armor seems to mean that they involve themselves actively in the struggle. They are not to leave the armor lying there, but must take it up for use. Once more Paul speaks of "the full armor of God" (see comments on v. 11). There should be no such misunderstanding as would lead us to rely on our own strength. In this battle we need all the help we can get, and Paul assures his readers that the best of all possible help is available. He begins with defensive armor and indeed puts most of his emphasis there. But he finishes with the sword, an offensive as well as a defensive weapon.

Again he puts emphasis on standing (cf. v. 11). His verb has the meaning, "set oneself against, oppose, withstand." There is the thought of conflict in which one stands firm (NIV, "stand your ground") against the enemy. Perhaps Paul's idea is that of holding one's position against strong opposition. He speaks first of standing "in the evil day," an expression found only here in the New Testament (though we have the plural "the days are evil" in 5:16). Paul does not explain what this "day" is, but he appears to mean that no matter how evil the times in which we find ourselves, we are to be able to stand. Anyone can hold firm when there is no opposition, but the apostle is saying now that when we are armed with the full armor of God, we will be able to "withstand" all the onslaughts of evil. The armor is available if we will but use it.

It is not clear whether the next expression means "and having accomplished everything" (as I have translated) or "having been victorious over everything." In the former case the meaning would seem to be that when Paul's readers have correctly used every piece of armor mentioned in the following section, they will "stand." In the latter case it would mean that, using the armor of a Christian, believers have had victory over every foe. "Stand" here will have the meaning "hold one's ground," or "withstand," as previously in this verse.

The Pieces of Armor

Paul proceeds to list the pieces of armor at the Christian's disposal, which will ensure ultimate victory if rightly used. Again he calls on his readers to "stand"—clearly it means a lot to the apostle that his friends do not fall down in the face of opposition. He begins with having the "loins" girded "with truth." People of that time did not normally wear a belt in the house, but when they faced some vigorous action such as running, or when a soldier was preparing for battle, they raised their loose robes above the knees and fastened them in place with a belt (NIV, "belt of truth buckled around your waist"). Thus the "girding" of the loins meant preparation for physical activity or, as here, for engaging in conflict. The "loins" are also often used for the place of the reproductive organs (e.g., Heb. 7:5), but there seems no reason for seeing this meaning here. It is preparation for conflict that Paul has in mind.

It is not clear why Paul has linked "truth" with the girding of the loins. Perhaps he does so because both are involved in the preparation for some task. We should bear in mind that "truth" is sometimes used as a summary of the Christian way (e.g., 2 Thess. 2:10, 12). Especially does it signify the truth of the gospel (cf. Eph. 4:21; Col. 1:5). At any rate, by putting it first in his list Paul makes it clear that "truth" is an important part of the Christian's equipment.

With that he links "the breastplate of righteousness." The breastplate was, of course, a most important part of the warrior's defensive armor, protecting his heart and lungs as it did. If the breastplate gave way, a soldier was in real trouble. "Righteousness" may be used in more ways than one. It may signify the righteousness that is the gift of God (e.g, Rom. 5:17), the right standing that comes when the sinner turns from sin and trusts Jesus Christ as his Savior. But it may also signify the righteousness that characterizes the way a true Christian lives (e.g., 2 Tim. 3:16). It is perhaps more likely that here Paul is speaking of the way the Christian is to live rather than the way the sinner becomes a Christian. But since both senses of righteousness are true and important, it is not beyond the bounds of possibility that the apostle deliberately uses an expression that may be taken in more than one way. And it is important in the present context that the "righteousness" in question is God's gift. Paul is not writing about armor forged by Christian achievement, but armor that is the gift of God.

Paul moves from defensive armor for the chest to protection for the feet (v. 15). His verb means literally "bind under" and may be used of either the sandal that is "bound under" the foot or the foot that has something "bound under" it. The meaning depends on whether the user of the verb wishes to put emphasis on the foot that is thus protected or on the sandal or shoe that protects it. In the case of a warrior, it would be a shoe rather than a sandal. Josephus speaks of a soldier who was "wearing, like any other soldier, shoes thickly studded with sharp nails" (*War,*

VI.85; a Latin dictionary speaks of *caliga* as meaning "a shoe of leather, esp. that worn by the Roman soldiers").

The protecting shoe is here described as "the preparation of the gospel of peace." We might not have expected "preparation" here, but perhaps the word is used in the sense of something that prepares the feet for making progress. "The gospel of peace" is the good news that tells of peace with God, which only God can give. We should perhaps recall the Old Testament words: "How beautiful upon the mountains are the feet of the messenger who announces peace, who brings good news, who announces salvation, who says to Zion, 'Your God reigns'" (Isa. 52:7).

The whole expression points to being fully prepared to preach the gospel. The Christian will function as a messenger, telling sinners that they must repent and believe the gospel if they are to enter the peace of God. Paul is far and away the most frequent user of "gospel" in the New Testament: he has the word 60 times out of a total of 76. He is also fond of the word "peace," which he has 43 times (it occurs in every one of his letters). But this is the only place where he joins the two words. The combination puts some emphasis on the truth that the gospel is good news about the way sinners are brought to peace with God.

"In all things" (v. 16) puts some emphasis on what follows; there is no place where "faith" is not necessary for the Christian. Or it may mean "With all of these" (NRSV); that is, along with all the other qualities mentioned. Faith may be viewed in any one of a number of ways. It is faith that brings people to God and initiates their spiritual life. It is faith that sustains believers day by day as they seek to serve God. It is faith that enables them to call on God in the difficult days. We recall that when a man asked Jesus if he could do anything to heal his son and Jesus said, "All things are possible to him who believes," the man replied, "I believe; help my unbelief" (Mark 9:23–24). We could go on with such examples. There is faith like a grain of mustard seed, and that faith moves mountains (Matt. 17:20). There is much more. Paul's statement here should perhaps be put alongside his other words: "The just shall live by faith," or "He that is just by faith shall live" (Rom. 1:17). For the apostle, faith is central to the Christian life, and something of this thought comes through in the present passage.

But the main thought here appears to be that of the value of faith as a means of assisting believers as they proceed along the path of Christian service. They will certainly meet a good deal of opposition, some of which they will be quite unable to counter in their own human strength or wisdom. But faith is a "shield." The word in Greek is connected with that for "door" and denotes the large rectangular shield that covered most of the body (not the small round one that a soldier might use on the left arm). Such a shield would give good protection from the blows

struck by the enemy. Paul is reminding us that we are not left to ourselves. The person who really believes does not expect to find an easy
path in this life. The forces of evil are strong, and from time to time we
find ourselves in situations where, left to our own devices, we cannot
cope. But faith shields us from the enemy and enables us to survive, no
matter what the difficulties.

The apostle specifies one such difficulty as "all the flaming arrows of
the evil one." Arrows were bad enough at any time, but when they carried flammable material they were even more dangerous. A good shield,
however, rendered them impotent. And believers had such a shield to
help them in the spiritual warfare in which they were engaged. Flaming arrows must have been a terrible sight in warfare, but Paul makes
it clear that the believer has no reason to fear the spiritual equivalent.
Faith is impervious to such weapons. Even though they come from "the
evil one," they are not to be feared. A genuine faith, a faith that puts its
trust in Jesus Christ rather than in any human effort, will always come
out on top.

Paul continues his list with "the helmet," the most important part of
any defensive armor, and "the sword," the most important weapon of
offense (v. 17). His verb mostly has the meaning "receive" ("Accept salvation as your helmet," REB), though it is sometimes used in the sense
"take." Paul's choice of word may be meant to bring out the truth that
salvation and the word of God are both gifts of God, freely given and
not in any sense the result of the Christian's own initiative.

For a warrior, the helmet was most important. If it was easily pene-
trated or if it was uncomfortable, the wearer was at a disadvantage. The
fight was lost if the head was badly damaged, so a helmet had to be
strong and well constructed. A helmet was made of metal or sometimes
of tough leather, and when well made it kept the warrior's head safe.
Salvation is aptly said to be the Christian's helmet and something
received from God. It is common for the New Testament writers to point
out that we do not merit our salvation by our own good deeds or our
own efforts of any sort. Salvation is the gift of God. And seen as part of
the Christian's armor it is that which keeps the believer safe against the
strongest blows of the enemy.

"The sword of the Spirit" is explained as "the word of God." Another
New Testament writer sees "the word of God" as "living and effectual
and sharper than any two-edged sword" (Heb. 4:12). In both passages
it is the effectiveness of God's word that is brought out. Here Paul speaks
of "the sword of the Spirit," the weapon by which the Spirit effects his
purpose. Jesus' use of Scripture in the temptation narrative provides us
with an example of how "the sword of the Spirit" may be deployed to
defeat evil (Matt. 4:4, 7, 10).

In earlier days "the word of God" might have been heard through divinely inspired prophets and then from the lips of the Son of God himself. For the church in modern times, it is the word of God set forth in Scripture that is important. This, of course, is why that word features in services of worship and is the basis of sermons, and why the Bible is the book that Christians study when they want to know what God is saying. It is our highest privilege to be able to study the word of God and see how it applies to Christian service in modern society, just as it has done to societies in earlier days. "The word of God" is indeed the sword used by the Spirit of God to effect his purposes in the church and the world.

From all this it is clear that Paul sees the Christian as adequately provided for in the conflict against evil. God has made available a complete set of weapons. It remains only for the believer to make proper use of what God has provided. Then the victory is secure.

21

Speaking for Christ

With all prayer and supplication praying at every season in the
Spirit and watching for this with all perseverance and supplica-
tion about all the saints, and for me that a message may be given
to me in the opening of my mouth, to make known boldly the
mystery of the gospel, for which I am an ambassador in a chain,
that therein I may speak boldly as I must speak (Eph. 6:18–20).

Paul now turns to the subject of prayer (6:18). This is often
taken to be part of his treatment of the Christian's armor (and so it may
be), but the apostle does not liken prayer to any piece of the soldier's
defensive or offensive equipment. It seems better to take this as separate from the armor passage and see it as continuing to deal with the
Christian's task—but this time Paul says directly what is involved. From
all his letters we see that the apostle considered prayer as most important in the life of the Christian. Foulkes reminds us that we all too readily take our difficulties to our friends rather than to God, but Paul is
stressing the importance of prayer in all circumstances.

There is a problem in the Greek construction used here. "Praying" is
a participle and it is not easy to see what it depends on. It may refer back
to the helmet mentioned in the previous verse: "Receive the helmet of
salvation . . . praying at every season," or it may continue the series
begun in verse 14: "Stand therefore, having girded your loins . . . having put on the breastplate . . . having shod your feet . . . having taken up
the shield . . . praying at every season." Perhaps it is more likely that this
is an example of using the participle in the sense of an imperative. It

will then mean "Pray at every season." Fortunately the sense is not greatly affected. Whichever way we take it, the expression emphasizes the importance of prayer in the lives of believers. In this passage Paul speaks of prayer, supplication, praying, and intercession, so he leaves no doubt about the varieties of prayer and the importance of using them all. The Greek word for "all" occurs four times in this passage (we can scarcely say in English "at all season," but Paul uses the word for "all" here, too), so the apostle is speaking of the scope of prayer as universal. "Prayer" is the general term, and it is used constantly in the New Testament for the prayers that Christians offer. It is always used of making requests to God. The word rendered "supplication" conveys the notion of entreaty and may be used of making requests to God or to people (in the New Testament it always refers to prayers to God). Paul looks for the Ephesians to be busy about their praying, and specifically he wants them to be praying for other Christians.

Prayer is to be "at every season" and "in the Spirit." The apostle does not regard prayer as an occasional activity but one to be engaged in constantly. There is no season at which prayer is inappropriate for the believer. "In the Spirit" is taken by some expositors as "in the spirit," that is, in the human spirit of the praying person. The idea then would be that prayer should be sincere and should issue from the innermost part of the person. But it seems more likely that we should see a reference to the Holy Spirit—"as the Spirit leads" (GNB) or "in the power of the Spirit" (REB). For Paul it is important that the Holy Spirit dwells in believers and that the Spirit guides and leads them in all that they do. So they should look for the Spirit to assist them when they pray. They will not pray effectively if they do so in their own strength and under the guidance of their own wisdom. It is still an important part of the Christian life that God enables us to pray powerfully by giving us the Spirit. Barclay points out that prayer "must be intense. Limp prayer never got a man anywhere." We should take more care with the manner of our praying than we so often do.

"Watching" points to the need for alertness as we pray; we do not drift into prevailing prayer by accident. The verb conveys the thought of keeping oneself awake as one watches over someone or something (cf. its use in Mark 13:33). The word translated as "perseverance" is a very rare one and some have regarded it as a purely biblical word. However, it has also been found in Jewish inscriptions near the Black Sea and elsewhere, so it was apparently more widely used than in biblical texts. It stresses the idea of continuity. Prayer for the saints is not to be halfhearted and occasional, but a continuing activity, one that goes on and on among believers. Paul speaks of supplication "about all the saints," and this will mean much the same as "for all the saints." The apostle envisages all

believers as bound together by intercession for one another. In view of
the military metaphors Paul has been using, we may well heed Hodge's
comment: "No soldier entering battle prays for himself alone, but for
all his fellow-soldiers also. They form one army, and the success of one
is the success of all."

As Paul considers the intercessory functions of the Ephesians, he asks
these believers to pray for him (v. 19). He particularly wants them to
pray for him as he proclaims the gospel. He does not ask for success for
himself, but simply that he may proclaim the gospel. "In the opening of
my mouth" may mean "when I open my mouth," but it is more likely
that we should understand the apostle to be saying that he wants God
to open his mouth, as, for example, the psalmist did when he prayed,
"O Lord, open my lips, and my mouth will declare your praise" (Ps.
51:15). The New Revised Standard Version renders this present verse,
"Pray also for me, so that when I speak, a message may be given to me."
Paul does not rely on human wisdom as he proclaims the gospel. He
looks to God to give him the right words.

If this letter was written from Rome while the apostle awaited the
trial that would follow his appeal to Caesar, he may have in mind the
possibility that he would be making his defense before Caesar himself.
The emperor, of course, would not necessarily hear the appeal in person, but nevertheless the apostle's defense would be before some very
high official. And even if at this point Paul had no thought of making
his legal defense, he would have seen any opportunity of setting forth
the saving truth of the gospel as very important and therefore be the
kind of speaking in which he would wish the Ephesians to support him.
We should notice that Paul asks for prayer "that a message may be given
to me"—he did not regard his speaking as resulting from his own earnest
preparation (though we have no reason for thinking that he did less than
the very best preparation he could make). He saw it as the result of a
divine activity, so that the words he would speak would be the words
God intended to be spoken in that situation.

The expression translated "boldly" comes first with some emphasis:
"in boldness to make known. . . ." The word for "boldness" is made up
of two words meaning "all" and "speech." It signifies the attitude when
one is completely at home and the words flow freely. Thus it may mean
"outspokenness," or "frankness." When a person is speaking in this way,
he or she is not in the least afraid, and thus the expression comes to signify "boldly." In Rome Paul faced a situation in which he might well feel
fear and therefore be unable to present the gospel as convincingly as he
would like. He looks for his friends to uphold him in prayer, so that when
he came to speak, no matter what his audience, he would speak frankly
and fearlessly.

The Gospel

The content of the message Paul would bring was "the mystery of the gospel." The Greek understanding of "mystery" was something very different from our use of the term and denoted not something merely hard to work out, but something *impossible* to work out (see the comments on 1:9 for "mystery" and on 1:11 for "gospel").

That sense of the word applies especially to the gospel, as here, though this is the only place in the New Testament where the expression "the mystery of the gospel" is found. But it is singularly appropriate. Who would ever have guessed that our salvation does not depend on our prayers, our devotional life, our good deeds in general and even those that may be comprehended under the heading "religious virtues" in particular? Who would have worked it out that salvation depends on the coming to this earth of the Son of God and on his living in lowliness and humility, "despised and rejected of men"? Who would have thought that the culmination of all this would have been a death like that of a criminal on a cross? And if he was to die in this way, who would have reasoned that on the third day he would rise again? All this is in the plan of God, a plan that we could never have worked out for ourselves. Well might the ancients speak of it as a "mystery." This "mystery," says Paul, is "the mystery of the gospel." The good news that God has worked out our salvation himself and that it involved the sending of his Son to live in obscurity and to die on a cross is certainly something that is not the product of human ingenuity.

"For which" (v. 20) refers to "the mystery," and the apostle claims that it is for this that he is "an ambassador." The lexicon says that the word translated "for" may signify "be for someone, be on someone's side." Paul is wholeheartedly for the gospel. When he says he is an "ambassador," he is using an unexpectedly exalted title for a man in such a lowly earthly station as his. The term was used, for example, of the Emperor's legates, so Paul is in no doubt as to the importance of his position. To men he might appear an insignificant figure, but where it counted—in the sight of God—his function mattered a great deal.

Paul has a striking contrast when he speaks of being an ambassador "in a chain." The word he uses can mean a literal chain (e.g., Mark 5:3–4; Acts 28:20), but it sometimes seems to signify something like "imprisonment," which may well be the meaning here. On occasion the Romans would attach one end of a chain to a prisoner and the other to a soldier, and this may be what Paul has in mind. Whichever way we take it, Paul is speaking of something incongruous in an "ambassador," and in doing so he brings out the very different standards the world has over against God's eternal truth. We may profitably reflect that, whether or not it uses literal chains and literal prisons, the world has a way of belittling God's ambassadors and thereby showing its own blindness to ultimate reality. And there is a further thought, which McDonald puts this way: "He is seated in his cell handcuffed to a soldier; but he is no less seated in the heavenly places in Christ. He is down in the dungeon, but he is up in the glory."

We could take Paul's next words as referring to either the purpose or the content of the prayer he wants the Ephesians to offer for him. He may be saying, "Pray for me in order that I may speak . . ." or alternatively, "May your prayer for me be that I may speak. . . ." In the end there is no great difference, for Paul is certainly asking the Ephesians to pray that he may preach the gospel and do so courageously. Since he was a prisoner in a hostile environment, there can have been no doubt but that it required courage for him to speak up for Christ.

But not only was it desirable that Paul proclaim the gospel boldly; he says, "I must speak." As the apostle saw it, there was a compelling divine necessity laid upon him. He would be in a place where no Christian preacher before had been able to proclaim the gospel. And in that place it was imperative that the gospel be preached. He does not say, "it would be advisable for me to speak" but "I *must* speak." Simpson sees a magnificent fulfillment of these words: "Was not Paul rendered cosmopolitanly vocal in his prison-Epistles, whereof this one is not the least resonant? In these pages he speaks in reverberant tones across the centuries to every subsequent generation a message of certainty and energy divinely sealed and verified."

News of Other Christians

But so that you also may know my affairs, what I am doing, Tychicus, the beloved brother and faithful servant in the Lord, will make everything known to you. Him I have sent to you for this very reason, so that you may know our affairs and that he may comfort your hearts (Eph. 6:21–22).

It is Paul's habit to have a little "chatty" section toward the end of his letters as he passes on to his readers news of other believers and of his own doings. In this case it largely concerns "Tychicus" (v. 21), who evidently was to take the letter to the Ephesians and who could bring news about Paul in person and thus save the apostle from writing about himself. Tychicus (the name means "chance") came from the province of Asia (Acts 20:4), which was situated in the western part of what we call Asia Minor. He was evidently a trusted colleague and one whom Paul sent on unspecified missions on more than one occasion (2 Tim. 4:12; Titus 3:12). Paul can speak of him elsewhere as "the beloved brother and faithful minister [or "deacon"] and fellow-servant [or "fellow-slave"] in the Lord" (Col. 4:7). Here he is "the beloved brother and faithful servant ["deacon" again] in the Lord." Tychicus had apparently been with Paul for some time, for the apostle is confident that he will make "everything" known to the Ephesians.

Paul is anxious that his friends at Ephesus ("you also" means "you as well as others") should know all about what was happening to him, and he tells them that this was the reason he was sending Tychicus to them. "I have sent" (v. 22) is an example of what the grammarians call "the epistolary aorist." We would say, "I am sending" (as in NIV), but Paul has in mind the time frame when the Ephesians received the letter; then the sending would be in the past so Paul writes, "I have sent." But in addition to bringing news, Tychicus was to "comfort your hearts." This may mean that Paul felt that Tychicus would put them right. Or, of course, he may simply mean that Tychicus was an encouraging and comforting person. Clearly Paul saw this man as an outstanding Christian, one who would be able to bring help and comfort to other believers. There was much to discourage members of the early church, especially the strong opposition they met from so many people who would not trouble to understand their message nor the work they were doing in the Lord's name. An encourager like Tychicus must have been greatly needed.

Closing Benediction

Peace to the brothers and love with faith from God the Father and the Lord Jesus Christ. Grace be with all those who love our Lord Jesus Christ in uncorruptness (Eph. 6:23–24).

"Peace" (v. 23) is a frequent New Testament greeting (see comments on 1:2). Although we often encounter "Peace to you" or the like, this is the only place in the New Testament where we read, "Peace to the brothers." Paul is very fond of referring to Christians as "brothers." He uses the expression in all 133 times, but in this letter it occurs only in 6:21 and here. Some have thought that "the brothers" refers not to believers as a whole, but to church officials of some kind, but this seems unlikely. It is much more probable that Paul has in mind the believers in general as he sends farewells to the church at Ephesus.

"Love" is one of the great Christian words, and it is especially frequent in Paul's writings. In a final benediction he can use it to refer to God's love (2 Cor. 13:14) or to his own love for his readers (1 Cor. 16:24). It is not clear which meaning he intends here, but either would make good sense. "Love with faith" is an unusual expression, but each term points to an important Christian concept. Paul is here emphasizing two great truths at the heart of the Christian way. "Love with faith" seems to point to the love that Paul wishes the Ephesians to display in conjunction with the faith that is the basic Christian attitude. The linking of the Father and the Lord Jesus is characteristic: Christians must not forget the close relationship between the two.

The prayer for "grace" to be with his correspondents (v. 24) is a feature of the closing of all Paul's letters, and it is thus natural that here he should pray for the Ephesians. Barth has a note on the importance of grace in this epistle: "'Grace' as an attitude of God is as eternal as his decision to unite Jews and Gentiles in Jesus Christ and to reveal his secret at the proper time (1:6–10). Grace as a manifestation of God calls and saves those who had been dead in sin and unites them with Christ and one another (1:15; 2:5–8). Grace as a 'gift' of God equips men to be witnesses to his mighty deeds before all the world (3:2, 7–8; 4:7–12, 29). Grace as the abiding 'power' of God conveys to mortal men a share in eternal life (6:24). Thus the end of Ephesians points back to the source of 'peace.' Those given peace and proclaiming it participate in the very 'life of God' (4:18), from here to eternity."

Paul describes the recipients of grace as "all those who love our Lord Jesus Christ in uncorruptness," and this may well mean that he is including others than the Ephesian believers in this comprehensive prayer. But clearly he has the church at Ephesus mainly in mind. That he speaks of "all those who love our Lord Jesus Christ" points us yet again to the centrality of love. Because it is at the heart of Christian thinking and living, we can never overestimate its importance.

Although a closing prayer and such concepts as peace, love, faith, and grace are to be found throughout the Pauline correspondence, it is otherwise with the term "uncorruptness." This is not a common word in the New Testament; it occurs only seven times, all in the Pauline writings. It is mostly used in the sense of "immortality," which would seem to be the sense here (NIV, "Grace to all who love our Lord Jesus Christ with an undying love"). Abbott comments that the word "does not point merely to time but to character, and that suits very well here as an attributive of love." Christian love does not cease at death but goes on in the eternal realms. Paul prays for his Ephesian friends.

References Cited

There is, of course, an enormous literature on Ephesians.
I have made no attempt to cull through it all, but have referred from
time to time to each of the following books by the author's name.

Abbott, T. K., *A Critical and Exegetical Commentary on the Epistles to
the Ephesians and to the Colossians* (Edinburgh: 1953).

Barclay, W., *Letters to the Galatians and Ephesians* (Edinburgh: 1974).

Barth, Markus, *Ephesians*, 2 vols. (New York: 1974).

Bruce, F. F., *The Epistle to the Ephesians* (New Jersey: 1974).

———. *The Epistles to the Colossians, to Philemon, and to the
Ephesians* (Grand Rapids: 1984).

Calvin, John, *The Epistles of Paul the Apostle to the Galatians,
Ephesians, Philippians and Colossians* (Edinburgh: 1965).

Foulkes, F., *The Epistle of Paul to the Ephesians* (London: 1963).

*A Greek-English Lexicon of the New Testament and Other Early Chris-
tian Literature,* translated and adapted from the fourth revised and
augmented edition of Walter Bauer's *Griechisch-Deutsches Wörter-
buch,* by W. F. Arndt and F. W. Gingrich; second edition revised
and augmented by F. W. Gingrich and F. W. Danker from Walter
Bauer's fifth edition, 1958. Published 1979.

Hodge, Charles, *A Commentary on the Epistle to the Ephesians* (London: 1964).

Lock, Walter, *The Epistle to the Ephesians* (London: 1929).

Mitton, C. Leslie, *Ephesians* (London: 1981).

McDonald, H. D., *The Church and Its Glory* (Worthing: 1973).

Moule, H. C. G., *The Epistle of Paul the Apostle to the Ephesians* (Cambridge: 1923).

Robinson, J. Armitage, *St. Paul's Epistle to the Ephesians* (London:
1907).

Simpson, E. K., and F. F. Bruce, *Commentary on the Epistles to the
Ephesians and the Colossians* (Grand Rapids: 1957)

References Cited

Stott, John R. W., *God's New Society* (Downers Grove: 1979).

Strelan, John G., *Chi Rho Commentary on Ephesians* (Adelaide: 1981).

Theological Dictionary of the New Testament, edited by G. Kittel and G. Friedrich; translated and edited by G. W. Bromiley, 10 vols. (Grand Rapids: Eerdmans, 1964–76).

Westcott, Brooke Foss, *Saint Paul's Epistle to the Ephesians* (London: 1906).

Wood, A. Skevington, "Ephesians," in *The Expositor's Bible Commentary,* vol. 11 (Grand Rapids: 1978).